Students In Conflict

L.S.E. Research Monographs 5

This series is published jointly with the London School of Economics and Political Science. It aims to make available research of originality and quality from the whole range of the social sciences, including all the fields and disciplines which are studied at the school. The intention is to provide a continuing outlet for serious scholarly work, and relatively quick publication. The books will be of interest to specialists in the various fields, irrespective of whether they are in universities, government departments, industries or elsewhere, as well as to libraries throughout the world.

Each monograph will be introduced with a foreword by a distinguished authority on the subject, whose aim will be to set the particular research in to the wider framework of the appropriate discipline. The following monographs have already been published:

Changes in Subject Choice at School and University
Celia M. Phillips

The Criminal Liability of Corporations in English Law
L. H. Leigh

Industrial Demand for Water: A Study of South-East England
Judith Rees

The Politics of Decontrol of Industry: Britain and the United States
Susan Armitage

Forthcoming titles:

The Administrative Functions of the French Conseil d'Etat
Margherita Rendel

The Concept of Responsibility in the Criminal Law
F. G. Jacobs

Six Studies of Indian Industry
Angus Hone (Editor)

Students
in Conflict
L.S.E. in 1967

Tessa Blackstone
Lecturer in Social Administration, London School of
Economics

Kathleen Gales
Senior Lecturer in Statistics, London School of Economics

Roger Hadley
Lecturer in Social Administration, London School of
Economics

Wyn Lewis
Lecturer in Statistics, London School of Economics

London School of Economics and Political Science

Weidenfeld and Nicolson
5 Winsley Street London W1

SBN 297 00028 4

Printed in Great Britain by Bristol Typesetting Co Ltd, Barton Manor, Bristol

Contents

All four authors worked together closely in planning this study and in writing up the results. However, the main responsibility for drafting the different chapters was allocated individually. Chapter 1 was written by K. Gales and R. Hadley, Chapter 2 by W. Lewis, Chapter 3 by R. Hadley, Chapter 4 by T. Blackstone, Chapters 5 and 6 by K. Gales and Chapter 7 by R. Hadley. Chapter 8 was written by W. Lewis. Chapter 9 was written by K. Gales, incorporating sections on student participation and political attitudes by T. Blackstone and R. Hadley. Chapter 10 was written by T. Blackstone and K. Gales. Appendix B was written by K. Gales and W. Lewis.

List of tables

A*

Terms and abbreviations

Rounding

In tables where percentages are shown each figure has been rounded individually. Where necessary the largest figure has been adjusted to make the rounded figures add to one hundred.

Small Subgroups

Where percentages in tables are based upon a number of cases less than thirty attention is drawn to the small base by enclosing such percentages in parentheses.

Glossary of Terms

U.G.s	Undergraduates
P.G.s	Postgraduates
H.U.G.s	Home Undergraduates
O.U.G.s	Overseas Undergraduates
H.P.G.s	Home Postgraduates
O.P.G.s	Overseas Postgraduates
Left Wing Groups	Anarchists, Marxists, Trotskyites, Communists and those who describe themselves as Left Wing Labour
Other maintained Schools	Secondary modern, technical and comprehensive

Acknowledgements

We should like to thank the following people for the help we received at various stages in this study. We are particularly grateful to Professor David Donnison and Professor James Durbin for their support and advice. The arduous job of preparing and mailing the 3000 questionnaires was carried out by the staff of the L.S.E. Registry and Graduate Office. We also wish to thank the school authorities for their grant of £500 for data-processing, the Statistics Research Division for a further grant of £100 for research assistance, Mr Frank Land and his assistant, Miss Marjorie Cowell, for their unstinting help in the use of the L.S.E. computer, and our research assistant, Mrs Susan McQuail, who helped us with the analysis.

We are grateful to Dr Walter Adams, Sir Sydney Caine, Mr Harry Kidd, Professor Robert McKenzie, Mr Patrick Davis and Mr Peter Watherston for their comments on earlier drafts. And, finally, we should like to thank all the students at L.S.E. whose cooperation in completing the survey questionnaire made the study possible.

Preface

The disturbances which began at the London School of Economics in the autumn of 1966 led, next spring, to the first strike called by students against the authorities of a British university. Students and teachers were bitterly divided – among themselves, rather than against each other. It was not a propitious moment for objective research upon the life of the School. But the authors of this book were determined, despite much opposition, to find out what students did and how they felt during these disturbances, and the Director of the School agreed to give them the help they needed for their study. This book presents the findings of research which had to be mounted at great speed in the immediate, uneasy aftermath of the events to be studied. It will interest all concerned with the evolution of higher education, for it throws light on many things besides ‘the revolt of the privileged’. That the study could be made at all is a compliment to the vast majority of L.S.E. students who were prepared to participate in it and to the authorities whose support made the work possible. That its findings cover so much ground and are presented in a form so clear, fair and readable is a compliment to the level-headed professionalism of its authors.

The authors resolved from the start to confine themselves to description and analysis of the behaviour they were studying. They do not tell us what to do. Indeed, they make it clear that unrest among students is a much more complicated affair than most commentators would have us believe, and we must learn a great deal more before we can convincingly explain it or confidently tell anyone what to do about it.

But we cannot wait for wisdom. All of us who work in universities – whether as teachers, students, administrators or governors – have to decide how to behave, whether we understand our predicament or not. Some readers will turn straight to the findings reported in this book, for they are its unique and special contribution. But to those who come to it in search of suggestions for action I offer an essay on the government of universities which may carry the discussion forward, if only by provoking fruitful disagreement.

This essay has been informed by the opportunity of following the research reported in this book, and improved by the authors' critical comments. But it is not derived directly from their research: it draws on the experience of other universities and on more recent events at the L.S.E., and it is addressed to all concerned with the future of British universities – not just to the College I happen to know best. The responsibility for it is entirely mine. Each of the authors of this book would probably dissent from parts of it.

Anyone who has spent the last three years at the L.S.E. must recognise that he can tell others nothing about the government of universities, unless it be a few cautious lessons, painfully learnt from his own and others' mistakes.

Consider the record. Militant students sought to reject the man chosen to be their Director, to make radical changes in the government of the School, to get some of the School's investments sold, to prevent disciplinary proceedings from being taken against teachers and students, and to remove gates that control movement within the buildings. None of these objectives has been achieved. Some things have changed: teaching has probably improved, and students are less apathetic about the politics of the School and of the country at large. But these changes could have been achieved more effectively in other ways.

Meanwhile teachers, administrators and governors have repeatedly tried to keep the work of the School going smoothly. And they too have failed. The disturbances studied in this book were followed, two years later, by further boycotts of teaching, destruction and defacement of property, interruption of lectures and temporary closure of the School. The opportunity for achieving the one new development to which nearly everyone in the School would give first priority – the building of a new library – has been threatened by these events and may be lost. A College which used to be one of the happiest and most productive in the country is now top of the poison ivy league.

We hope that events are about to take a more constructive turn, and it would be a mistake to exaggerate the School's predicament. There is nothing in this record to compare, in extent or cost, with the disturbances which have afflicted universities in America, Japan, France, Italy and other countries. It is clear, nevertheless, that all concerned in the life of the School have failed to achieve what they hoped for. Other universities and colleges in this country have had similar experiences.

Against this background of failure, recriminations and confident prescriptions of any kind would be out of place. I want only to offer some suggestions about the government of universities which may help all concerned to make progress towards common objectives, to recognise that disputes will occur, and to find ways of conducting disputes more productively. It is politics – the constructive management of conflict – that I am writing about.

In universities power operates in peculiarly unexplicit ways. There can be few institutions whose written constitutions and rules tell less about the reality of their government. But if we exclude the Scottish universities and Oxbridge, products of different traditions, some fundamental trends are clear.

Professors steadily gained power in their universities during the first half of this century. They secured seats on their governing bodies, undisputed control of academic matters, and an enlarged definition of what was ' academic '. But in the last fifteen years the power of professors has been challenged and eroded by pressures converging from all sides. The public funds poured into universities have compelled government to exert, first a reluctant but now an increasingly determined, influence on their development. The growing scale and complexity of higher education have brought into being a corps of administrators upon whom academics have come to rely for the guidance which only an experienced official can offer. A growing staff of lecturers – many of them young and recent recruits – has gained increasing influence over the development of teaching and research, and secured seats on the more important committees. Now students are emerging as the latest contenders for power in the universities. The latest, but certainly not the last: the technicians who run the universities' laboratories, computers and workshops are already mobilising their forces.

These pressures are neither sinister nor surprising; they follow inevitably from the transformation of a collection of local academic guilds and colleges into a major national industry. But the pressures are converging upon a power structure of unspoken conventions which no one has ever had to clarify. The conflicts that ensue have no consistent strategy or battle front; they are skirmishes in a fog. Before examining the drama we should pause to consider the cast, though any brief description of their roles must be something of a caricature.

Let us start with students. Among them will be found the militant left, the student loyalists, the apathetic, and the militant right. In 'normal' times, most students are apathetic about university politics – for all sorts of, generally good, reasons. They are working very hard, or playing football or music, or courting, or doing other things. Far the most important in university politics are those I described as the loyalists. They are actively concerned about their own needs and the university's affairs; they give their allegiance to those who appear to appreciate and defend them, their hostility to those who appear to threaten their interests or frustrate their aspirations. In times of crisis many of the apathetic adopt an active loyalist role, and loyalists grow increasingly militant. Those who have the loyalists' support can ultimately run the university— or prevent anyone else from running it. The militant left consists of continually changing groups, often at odds with each other, but two sections should be distinguished. Some are mainly and passionately intent on changing the university, while others regard the university as a base, ultimately expendable, from which to change the world at large. Those concerned mainly with the university will never be completely satisfied, but it is possible to reach serious agreements with them and they are prepared to participate consistently and constructively in the management of the university. Those primarily intent on revolution in society at large aim to discredit and destroy all established authority, since they regard it as corrupt beyond redemption. Responsibility within the university is the last thing they want; any concession offered to them by authority will be met by more extreme and deliberately unacceptable demands. In British universities the militant right has not recently appeared in force. Many of the opponents of the militant left, described in this book as the 'opposition', were not right-wingers, but student loyalists, prepared to take an active part on the side of moderation because they felt that was the best way to serve the interests of students. But a more authoritarian backlash is likely to emerge as the first enjoyment of militancy wears off and its failures become more apparent.

Teachers in the university adopt rather similar roles, but in different proportions. Most of them, most of the time, want to be spared involvement in university politics so that they can get on with their research and teaching, and have some time to spare for other activities and for their families. The loyalists rally more actively to defend the interests of the ordinary teacher, and that may align them against professors, students, governors, or whoever appears for the moment to be frustrating the work and aspirations of lecturers. As with students, these are the crucial part of the political spectrum without whose support it is impossible to run the university. The militant left and right resemble their opposite numbers among students, except that the right is numerically stronger and its thinking informed by more sophisticated argument about the dangers of disintegration and mob rule within the university.

Administrators in the university are more honestly and wholeheartedly devoted to serving their committees (rather than manipulating or dominating them) than administrators in any other setting I know. They also have more at stake than other members of the cast. Students will leave the university before long, and even if they leave prematurely many of them could take an external degree. Teachers rely for their security on their Ph.D.s, their publication lists and their academic reputations. But the administrators' life and work is confined more completely to the university, and they depend more heavily on it for their living. They cannot do their work or look with any confidence to the future unless the university gives them an effective decision-making machine to serve.

The university's governing body, consisting mainly of laymen, has been accustomed to giving advice when asked for it, and taking decisions about new investment in buildings and capital equipment, the allocation of major resources, and the evolution of the framework that facilitates research and teaching. The laymen often have an exaggerated respect for senior teachers, keep well clear of any decision that could be classified as 'academic' and have no wish to involve themselves in the day-to-day running of the university. When events compel them to do this they are ill-prepared for the task.

Outside the university – particularly if it stands in a great city – there is a fringe of hangers-on; a motley collection, ranging from revolutionaries and cranks to dope-pedlars and the deranged, who will move in to share and stoke the uproar if opportunity arises. It is as easy to walk into a city university as to walk into Kings Cross station. Anyone who has seen these characters at large in the university and in his own lecture audiences must be aware that he is living on the margins of chaos – chaos generally prevented, and only preventable, by students themselves.

These caricatures describe roles, not individuals. Many in the cast shift from one role to another under the pressure of events. In the face of militancy, the university can work only if it has enough loyalists, and only if the loyalists among students and teachers are sufficiently convinced of each other's basic goodwill and competence to make common cause most of the time. Universities have always had their militants – fortunately – and militants only become destructive if they secure the support of a sufficient number of loyalists, for to disrupt the work of the university without this support is to reveal themselves as the small minority they are and to alienate the very people whose backing they most need. So much for the cast; next for the action.

Government that is 'responsible', in the sense that its decisions are consistent and produce co-ordinated and effective action, must be conducted by fairly small groups of people. It cannot be conducted in mass assemblies or by groups whose members continually change. If government is also to be 'responsible' in the sense that its decisions are questioned, criticised and ultimately backed by a consensus among the governed, it must be conducted by groups which have a legitimate claim to speak for the governed and regularly account for their decisions before the governed.

In a university this means that fairly small, continuing groups of decision makers must be organised at various levels (departmental, college and university) for various purposes (teaching, research, admissions, building, etc.). Students must be represented, in ways which they and others accept as legitimate, at all levels where major decisions of policy are taken, and on any tribunal which can impose disciplinary sanctions on students. It has long been accepted that students should play a major part in the management of halls of residence, athletic unions, catering and other services intended principally for them. But those who believe their participation should be confined to these matters have failed to grasp the issues now at stake.

I believe there are two main issues. The first affects all young people to some extent. For many reasons, not worth exploring here, they have shed much of the deference towards those with superior status which marked an earlier generation. People who are older, better qualified, richer or in authority are expected, more often than hitherto, to make good their claims to power and influence by demonstrating their superior knowledge and capacity and exposing themselves to questions and criticism. Universities have always prided themselves on conducting their affairs in this way, but although they approach the ideal more nearly than most institutions they still fall far short of it. This change in the attitudes of the young can be a bruising affair, but it gives us opportunities which must not be missed.

The second issue arises from changes in the universities themselves. They contain many of this new, irreverent generation. They have embarked on an expansion which will go on till all who are capable of continuing their studies beyond school in a systematic fashion will enter higher or further education of some kind. That may take a long time to achieve, but there is no stopping point on the way. We have decided – partly as a matter of ideology, partly for lack of better criteria – to use the demands and capacities of young people seeking university places as our main guide to the pace and directions of university expansion. For graduate work the rules are different, but for the bulk of the universities' growth 'social demand' is to be our criterion. If students themselves have no say in decisions about the kind of work they are to do, the way in which they are to do it, and the ways in which their performance is to be assessed, then 'social demand' will simply be a fancy name for academic syndicalism – a pretence which the nation and its government will soon see through. There are other reasons for what is sometimes called democratisation of the university; some believe that participation in these responsibilities can be an important part of a university education; others believe there is no other way of keeping the university's work going smoothly. But the essential point is much simpler. Universities must serve the labour market (but not *only* serve the labour market) if they are to make their contribution to the growth of higher education. Students have an eye on the opportunities awaiting them in that market; and the universities' links with it will only evolve effectively and humanely if they develop as a response to students' aspirations and interests. The alternatives – to disregard the needs of the market, or to rely on government and the employers to call the tune – will in their different ways prove equally destructive.

The right to question the university's policies and procedures must begin in tutorials and seminars, and continue through departmental and college levels to the governing body of the university itself. From the departmental level upwards, representation in small policy-making committees and regular opportunities for debate in larger assemblies are both required; neither can substitute for the other.

How many students should serve on such committees? They should be numerous enough to make themselves heard, but on the more important policy-making bodies they should not have a majority. A university is concerned with a great deal more than teaching; the principal (but never the only) voice in their government must therefore be that of the people responsible for developing and applying their disciplines in collaboration with colleagues engaged in similar work throughout the world. The universities are ultimately responsible to the nation at large, and cannot hand this trust over to the small group of privileged young people from middle-class homes who form the majority of their students. Procedures for the selection of students to serve on representative bodies deserve careful thought – *before* they become an emotionally charged issue. Secret ballots, by an electorate subdivided to represent the different faculties, subjects and year-groupings in proper proportions, make better sense for most purposes than elections from an undifferentiated Union body.

In some decisions, students should play no part at all. They should not decide on the recruitment and promotion of staff, or the selection, assessment and grading of students. But they should be entitled and encouraged to ask what criteria are used for recruitment, promotions and admissions, and to discuss the content and character of teaching and the purpose and procedure of examinations – and be given serious answers.

However carefully we organise and reorganise the government of universities, there will still be times when students, teachers or other members of the university find that constitutional procedures cannot adequately express their views or secure the action they want. How should we behave if such pressures burst the banks of constitutional channels and spill out into demonstrations or disorder?

The first lessons to be learnt from tumult are obvious enough to anyone with experience of politics or industrial relations. Keep all the communication systems working – particularly in peaceful times when there seems to be no great need for them. When trouble comes, meet the opposition (whoever your opposition happens to be) listen seriously to what they have to say, don't lose your sense of humour, and don't panic. Never make unenforceable threats or rules. Keep your eye on the loyalists or active moderates: neither side can get its way without support from loyalists on the other side. Give the responsible militants responsibility. Every large community has its share of irresponsible militants and a few madmen, they will be harmless so long as they do not get the support of the loyalists.

If more serious disorder begins, remember that many of those involved are *enjoying* themselves – however painful the situation may seem to you. (Anyone who observed students during the sit-in described in this book will have an abiding memory of young people bearing sleeping-bags and guitars into the School, sharing food and drink and talking endlessly, and making a lot of friends in what had previously been, for many of them, a crowded but exceedingly lonely institution. It was like the comradely and heartwarming parts of the blitz, with none of the danger or misery. Anyone who observed teachers during the same weeks will recall that scholars who have spent half a lifetime studying and re-living the deeds of men of action enjoy the opportunity of acting out their own fantasies for a while: they, too, can harangue the masses, stage a strike or a lock-out, hold press conferences, convene emergency committees in the small hours, unmask villainies or defend the martyred.) Many of those who are enjoying themselves, like many others who are not, will also be doing their honest best to resolve conflicts and heal the wounds of strife. But people who are enjoying themselves will go on raising hell of some sort until they have had enough of it. They must therefore be given purposeful things to do which lead to practical results, and the sense that authority is concerned and decisive. Disorder cannot simply be put down; and if it continues indefinitely without results it is apt to turn nasty.

How much disorder can the university tolerate? University authorities now have the task of drawing the line between the tolerable and the intolerable. That line will not be respected unless students play a part in defining it. The line must then be made tactfully but abundantly clear at every opportunity.

Most of the frontier between tolerable and intolerable forms of political pressure can be agreed without much trouble if the problem is faced before hysteria takes command. For example a lecturer may be interrupted and questioned about the subject of his lecture for as long as he is prepared to give the floor to his questioners, but he may not be questioned during his lecture about altogether different issues, and must not be prevented from doing the teaching which some of his audience have freely come to hear. (For no one is compelled to attend lectures.) Students may boycott teaching, provided they show evidence of having done serious work when asked for it. (Their local education authorities have a right to know if any is being done.) People may sit down in and around university buildings but must not prevent those who wish to enter libraries, teaching-rooms or administrative offices from doing so. The right to boycott teaching and the right to teach and be taught without interference or intimidation are alike essential parts of freedom within the university. Once rules on these and other matters have been agreed with the representatives of students and teachers, they should form part of the contract which every student and every teacher entering the university agrees to be bound by.

In seriously troubled times the university will be compelled to use sanctions against those who pursue political action to a point at which it brings work to a halt. Civil disobedience intended to compel government to use sanctions which ultimately alienate the governed is a recognised political device. It helped to win India and Ireland their freedom, and women the vote. If the university has done its best to ensure that all concerned know precisely where the frontier between the tolerable and the intolerable lies, and this frontier is then deliberately crossed, disciplinary action must follow. That is the intention of those who cross it and, since they must eventually get their way, action is better taken soon than late.

But traditional disciplinary procedures, which were designed to deal with offences such as the theft of books from libraries, will no longer do. Offences intended as a deliberate challenge to the authority of the university cannot be tried by the very authorities whose jurisdiction is in question. For serious offences – and *any* deliberate action which prevents people doing their work in a university is 'serious' – new procedures are needed which ensure clear statement of the charges and their supporting evidence, cross-examination of witnesses, help for the accused from a friend or advisor he chooses for himself, reasoned decisions, and rights of appeal. The tribunal, and any tribunal dealing with appeals from its decisions, must be recognised as impartial: for charges against students, an independent chairman, a representative of teachers and a representative of students seem appropriate, and it may be wiser to choose these representatives from another college or university not involved in the conflict.

If, despite all attempts to prevent it, the work of the university is genuinely brought to a halt with scant prospect of an early return to conditions in which research and teaching can proceed, then the place must be closed. Such closures can provide a breathing space in which all concerned may cool off and sanity be restored. But the device cannot be repeatedly used; whatever it may intend, a university that is repeatedly closed will find that local authorities will withdraw grants from students who can no longer pursue their studies there – and rightly, too. Considerable changes would then have to be made before anyone would send students to such a university again. All concerned should know that they are in the same boat; and it is a boat which will actually sink if they cannot contrive to keep it afloat.

The ultimate winners in a struggle for power within the university will be those who gain the support of public opinion: opinion in the university itself (particularly among the active moderates whom I described as student and teacher loyalists) opinion in other universities, opinion in the local authorities and in Parliament, and opinion among newspaper readers and voters throughout the country. The public can readily understand young people's hostility to authority, and will sympathise with them if authority seems unreasonable, oppressive or inept. But they expect students to study and resent anyone who wilfully throws this privilege away or prevents others from exercising it.

Students at odds with university authorities should therefore take every opportunity they are given of participating in university government. They can ask for more later if they are not satisfied with what they are offered at first. Their demands for change should then be focused on the improvement of teaching, the improvement of libraries and the laboratories, the opening up of new opportunities for learning and the reappraisal of examining procedures. Here they are on strong ground, for all can appreciate that they know a good deal about these things and have a right to be heard.

Teachers must find ways of engaging students in the development of the university's work at all levels of its structure, and particularly at the lowest levels where a foundation of good human relations and the habit of serious, open discussion can be built. They must work out agreed codes of discipline with their students and make sure they are understood by all. They, like students, must be prepared to give honest and precise evidence when it is alleged that the codes have been flouted.

Governing bodies must insist that progress is made in these directions, despite the rebuffs they may at first experience from students and teachers alike. They must also ensure that disciplinary procedures command the confidence of all concerned and relieve governing bodies of the task of acting as court of appeal in cases where their own decisions and policies are challenged. When they have got these things right, they must be determined to seek the help of students in running the university, tolerant of orderly demonstration, endlessly willing to answer questions, but severe in dealing with those who deliberately prevent others in the university from doing their work.

These proposals offer no assurance of universal peace and goodwill, nor are they intended to. They are designed to help us conduct our disputes in a more productive fashion.

DAVID DONNISON
Professor of Social Administration
London School of Economics

Chapter 1

Introduction

At about five o'clock on 13 March 1967, two hundred or more students streamed out of the main lecture theatre of the London School of Economics, where they had been holding a meeting of their union, and sat down in the lobbies and corridors of the School. The sit-in continued, accompanied by a boycott of lectures and classes and with increasing student support, for the following eight days and nights, and became the first major student strike this country has known. The immediate cause of the strike was the decision of the L.S.E.'s Board of Discipline to suspend two student leaders until the end of the summer term 1967 for disobeying an instruction of the Director. The boycott and sit-in were called to back student demands that the sentences of the Board should be quashed.

The origins of the affair can be traced back ten months to the announcement in June 1966 that Dr. Walter Adams had been appointed to succeed the retiring Director, Sir Sydney Caine, in October 1967. Some of the students at L.S.E. were highly critical of what they believed to be Dr Adams's record in Rhodesia, and questioned his suitability for the post of Director of the School. In the autumn term 1966, the appointment was hotly debated and the Students' Union clashed with the School authorities on the legitimacy of regulations which limited their freedom to write to the Press on the issue. Early in the following term a meeting was called to discuss direct action to stop the appointment of Adams. Although the Director subsequently banned the meeting, many students thought it should still take place, and a large number of them gathered outside the lecture theatre in which it was to have been held. A confused and excited debate took place as to whether the lecture theatre should be used inspite of the Director's ban. Eventually a number of students pushed past the porters guarding the doors to the room with the intention of holding the meeting as planned. In the excitement one of the porters had a heart attack and died. He had not been physically assaulted in any way, and no blame for his death was attached to any of the students concerned. Nevertheless, the Board of Discipline was convened to hear charges against a number of the students involved, including the President of the Student's Union and the President of the Graduate Students' Association. The charges against the other students were dismissed but both student presidents were found guilty of disobeying the instruction of the Director and were rusticated until the end of the summer term 1967.

The March boycott and sit-in continued until the end of the Lent Term. Although on appeal to a committee of the Board of Governors the two leaders' period of suspension was reduced, the students were not satisfied, and decided to reinstitute the strike at the beginning of the summer term if negotiations had not produced a more satisfactory settlement by then. During the vacation, however, the governors decided to suspend the sentences altogether, subject to the satisfactory conduct of the two students concerned, and the strike was finally called off.[1]

Our decision to make a study of the boycott and sit-in was in no way inspired by long-term research interests in the field of student protest. We simply had a common desire to gain some understanding of the social upheaval that was happening on our own doorstep and which had wide implications for anyone who taught in the School. It is worth emphasising how much confusion the strike created in the L.S.E. Not only were most people ill-informed of the latest developments in the conflict, but the air was full of contradictory reports about the extent and character of student involvement, while theories of the underlying causes of the affair abounded. The confusion can be well illustrated from the conflicting statements made at the time about the number of students who took part in the boycott and sit-in. For example, the Director was reported by *The Times* (15 March 1967) as saying, at a press conference on the second day of the strike, that the number of agitators at the L.S.E. was about fifty and that there might be two hundred willing to support them. At the same press conference he claimed that lectures were not seriously affected, being only 10% or so below normal attendance.[2] The next day, however, *The Times*'s own correspondent estimated support at 'more than 500', and another newspaper thought more than twelve hundred were backing the strike.[3] Later in the week, a member of the staff of the L.S.E., in a letter to *The Times*, hotly denied that student support was widespread. Referring to the second day of the disturbance, he wrote: 'while your photographers and reporters were devoting their attentions to the two hundred or so victims of a few demagogues, I held a seminar and gave a lecture and tutorials, all in normal fashion and with normal attendance.' But other reports continued to suggest much stronger student backing, and later, when the strike was over, the students claimed that the count they had made every day of the numbers attending lectures and classes showed the boycott was between 69% and 75% successful each day,[4] and a count of those sleeping in the School on one night during the sit-in showed seven hundred students were in the building.[5] Although some of the discrepancies between the figures quoted by different sources could be explained by the fact that they referred to different periods in the strike and reflected fluctuations in support, other differences were too large to be fully accounted for in this way, and the *Sunday Times* 'Insight' team tried to establish the extent of support on a firmer basis. The team adopted what it called 'the only method suitable for the analysis of a dispute at the legendary home of the social sciences', initiating a survey of student opinion. In the survey, which was said to be based on a random sample of all students, they found that not only did most of those who completed their questionnaires feel the sentences on the student leaders were too harsh and that the boycott and sit-in were justified, but that a clear majority had themselves taken part in the demonstrations. However, this report was received with some scepticism in the 'legendary home of the social sciences', not simply because the methods used to draw the random sample were obscure, but also because the response-rate from those who were sent the questionnaire was only 30%, a level far below that normally regarded as acceptable in such surveys.[6]

Theories on the underlying factors in the dispute were also in plentiful supply and added to the atmosphere of confusion, not so much because they were contradictory, as because of the multiplicity of causes they invoked. Again, newspapers and journals published during the nine days of the boycott and sit-in provide good examples. Two levels of causation were suggested by most writers: local difficulties peculiar to the L.S.E., and major developments affecting the position of the student in society. A leader in the *New Statesman* (17 March 1967) included many of the factors presented under the first heading.

The students' union, a vital forum for self-expression and service, is starved of funds and denied freedoms granted elsewhere. The chain of command still reflects the authoritarian bias of the Webbs, who founded the L.S.E., and the present clashes reveal a long-felt need for reform ; for instance the Olympian board of discipline compares poorly with the disciplinary committee, functioning well with a student majority, at the University of Sussex. The curriculum, in whose shaping the students have no say, is narrowly orientated toward examination demands, and students complain that new ideas are seldom admitted for debate.

The second level of explanation sought to link the strike to broader changes in the relationship of students and society. For instance, *The Times* (15 March 1967) saw the emergence of a 'self-conscious student class' reminiscent of the emergence of a self-conscious working class in the nineteenth century. 'They pursue a separate "youth culture". They possess collective grievances. Although some of these are cosmic, being concerned with nuclear armaments, Vietnam, or apartheid, others are of an earthier desscription — the size of grants, lodgings, crowded quarters.'

Pursuing a similar argument and comparing the disturbances at L.S.E. with those in the Free University of Berlin, Timothy Raison wrote in the *Sunday Times* (19 March 1967):

In the broadest terms the disorders in both universities are part of what has come to be known as the inter-generational conflict—brought about by the world-wide tendency on the part of the young to say, not as in the past that 'I accept your values but I am going to break them', but rather simply 'I think your values are wrong'.

The survey
The four authors of this report felt that the L.S.E. student strike should not be allowed to pass into the hands of the historians of higher education before some attempt had been made to reduce the confusion over the extent and nature of student involvement by a systematic study, and to provide factual evidence for use in testing theories of underlying causation. We were aware that any study must be limited in scope and method, given the need to act quickly before memories faded and many of the students had dispersed. Nevertheless, we felt that a worth-while

project could be carried through and decided to ask the Students' Union for its co-operation. This was willingly offered, but union officials informed us that they did not keep lists of students' names and addresses which we needed if we were to draw a random sample for our study. This information could only be obtained from the school administration. Consequently, we next approached the Director, Sir Sydney Caine, to seek his permission for access to these records. The Director, though not opposed in principle to a study of the sit-in and boycott, expressed grave doubts as to whether it should be carried out by members of the staff of the School when the object of the study was relations within the School itself. He proposed that an outside research-body should be retained to conduct the study, and we reluctantly agreed to co-operate with such a body if it could be found in the short time available, but stressed that we would prefer to go ahead with our own project. In the event, the school authorities finally abandoned the idea of an independent investigation. The Director then referred our request to the Committee on the Relationships between the School and its Students and, following the recommendation of this committee, the four authors were given permission to carry out the study under certain conditions. The first of these was that the survey should cover all students and not simply the 15% or 20% sample we had suggested. The second was that the data would not be reported upon unless a response-rate of at least 70% was achieved. The third was that no report of any kind would be published until the school authorities and the President of the Students' Union had been given the opportunity to comment upon it. Two senior members of staff, the conveners of the two departments in which the authors taught, were asked to act as advisors and sponsors for the project. The School agreed to provide the clerical assistance needed in duplicating and sending out the questionnaires and reminders, and to pay the cost of having the questionnaires coded and the computer cards punched by an outside market-research agency.

The primary objective of the survey was to discover the facts in regard to the extent and nature of student support for the demonstrations, measured both attitudinally and in terms of actual participation. Methodologically, the first major decision was whether the information should be obtained by interviewing students or by means of postal questionnaires. There were many arguments in support of personal interviews, but the mail questionnaire was ultimately accepted as the better method, mainly because of the prevailing attitude of distrust within the student body at the time of the survey, which we believed would militate against a satisfactory response-rate in an interview survey. A further consideration was the imminence of both examinations and the summer vacation, which we expected would have a greater effect in lowering the ultimate response-rate to an interview as compared with a postal survey. In previous postal surveys of students of the School satisfactorily high response-rates of 80% or more had been achieved and although special problems were anticipated, due both to the need for student assurance of complete anonymity and the pressure of examinations, we believed that an adequate response-rate would be obtained. Having decided on the postal questionnaire as the only feasible approach, we were then led to consider what size of sample should be used. However, as the School authorities in giving permission for the survey to be carried out asked for complete coverage of all full-time students, no sampling was required.

The coverage of the questionnaire (see Appendix A) was dictated by the objectives of the survey and the fact that it was to be administered by post. The questions fell into three main areas: participation in most of the important events during the crisis weeks, attitudes towards these events, and those attitudes and characteristics of students potentially associated with support for the demonstrations. In the latter category we covered in some detail the family and educational backgrounds of students, their political views, their participation in student societies, their courses of study and their attitudes towards the Students' Union and other aspects of life as a student at L.S.E. One major omission from the questionnaire was any direct questions concerning the reasons for the demonstrations or the participant's own reasons for supporting them. We were, perhaps, too ready to accept the view put forward by many of those who opposed the survey that no useful information on this complex matter could be obtained from a postal questionnaire. Other questions of potential interest were not asked because of the need to limit the length of the questionnaire.

Most questions were precoded and although the questionnaire was eight pages in length it could be completed fairly quickly.

Only about 5% of respondents took advantage of the suggestion that qualifications to answers could be written on the reverse sides of pages. The specific areas covered in the section on political attitudes, such as views about Vietnam and comprehensive schools, were determined by a small pilot-study in which students were asked to specify the political issues they considered to be of most importance internationally and nationally. The questionnaire was piloted before being sent out, though only a small pilot-study was attempted due to the intention to cover all full-time students in the main survey.

In order to maximise the response-rate to the survey, the active co-operation of the Students' Union was sought and obtained. A special procedure (see Appendix B) was devised to guarantee the anonymity of respondents, whilst ensuring that initial non-respondents could be contacted later. After two follow-ups of non-respondents the final response-rate from all full-time students was 80%. Seventeen per cent of undergraduates, 26% of postgraduates and 24% of students on diploma courses did not complete the questionnaire. Among undergraduates a slightly lower response was obtained from third years than from other students. A full analysis of non-response is given in Appendix B.

In considering the limitations of the information obtained, the 20% of non-respondents must be borne in mind. We have no information about the involvement of these students in the demonstrations or their attitudes towards them. Although it seems probable that the non-respondents were on the whole more apathetic and uninvolved than the respondents, mistrust of the anonymity of the survey procedure may have led to some non-response on the part of participants. In spite of the special precautions we took to ensure anonymity and our explanation of them in the covering letter sent out with the questionnaires, some participants still objected to the identifying code-number and others removed it.

An analysis of the attitudes and participation-rates of respondents by the date of return of their questionnaires was carried out in order to discover whether there was any trend which might throw some light on the nature of non-respondents. Some of the results are shown in Appendix B. Neither for undergraduates nor for postgraduates was there any consistent trend in the nature of the reported support for the demonstrations over the eight-week period during which questionnaires were returned. The respondents who replied at the end of the period and who would have been non-respondents had an earlier closing-date been set, differed little in their replies from those who had replied much earlier. The analysis therefore provided no basis for assuming non-respondents to be in any way different from respondents in their support for the boycott and sit-in.

Because of the delay in obtaining access to the student lists, seven weeks elapsed between the end of the sit-in and the sending out of questionnaires. This delay may have resulted in some memory errors in the factual information concerning behaviour during the week of the sit-in, although the 'don't remember' answer-categories were resorted to by only a small percentage of students. Memory errors may also have entered into the information provided on attitudes towards the boycott and sit-in at their start and at the end of the Lent term. The possibility that some respondents deliberately gave false answers to the questions concerning the demonstrations also exists. There were, unfortunately, no external checks which could be applied to test the validity of the information.

The uniqueness of the events during the period of crisis and the high degree of emotional involvement of most students, leads us to expect, however, that memory errors in information concerning actions in this period would be of negligible importance. And, although individual errors due to memory failure or to deliberate lying may have occurred, these could operate in different directions and we would expect net errors to be small. The timing of the survey must, however, be regarded as a potential source of bias in the information collected concerning attitudes towards the School and the Union. We accept that attitudes of satisfaction or dissatisfaction towards aspects of the School or the Union, and views concerning student representation, were measured at a point in time when students could be expected to feel more strongly than either earlier or later. In reporting the survey results in these areas (Chapters 4, 5 and 6) our emphasis is therefore upon the differences in the expressed attitudes of the various sub-groups of students on the questions covered. Without comparative data from other universities or from L.S.E. in earlier years, the absolute figures are in any case of limited value.

The survey report falls into two distinct parts and the reader whose concern is primarily with student unrest may wish to read only Part 2, in which the main facts and findings concerning the 1967 student protest at the School are discussed. However, in the course of the survey a wealth of information about students' background characteristics, political views, participation in student activities and attitudes towards the School was obtained in order to relate these factors to support for the demonstrations. Because of the shortage of data of this type, together with the growing national concern with the student problem, we decided to devote Part 1 of the report to a discussion of our findings in each area, quoting comparable data from other universities whenever these could be obtained.

The nature of the report is predominantly descriptive rather than explanatory. Some of the relationships found may appear to be casual but, without more information and more sophisticated methods of multivariate analysis, inferences from the data concerning the causes, either of the conflict at the School, or of student unrest in general, must remain speculative. In describing L.S.E. students in 1967 and the nature and extent of those in support of the boycott and sit-in we hope, however, to have provided a factual record of those events which may, in conjunction with similar studies carried out in other universities, contribute towards an understanding of the phenomenon of student protest.

No more up-to-date data on the attitudes of all L.S.E. students are available than those reported here. The authors sought permission from the School authorities in November 1968, after a week-end 'occupation' of the school buildings by students, to carry out a further survey on a sample basis.[7] Permission was not obtained because of the potential effect which the school authorities believed such a survey might have on the response to another survey, on teaching-methods, planned for January 1969. This survey did not in fact take place at the time intended owing to the closure of the School for three weeks in February 1969, following further student protest.

B*

Part 1

L.S.E. students in 1967

Chapter 2

Characteristics of L.S.E. students

The London School of Economics is in many ways a unique university institution. It was founded in 1894 by a group of Fabian socialists, largely in an attempt to remedy the lack of provision for research and training in the social sciences that then existed in the country. It has since gained a world-wide reputation in these fields, and is still essentially a ' one-faculty' institution, studying and teaching every branch of the social sciences. It was planned from the start to attract more mature students, especially those in employment, and students from overseas and to become a centre for research and postgraduate study; it has in these respects, also, largely kept to its founders' intentions.

This chapter discusses the composition of the School's student population in terms of these and other factors, drawing, where possible, on comparative information from other universities; its main purpose is to provide a framework for the interpretation of the remaining chapters. The chapter begins with a description of student numbers, nationality, fields of study, sex and age; this is followed by a consideration of the social and educational background of home students, and the chapter ends with a brief account of students' living accommodation. Except in the short section on student numbers the discussion is confined to full-time students. Almost all the data are drawn from the 1967 student survey and relate to the academic year 1966/7.

Student numbers[1]

In terms of student numbers, the School is a medium-sized university institution. In 1966/7, there were 3,833 students, more than in any previous or subsequent year.[2] The majority, 77% of students, were on full-time courses, and the remainder were on part-time courses.[3] Of full-time students, almost two-thirds (62%) were undergraduates and 38% were postgraduates. Thus, the long-standing emphasis on part-time study and on postgraduate study at the L.S.E. continued to be much greater than at other universities, for only 8% of all students at universities in the United Kingdom were on part-time courses, and only 17% of full-time students were on postgraduate courses.

There has been a rapid expansion in student numbers at the L.S.E. in the sixties, with the number of full-time students increasing by 30% between 1961/2 and 1966/7. While such growth has not been unusual in British universities during this period, it has at L.S.E., unlike other universities, been characterised by a relatively greater emphasis on postgraduate than on undergraduate studies, with the number of postgraduates increasing by 38% and under-graduates by 25% over the period.

Nationality
The L.S.E. has always attracted large numbers of overseas students. They have usually formed approximately a third of all full-time students, and in 1966/7 the proportion was 31%, with roughly equal numbers coming from Commonwealth and other countries. This proportion has always been about three times the com-parable figure for all universities in the United Kingdom, which in 1966/7 was 9%.[4] The majority (69%) of overseas students at the L.S.E. study at postgraduate level; thus, overseas postgraduates form over a half (52%) of all postgraduates at the School, but only 14% of undergraduates come from overseas.

Table 2.1 Overseas students: by country of origin

Percentages

	Australasia	Canada	Europe	U.S.A.	Africa	Asia	Central or South America	West Indies	Total	N
Under-graduates	1	2	16	21	23	32	1	4	100	205
Post-graduates	5	15	11	35	12	16	4	2	100	421
All	4	11	13	30	15	21	3	3	100	626

Note: The nationality of 1% of overseas students was unclassifiable. These are excluded from the table.

In the 1967 student survey, 28% of all students were from overseas, and their country of origin is shown in Table 2.1.[5] The largest proportion of students comes from the United States, followed by Asia, Africa, Europe and Canada. The composition of overseas students in terms of nationality differs for undergraduates and postgraduates, and it is perhaps noteworthy that, whereas 60% of overseas undergraduates come from developing countries, they account for only 34% of postgraduates, the majority of whom are from industrialised Western countries.

Fields of study
As has been mentioned, perhaps the best-known feature of the School is that it is an institution devoted almost exclusively to the social sciences. No more than 6% of its students are classified by the University Grants Committee as being in an Arts faculty, and no pure science or technological subject is taught. The School has always trained a very large proportion of all United Kingdom students in the social sciences. At one time, this almost amounted to a monopoly, but in the last decade, with the rapid expansion of Social Sciences in other universities and institutions,[6] its predominance in this respect has declined. Even so, in 1965/6, L.S.E. had only 1.5% of all full-time students at universities in the United Kingdom, but 11% of those studying economics, 29% of those studying politics and 15% of those studying sociology.[7]

The majority of undergraduates (65%) are studying for the B.Sc.(Econ.) degree, in which students take a general first-year course including compulsory papers in economics, government and history, but specialise in the remaining two years in one of a number of subjects including various aspects of economics, history, politics, sociology and statistics. The remaining students study for specialist degrees in anthropology, geography, law, history, philosophy and economics or sociology.[8] Table 2.2 shows the distribution of undergraduates by field of study.[9] The largest proportion (31%) study economics, followed by 23% studying politics and history and 18% sociology. Some 9% are classified as being in 'other' fields of study and, of these, 6% are on a one-year 'general' course not leading to a degree. Almost all those on a 'general' course are overseas students, which is one of the reasons for the marked difference between home and overseas students in fields of study.[10] Economics is the largest group among home

Table 2.2 Distribution of students: by field of study

Percentages

	Economics	Geography	Law	Politics	Social Administration	Sociology	Other	Total	N
Undergraduates									
Home	29	10	12	25	19		5	100	1197
Overseas	39	(–)	9	12	7		33	100	206
All	31	9	11	23	18		8	100	1403
Postgraduates									
Degree									
Home	30	7	4	22	4	27	6	100	227
Overseas	34	4	11	28	2	15	6	100	346
All	32	5	8	26	3	20	6	100	573
Diploma									
Home	5	0	0	0	91	2	2	100	159
Overseas	5	0	0	0	82	6	7	100	38
All	5	0	0	0	89	2	4	100	197
All students	29	7	10	22	26		7	100	2175

Notes: 1. The field of study of 3% of students is not known; these are ex-
cluded from the table.
2. Departments have been grouped to form fields of study as fol-
lows:
Economics – Accounting, Economics and Statistics (which includes Computing, Demography, Operational Research and Mathematics)
Geography
Law
Politics – Economic History, Government, International History
and International Relations.
Social Sciences and Administration
Sociology – Anthropology, Social Psychology and Sociology
Other – Industrial Relations and Philosophy, Logic and Scientific
Method; also included are undergraduates on a general
course and postgraduates not attached to a department
or who were attached to more than one department.

undergraduates, but there are reasonably large numbers in each field of study. Among overseas students, 33% are classified as ' other '—30% of whom are on a general course. If these are excluded, then economics is by far the most dominant subject. In terms of country of origin, almost all students from the United States and a third of those from Europe are on a ' general ' course, but almost all from Africa and Asia and other countries are studying for first degrees.

Postgraduates, as defined in the survey (see Appendix B), study for a number of different qualifications. The largest group (39%) study for the one-year M.Sc., while 17% are Ph.D. students and 15% study for other Masters degrees. Almost a quarter (23%) are on diploma courses. As can be seen from Table 2.2, the large majority of both home and overseas diploma-students are studying social administration. Among postgraduate degree-students, the largest fields of study are economics, followed by politics and history, and sociology; home and overseas students follow much the same pattern in this respect.

Sex, age and marital status

As at most universities, some three-quarters (76%) of students at L.S.E. are men, with the proportion being rather higher among undergraduates (77%) than among postgraduates (68%), and also higher among overseas students (79%) than among home students (72%).

The higher-than-average numbers of overseas and postgraduate students leads one to expect that L.S.E. has a relatively high proportion of older and mature students. In 1966/7, the median age of all full-time students at universities in the United Kingdom was 20.7 years, and 11% were aged 25 or over; but at the L.S.E. the median age was 21.9 and 26% were aged 25 or over.[11]

The age distribution of students in the survey is given in Appendix C, Table 2.1A, and Table 2.3 summarises this information. Undergraduates are, of course, younger on average than postgraduates, and home students are younger than overseas students, with over a half of overseas postgraduates being aged 26 or over. The ages of students by country of origin is shown in Appendix C, Table 2.2A, and quite wide variations are apparent. It is particularly noticeable that, while students from the United States have much the same age structure as that of home students, undergradu-

ates from Africa and Europe and postgraduates from Asia and
Europe are on average much older than others.

Table 2.3 Age of students

	Median age (in years)	Percentage of students aged 26 or over
Undergraduates		
Home	20.7	8
Overseas	22.0	21
All	20.9	10
Postgraduates		
Home	24.5	27
Overseas	26.0	50
All	25.2	39
All students	22.0	21

Note: The age distribution of students is given in Appendix C, Table 2.1A

Given a student population with this age structure, it is not
surprising to find that 17% of all full-time students are married;
the proportion is higher among postgraduates than among undergraduates and is higher among overseas students than among home
students. (See Appendix C, Table 2.3A.)

Social and educational background of home students
This section considers the social and educational background of
home students and, where possible, introduces comparative information for other universities. In the student survey some comparable but much more limited information was collected for overseas students and is included in footnotes in this section and in
tables in Appendix C.
Social background
In the United Kingdom, entry into higher education is closely
related to social background. Relative to their numbers in the
population as a whole, students from middle-class, higher-income
backgrounds are over-represented in universities, and students at
the L.S.E. conform to this general pattern.

In the survey, students were asked to place their father's current
occupation into one of a number of occupational categories,[12] and
Table 2.4 shows the occupational distribution of those who were

in employment.[13] As can be seen, students at L.S.E. were much more likely to come from middle- rather than working-class backgrounds. Over all, only 20% came from homes where the father is in a manual occupation, although some two-thirds or more of the employed population of the United Kingdom can be classified as manual workers. This social class bias tends to be stronger among postgraduates than undergraduates, as only 15% of the former but 22% of the latter came from manual backgrounds; diploma courses, in particular, seem to attract very few working-class students. A further feature of the table is that more students, particularly among those on diploma courses, came from ' professional' backgrounds than from any other single group. This is perhaps to be expected, since most professional people are themselves likely to have taken a course in higher education, and to be more likely than others to encourage their children to follow their example.

Table 2.4 Social Class (Father's Occupation)

Home students

Percentages

	Non-manual				Manual				
	Professional	Managerial	Own business	Clerical	Skilled manual	Semi-skilled manual	Unskilled manual	Total	N
Undergraduates	29	22	14	12	13	5	4	100	999
Postgraduates									
Degree	36	20	14	12	12	3	3	100	181
Diploma	47	17	19	7	5	4	1	100	103
All	40	19	16	10	10	3	2	100	284
All students	32	22	15	11	12	4	4	100	1283

Note: The table includes only those fathers currently in the employed working-force. It excludes those who are dead or retired, or where the answer was unclassifiable or where the student did not know or gave no answer. For all home students these proportions were respectively 16%, 3%, 1%, 2%. The proportions dead or retired were much higher for postgraduates (26%) than for undergraduates (12%).

Among undergraduates, men and women were almost equally likely to come from non-manual backgrounds; the only marked difference was that far more women (40%) than men (28%) came from professional backgrounds. (See Appendix C, Table 2.4A.) Among postgraduates, however, there are major social-class differences between men and women, as 19% of men but only 10% of women came from manual backgrounds. This difference is only partly explained by the inclusion of diploma students (the large majority of whom were women on social administration courses) in the postgraduate group since postgraduate degree students follow the same pattern.

The preponderance of middle-class students is, of course, a general characteristic of the United Kingdom higher education system and particularly of its universities. Comparable data for other universities are not easily obtained, but some are shown in Table 2.5. The latest national figure for the percentage of undergraduates from manual backgrounds, 25%, relates to 1961/2, and has not changed to any great extent for some thirty years.[14] The L.S.E. figure is near this national average and falls more or less in the middle of the later figures given for other universities.

For postgraduates, the latest national figure again relates to 1961/2, and in this case the L.S.E. figure for postgraduate degree-students is only half the national average. Thus, while nationally there are proportionally more postgraduates than undergraduates from manual backgrounds, implying that working-class undergraduates are more likely than others to proceed to postgraduate work, the reverse is true at the L.S.E. Why this is so is rather difficult to discover. The national data refer to a period prior to the big expansion in the number of postgraduates in the 1960s, and the position could have changed by 1966/7. They also refer to students in all faculties, whereas L.S.E. competes for students only in the Social Sciences. There is some evidence that nationally at undergraduate level the Social Sciences recruit fewer than the average proportions of students from manual backgrounds[15], and it is possible, of course, that this is also true at a postgraduate level. One reason, probably specific to the L.S.E., is that it attracts as many as 25% of its postgraduate degree students from Oxford and Cambridge, and very few (7%) of these students come from a manual background.

Table 2.5 Percentage of students from manual backgrounds at L.S.E. and other universities

Home students

	Percentage of students from manual backgrounds
Undergraduates	
L.S.E. 1966/7	22
Essex 1966/7, entrants	29
Sussex, 1966/7, entrants	23
Manchester 1963	33
Edinburgh 1964	15
Durham 1964	21
Newcastle 1964	20
Brunel 1964/5, entrants	34
All universities 1961/2	25
Postgraduates	
L.S.E. 1966/7 (degree students only)	18
All universities 1961/2	25

Sources: All universities 1961/2 – Committee on Higher Education, 1961/3, *Higher Education,* Appendix II B.

Essex and Sussex 1966/7 – private communication from the Socio-educational Research Unit, Sussex.

Edinburgh, Durham and Newcastle 1964 – J. Abbot, Social Class in Three Northern Universities, *British Journal of Sociology,* Vol. 16, No. 3 (1965).

Brunel 1964/5 – Private communication from D. Marsland, Department of Social Science, Brunel University.

From the social class composition of home students, it is a reasonable prediction that they also come from relatively wealthy backgrounds. According to information obtained in the student survey,[16] the median annual income of students' fathers was approximately £1680, with 26% earning more than £2500 per annum and only 20% earning less than £1000 per annum. This income distribution is obviously quite untypical of the population as a whole, and might be compared with the annual incomes of all heads of households in Great Britain between the ages of forty and sixty-five: these, in 1965, had a median annual income of £936, with only 3% earning more than £2500 per annum and as many as 59% earning less than £1000 per annum.[17]

In view of the importance attached to students' political views in any study of student protest, it was felt necessary to obtain some idea of the political allegiances of students' parents. In the survey, students were asked to indicate which, if any, political party their parents had voted for in the last national election, which had taken place on 31 March 1966, and had been won, with a large majority, by the Labour Party. A very strong relationship exists in the United Kingdom, as in any society, between social class and political views, and given the largely middle-class nature of the L.S.E. student body one could not expect the national voting-pattern to be reproduced. Table 2.6 shows the extent of the difference, with the parents of students at the School being more likely to vote Conservative, slightly more likely to vote Liberal and less likely to vote Labour than the electorate as a whole.[18] On average, the voting pattern of undergraduates' parents is much the same as that of postgraduates' parents; but within the latter category distinct differences are apparent between diploma and degree students, with

Table 2.6 Voting of students' parents in the 1966 General Election

Home students

	Parents who voted				Percentages	
	Con.	Lib.	Lab.	Other	Total	N
All parents						
Undergraduates	47	12	40	1	100	1857
Postgraduates						
Degree	43	10	46	1	100	350
Diploma	50	18	31	1	100	219
All	46	13	40	1	100	569
All students	47	12	40	1	100	2426
All students						
Fathers only	45	11	42	2	100	1155
Mothers only	47	13	38	2	100	1271
National	42	8	48	2	100	—

Source: National data from D. E. Butler and A. King, *The British General Election of 1966.*

Note: The table includes only those parents reported as having voted in the General Election held in March 1966. Four per cent of parents had not voted, compared with 25% nationally; 5% were dead; in 6% of cases the student did not know his parents' vote (these were largely women who did not know their father's vote) and 2% did not answer this question.

the parents of diploma students being much more likely to vote Conservative and especially Liberal. Generally, as shown in the table, there was little difference between the voting-pattern of mothers and fathers.

Thus the difference between L.S.E. parents and national voting figures is in the anticipated direction, with the relatively larger middle class composition at L.S.E. leading to a tendency to vote more to the right than left of the political spectrum. But what is surprising is that the difference is much smaller than one might expect, and leads to a suspicion that parents' political opinions within each social class are quite different from those nationally. Table 2.7 makes this comparison and shows that the suspicion is confirmed; for within manual and particularly non-manual categories L.S.E. parents were much more likely than the population as a whole to vote Labour and less likely to vote Conservative.[19] If four rather than two social-class categories are used (i.e. middle, lower middle, skilled working and other), the same result is found within each category.

Table 2.7 Voting in the 1966 General Election: by social class

Home Students

	Con.	Lib.	Lab.	Other	Percentages Total
L.S.E. parents					
Non-manual	51	14	34	1	100
Manual	24	7	68	1	100
National					
Non-manual	63	11	25	1	100
Manual	30	7	62	1	100

Source: National data from D. E. Butler and A. King, *The British General Election of 1966.*
Notes: 1. The data for L.S.E. parents include only those parents reported as having voted in the national election of March 1966.
2. The true national voting-pattern in the election by social class is of course not known. The data above are estimates based on voting intentions immediately prior to the election.

Of course, from these data one should not immediately conclude that L.S.E. students are more likely than others to come from relatively left-wing backgrounds. It is unlikely, but not impossible, that this is a characteristic of all university students or perhaps all social-science students. More probably it is at least partly a function of other factors, such as age, education or regional distribution, which have not been introduced.[20] Many hypotheses can easily be constructed to explain the differences found, but are almost impossible to test since no comparable data are available for students at other universities, and insufficient data exists on the characteristics of both the parents of L.S.E. students and national voting-pattern by age, education and other factors.

Educational background
Secondary schooling

Secondary schooling is highly correlated with entry into British universities; in general, all the evidence points to the fact that children, even within the same ability categories, are much more likely to gain a university place if they attend a non-maintained rather than a maintained school.[21] In the survey, students were asked to record which type of secondary school they had last attended, and the results are shown in Table 2.8.

Table 2.8 Secondary schooling

Home students

Percentages

	Maintained					Direct Grant	Independent	Other	Total	N
	Grammar	Technical or Central	Secondary Modern	Comprehensive						
Undergraduates	66	4	2	2	10	13	3	100	1191
Postgraduates									
Degree	50	3	(–)	2	20	22	3	100	239
Diploma	42	2	3	1	13	34	5	100	155
All	47	2	1	2	17	27	4	100	394
All students	61	4	2	2	12	16	3	100	1585

Notes: 1. Students were asked to indicate the last secondary school they had attended.

2. 'Other' includes schools which were unclassifiable and schools outside the United Kingdom.

3. The secondary schooling of 1% of home students is not known. These are excluded from the table.

In all, 69% of L.S.E. students had attended a maintained school, 12% a direct-grant school and 16% an independent school. This distribution differs quite markedly for postgraduates and undergraduates, with a much higher proportion of the former coming from the non-maintained sector. Given the strong relationship between social class and schooling, and the already discussed social-class composition of L.S.E. students, this postgraduate–undergraduate relationship is to be expected.

It is again difficult to obtain comparable data for other universities. As regards undergraduates, the latest national data, collected by the Robbins Committee, relates to 1961/2 and, as shown in Table 2.9, 63% of all students came from maintained schools. There is some evidence that this proportion had probably risen by 1966/7,[22] so that the schooling of L.S.E. undergraduates is probably much the same as for all undergraduates. As regards all university students in Social-Science faculties, there is no current information available, but the 1961/2 figure was only 55%; if this differential has been even only partly maintained over the intervening years, then it is likely that L.S.E. attracts at the undergraduate level a larger proportion of students from maintained schools than is average for the Social Sciences.[23] Some data are shown in the table for other universities over the same time-period, and of these L.S.E. has the highest proportion of maintained school students; one would, however, *a priori* expect the other universities to be below the national average.

It is not possible to decide whether the differences in the secondary schooling of undergraduates and postgraduates at L.S.E. holds for all universities. The only data on postgraduates again relates to all students in 1961/2 and shows that 69%, a higher proportion than for undergraduates, came from maintained schools. This pattern obviously follows that already found for the social class of students, and, again, problems arise due to the possibility of faculty differences and changes over time. As with the social-class differential, the large numbers of Oxford and Cambridge graduates in L.S.E. postgraduate school provide a partial explanation—as only 27% of these students come from maintained schools.

Qualifications—undergraduates

Entry to universities in England and Wales is usually based on the number and quality of passes obtained in the Advanced level examination of the General Certificate of Education.[24] At the

**Table 2.9 Percentage of students from maintained schools at L.S.E. and
other universities**

Home students

	Percentages from maintained schools
Undergraduates	
L.S.E. 1966/7	74
Sussex 1966/7 entrants	63
Essex 1966/7 entrants	69
Oxford 1966/7 entrants	40
All medical faculties 1966/7 entrants	54
All universities, entrants 1965/6	70
All social science faculties 1961/2	55
All universities 1961/2	63
Postgraduates	
L.S.E. (degree students) 1966/7	55
All universities 1961/2	69

Sources :	All students 1961/2	—Committee on Higher Education, 1961-63. *Higher Education,* Appendix II-B.
	Essex and Sussex 1966/7	—Private communication from the Socio-educational Research Unit, Sussex University.
	Oxford 1965/6	—University of Oxford, *Report of Commission of Inquiry,* vol. II.
	All medical faculties 1966/7	—*Royal Commission on Medical Education 1965-8 Report,* Cmnd. 3569 (H.M.S.O., 1968).
	All university entrants	—*Statistics of Education,* vol. II (1956-66).

Note : The data on all university entrants 1965/6, relates to school-leavers
in 1964/5 who were known to be entering university in October
1965.

L.S.E., entry standards and procedures are considered by the Admissions Committee, but each degree has its own sub-committee
to select its own entrants. By and large applicants need two Bs at
'A' level to ensure consideration. This is never a rigid requirement, particularly as the School accepts students with qualifications
other than 'A' levels, or on the basis of an entrance examination.
In the student survey 3% of undergraduates had no 'A' levels
and are excluded from consideration below.[25]

The large majority of students (86%) had three or more ' A ' levels, and almost all the remainder had two. The ' A ' level grades obtained are shown in Table 2.10, and 37% had at least three at grades A or B, 47% two grades A or B and 14% one grade A or B.[26]

These data are interesting in comparison with data for other universities, and the available evidence tends to show that L.S.E. attracts students of higher-than-average calibre (in terms of ' A ' level grades) and that competition for places is rather stronger than at other universities. Table 2.10 illustrates this, for the ' A ' level grades of both all L.S.E. undergraduates and of first years only, are very much better than those of all university entrants in 1966, with 84%, 87% and 55% respectively having two or more grades

Table 2.10 Number of 'A' levels at grades A or B
Home undergraduates

Percentages

| | Percentage with this number of 'A' levels at grades A or B | | | | |
	3 or more	2	1	0	Total
L.S.E., all students 1966/7	37	47	14	2	100
L.S.E. entrants 1966/7	36	51	12	1	100
All universities, entrants October 1966	23	32	26	19	100
All universities, entrants October 1967	22	30	29	19	100
All universities, entrants to social-science faculties, October 1967	18	37	33	12	100

Source : All universities—Universities Central Council for Admissions, *Fourth Report 1965/6, Statistical Supplement; Fifth Report 1966/7, Statistical Supplement;* U.C.C.A., London.

Notes : 1. See footnote 24.

2. The figures are based on all those with two or more 'A' level passes.

3. The figures for all universities relate to those who applied for entry through the U.C.C.A. Almost all entrants do so.

4. Entrants to Social Science faculties relate in the U.C.C.A. data to students who were accepted at a university and whose first choice was entry to a Social Science faculty.

A or B.[27] No information is available for 1966 entrants to all social-science faculties, but the figures are probably not too different to those for 1968 entrants; by comparison with these, L.S.E. students are seen to have on average far better 'A' level grades.

The only data comparing L.S.E. with individual universities relate to entrants in October 1964.[28] These data are given in Appendix C, Table 2.6, and show that, both in Social Science and Law faculties, L.S.E. had a higher percentage of entrants with 'good' 'A' levels than any other university.[29] The figure for Social Sciences (89%) is in fact as high a proportion as for any faculty in any university except for Pure Science at Bristol University.

Given the overall high standard of entry to L.S.E., the competition for places means that most sub-groups of students are not likely to vary significantly from the average standard. Some data are given in Appendix C, Table 2.7, and show that on average men have better 'A' levels than women; students from manual backgrounds have better 'A' levels than those from non-manual backgrounds and those from maintained schools have better 'A' levels than those from direct-grant or independent schools; in no case is the difference very large.

Rather more variation is found for students in different fields of study, with economics 40%, and politics 37%, attracting the highest proportions of students with three or more 'A' levels at grades A or B. If these combined fields of study are sub-divided, then the range increases quite considerably, with 58% of students in the Statistics Department compared with 23% in Accounting having three or more grades A or B; but most other departments still fall within the 30-40% range.

There are also quite wide variations between students reading for different degrees, with B.Sc.(Econ.) students having rather better 'A' levels than others. This probably reflects different entry requirements and perhaps the relative attractiveness to good applicants of a more general to a more specialised degree. The difference is confirmed if one looks at geography and sociology, for these subjects can be taken either in the B.Sc.(Econ.) or as a specialised degree, and in both cases one finds the quality of 'A' levels of B.Sc.(Econ.) students to be higher.[30]

Qualifications—postgraduate degree students

Entry to postgraduate degree-courses is dependent on the quality of a student's first degree; only in a very few cases, about 1%, are

qualifications other than a degree accepted. Numbers of home postgraduates accepted are also determined by the number of grants
made available to the School by the Social Science Research Council and the Science Research Council.

Table 2.11 shows the university which postgraduate degree
students had previously attended.[31] Four per cent had degrees from
a foreign university and 4% had degrees from non-university
institutions. The most striking feature of the table, however, is that
only a minority (26%) of postgraduates, graduated at L.S.E.;
nationally, the proportion is over twice as large.[32] L.S.E., in fact,
attracts more students from Oxford and Cambridge (29%) than
from any other university group. The relatively low proportion
of L.S.E. graduates seems to be consistent with other information
which shows that, over the last ten years, as the total number of
postgraduate students has increased, the proportion of L.S.E.
graduates among entrants has decreased from 67% in 1957/8 to
48% in 1960/1 to 40% in 1963/4.[33] The introduction of the one-
year M.Sc. degree in 1964/5 and the rapid expansion of the
graduate school have probably accentuated this trend.

Table 2.11   Previous university of postgraduate degree students
Home postgraduates

Percentages

Previous University	Percentage who took a degree at this university
L.S.E.	26
Other London	11
Oxford and Cambridge	29
Other United Kingdom	26
Non-university institution	4
Foreign university	4
Total	100
N	227

Note: The previous university of 5% of home postgraduate degree students
is not known: they are excluded from the table.

The social and educational background of postgraduates from
different universities is entirely consistent with the known characteristics of entrants to these universities. Thus, while 30% of the

postgraduates at L.S.E. from 'other' universities[34] were from working-class backgrounds, the comparable proportions are 22% for L.S.E. and only 7% for Oxford and Cambridge. In terms of secondary schooling, the relative proportions of students from maintained schools are 72%, 71% and 27%.

The quality of first degrees of postgraduates was predictably

Table 2.12 Class of first degrees obtained by postgraduate degree-students: by previous university

Home postgraduates

Percentages

	First	Upper Second	Undifferentiated Second	Lower Second	Third	Other	Total	N
			Class of degree					
Previous university								
L.S.E.	18	70	0	5	0	7	100	57
Other London	(17)	(60)	(0)	(17)	(4)	(0)	100	23
Oxford and Cambridge	11	29	50	6	3	–	100	62
Other United Kingdom	20	66	4	5	2	4	100	56
Non-university institution	(0)	(33)	(12)	(33)	(11)	(11)	100	9
All	15	54	17	8	2	4	100	207
All universities, students graduating in 1966								
Social Science, Arts and Language faculties	4	24	14	36	14	18	100	13403
All faculties	7	22	8	28	14	21	100	29964

Source: All universities—Department of Education and Science, *Statistics of Education 1966*, vol. 6. Universities (H.M.S.O., 1969).

Notes: 1. The data from the student survey excludes the 13% of home students who had no first degree, a degree from a foreign university or gave a university without giving the class of degree.

2. The data for students graduating in 1966 at all universities in the United Kingdom exclude those graduating in medicine, dentistry or health.

higher than average, as is shown in Table 2.12. Thus 15% of postgraduates had obtained first-class honours and 69% either a first or an upper second, as compared with 7% and 29% respectively of students in all universities in the United Kingdom graduating in 1966. The overall standards were much the same for students from each university group.

The proportion of entrants to higher degree courses who have first-class honours has fluctuated over the past few years, from 15% in 1957/8 to 24% in 1961/2 and 22% in 1963/4; the proportion with first or upper seconds has, however, declined from 74% to 76% to 64%.[35] The data from the survey which relate to all postgraduate degree students, and is not inconsistent with these trends and the drop in the proportion of firsts is probably due to the large increase in the size of the L.S.E. postgraduate school and also in the number of universities in the United Kingdom who offer postgraduate degrees in the Social Sciences.

Qualifications—diploma students

The pattern of qualifications held by diploma students was quite different from that of postgraduate degree students. This is to be expected, since diploma courses can be categorised into those requiring a degree or its equivalent as an entry qualification and those to which entry is based on qualifications other than a degree or through practical experience together with an entrance examination.

Thus a quarter of diploma students had no ' A ' levels. Thirty per cent had no qualifications at a higher-education level; 51% had obtained a first degree and 13% had qualifications other than a degree. Of those with a first degree, 5% had firsts and 35% a first or an upper second; very few (5%) had a degree from L.S.E.

There is a clear relationship between schooling and qualifications among diploma students. Of those with no qualifications at a higher education level, 59% had been to an independent school, and only 39% to a maintained school; of those with a qualification, only 27% had been to an independent school and 55% to a maintained school (the remainder in both cases had attended a direct-grant school).

Employment

Many undergraduates do not enter university immediately on leaving school. Some enter full-time courses at other institutions of further education, often to improve their 'A' level qualifications; others enter employment for a short period either for money or experience; and a further group only decide or are qualified to enter university long after leaving school.

It is therefore not surprising to find that as many as 38% of home undergraduates at L.S.E. had entered six or more months after leaving school;[36] this is rather higher than the comparable proportions of 30% for all universities in 1961/2 but less than that for social studies students (47%).[37]

Only a minority of these 'late' entrants (15%) had taken a full-time course in further education, with 10% obtaining some qualifications. The large majority (90%) had been in full-time employment, in most cases (47%) for less than one year, but in some (28%) for two or more years.

There was little variation in the proportions of students from different social classes who did not come to university straight from school, but their apparent reasons for not doing so were different. Two-thirds of late entrants from non-manual backgrounds had spent less than one year in employment; but of those from manual backgrounds almost a half had been employed for two or more years.

Late entry is also related to secondary schooling, with 69% of those from maintained grammar and direct-grant schools coming to university immediately, compared with 55% and 59% of those from other maintained and independent schools respectively. However, as one might expect, the employment-patterns of students from the latter types of schools is strongly related to their social origin, so that 65% of late entrants from independent schools had had less than a year's employment, compared with the 48% from other maintained schools who had been employed for two or more years.

The employment patterns of postgraduate degree and diploma students differed quite substantially as one might expect from the evidence on their ages and qualifications.[38] Almost a half (47%) of degree students had no employment experience, compared with 27% of diploma students; all the latter had taken first degrees. At the other end of the scale, 24% of degree students had spent two or more years in employment, compared with 48% of diploma students.

Living accommodation

Students' accommodation may be classified into homes of parents or guardians, halls or hostels, which are usually owned by the university, and lodgings. This latter category varies from lodgings with full board to self-contained flats or houses. The most important distinction, certainly from the point of view of the social life and corporate activity of a college, as well as of students' own freedom of movement, is perhaps between lodgings where week-day evening meals are included in the rent and those where they are not. This distinction is drawn in the survey results, and the categories are respectively called ' lodgings ' and ' flats '.

L.S.E. draws about a quarter of its full-time students from the Greater London area, but, as Table 2.13 shows, only 15% live at home, the majority opting to live elsewhere. A fifth (20%) live in either a hall or a hostel; L.S.E. itself owns two halls of residence, and there are a number of London University and private halls and hostels. The majority of students (53%) live in flats, and only a few (8%) live in the relatively restricted atmosphere of lodgings. A further 4% of students live in ' other ' accommodation, and these were usually older married students who owned their own homes.

This pattern of accommodation will obviously vary for different categories of students. More home than overseas students live with their parents, as do more undergraduates than postgraduates, but many more overseas students than home students live in hall; and for each category of students almost all the remainder appear to prefer flats of various kinds to lodgings. This latter category is only at all large (12%) for home undergraduates, and even here it varies markedly with year of course. First-year students are likely to be more conservative in their choice of accommodation and know little of the intricacies of the London accommodation-market. Thus, 20% of home first-year undergraduates lived in lodgings, but by the third year this had been reduced to 8%.

Apart from differences in costs and amenities, the various types of accommodation also tend to vary in terms of distance from L.S.E.[39] On average L.S.E. students had a thirty-three-minute journey from home to the School and 6% had over an hour's journey. Halls and hostels are almost all in central London, and here the median travelling-time was only twenty minutes. Lodgings seem on average to be substantially further from the centre than

Table 2.13 Living accommodation

Percentages

	Home of parent or guardian	Hall or hostel	Lodgings	Flat	Other	Total	N
Home students							
Undergraduates	22	20	12	43	3	100	1202
Postgraduates	13	9	4	64	16	100	397
All	20	18	10	48	5	100	1599
Overseas students							
Undergraduates	10	32	4	58	1	100	203
Postgraduates	2	26	4	66	2	100	424
All	4	28	4	62	3	100	627
All students	15	20	8	53	4	100	2226

Notes: 1. Lodgings is defined as accommodation with at least weekday evening meals included in the rent; other rented accommodation is included in ' flat '—in almost all cases this amounted to rented or leased accommodation without any meals.

2. The living accommodation of a small number (less than 1%) of students is not known. These are excluded from the table.

flats (forty-one minutes, compared with thirty-three minutes), but most students living with their parents had an even longer journey—with an average of fifty minutes, and 21% spending over an hour.

A student's living accommodation is also important from the point of view of his work, and in the survey, students were asked whether they had adequate facilities for study in their accommodation. Over all, 14% were dissatisfied with their accommodation in this respect. As perhaps should be the case, those living in halls, at home or in other accommodation were the least dissatisfied (8% in each case), with the proportions being much higher in flats (20%) and lodgings (18%).

Chapter 3

Political attitudes

This chapter examines the political attitudes of the L.S.E. students. We treat the subject in some detail here both because of its importance in understanding the student's role in society outside the university and because of its bearing on his attitudes and behaviour within it. The political attitudes of students have always attracted particular interest in the world beyond the university, if only because today's students are likely to furnish tomorrow's elites. Recently, events in Europe have given a more immediate significance to their political views by showing that they can have an important influence on national politics while they are still at university. When we turn to examine the more local problems of the students' relations with the academic institution it quickly becomes evident that their attitudes to the question of organisation and representation as well as their reactions to crises such as the sit-in and boycott are closely related to their political orientation. In the present chapter we confine ourselves to describing the nature of students' political views and considering some of the more important background characteristics which may have been related to their formation. In subsequent chapters on attitude to the School and participation in the sit-in and boycott, political orientation is used as one of the key variables in the analysis.

Home students
In this section we examine the students' party preferences and try to assess the importance of politics to them in terms of interest and party membership. We then consider views on particular political issues and the extent to which they are related to party preference.
Party allegiance and voting
Two questions were used in the survey to measure attitude to political parties. The first question allowed the respondent to be more discriminating, asking which political party or group most nearly reflected his views. The second question, which asked how he would vote if there were a general election on the following day,

made it possible to compare ideal choice with response to the
reality of a two-party system.

In the following analysis the first question has been used when
party attitudes are involved, unless otherwise stated. The various
small parties and groups to the left of Labour are combined into
a single category referred to as the 'Left-wing Groups'. When
Labour and the Left-wing Groups are combined they are referred
to collectively as the 'left'. When the terms 'centre' and 'right'
are used, they refer to the Liberals and Conservatives respectively.

Table 3.1 Party allegiance

Home students

Percentages

	Conservative	Liberal	Labour	Left-wing groups	Other	Total	N
			Party allegiance				
Undergraduates	20	16	42	9	13	100	1206
Postgraduates	12	14	53	9	12	100	400
All	18	16	45	9	12	100	1606

The popular view of the L.S.E. as a stronghold of the left finds
some support from Table 3.1, at least as far as the politics of the
British-born students there are concerned. Taking all home students
together, 45% stated a preference for the Labour Party and a
further 9% for the Left-wing Groups.[1] Only 18% were Conservatives and 16% Liberals. Postgraduates were markedly more inclined to the left than undergraduates: 62 per cent supported
Labour and Left-wing Groups, compared with 51% of the undergraduates.

When students were faced with the choice involved in a general
election there was predictably some polarisation of party preferences, but the changes involved were not large and the movement
from the centre was mainly to the left. Thus the proportion of
Liberal supporters dropped by almost a third, Labour picked up
by 3%, while the increase in Conservative support, which was con-

Table 3.2 Voting intentions

Home students

Percentages

	Conservative	Liberal	Labour	Communist	Other	None don't know	Total	N
				Voting intentions				
Undergraduates	20	12	45	3	12	8	100	1206
Postgraduates	13	10	56	5	9	7	100	400
All	18	11	48	3	12	8	100	1606

fined to postgraduates, was too small to show in the rounded percentage-figure for all home students choosing this party.

National opinion at this time was much more evenly divided between Labour and Conservative. A sample interviewed by National Opinion Polls in June 1967 found 46% would vote for Labour in a general election, 43% for the Conservatives and 9% for the Liberals.[2] However, unqualified comparisons with national data can be misleading, since the composition of the populations compared is different. In this case differences in the proportions in each social class in the two populations were very marked. As we have pointed out in Chapter 2, 78% of L.S.E. students came from non-manual backgrounds. This compares with 33% of the male working population as a whole.[3] Given that a large majority of those in non-manual occupations usually vote for the Conservatives, we might have expected L.S.E. students to be *more* Conservative as a body than a national sample rather than less. Comparison of the voting of professional and managerial, and semi-skilled and unskilled classes in the National Opinion Polls sample with data in the L.S.E. survey shows most strikingly the manner in which opinion at L.S.E. deviated from national trends. Students from the homes of semi-skilled and unskilled workers were no more inclined to vote Labour than those in the same class interviewed in the national sample, but students from professional and managerial homes were far more likely to favour Labour than voters in this class in the country as a whole. While 72% of the professional and managerial class interviewed by National Opinion Polls said they would vote Conservative, compared to 19% Labour and 9% Liberal, at L.S.E. 45% of the students from the same class chose Labour, 24% the Conservatives and 11% the Liberals. However, students differed less markedly in their voting-preferences from their parents. As we have shown in Chapter 2, there was a substantially higher level of support for Labour and lower level of support for the Conservatives amongst parents in professional and managerial occupations than in this class in the country as a whole.

Interest in national politics and party membership

Neither voting-intention nor party allegiance necessarily indicate the importance of politics to the student. It is, for example, quite possible to support a party without being engaged in political activities or even being particularly interested in politics. Consequently, to obtain some evidence of the nature of student involvement, questions were included on the level of interest in national politics and on party membership.

Table 3.3 Interest in national politics

Home Students

Percentages

	Interest in national politics					
	Very interested	Moderately interested	Slightly interested	Not interested no answer	Total	N
Undergraduates	42	45	9	4	100	1206
Postgraduates	40	47	10	3	100	400
All	42	45	9	4	100	1606

Most home students claimed to be moderately or very interested in national politics. The student who wrote in on his questionnaire that 'politics are a drag' and suggested the slogan 'tune in and drop out' was clearly in the minority. Nevertheless, it is difficult to give much meaning to these answers on their own and, unfortunately, no comparative data are available from other British student surveys. However, there is some evidence that the L.S.E. student was much more interested in politics than the electorate as a whole.

Replies to a similar question put to a national sample showed only 15% were very interested compared with 42% of home students at L.S.E.[4] It seemed that this substantial difference in interest level might be accounted for by differences in the class composition of the two populations compared, but the separate data for middle- and working-classes in the national sample show this was not the case: taking middle-class respondents alone the proportion 'very interested' in politics was 17%, only 2% more than in the sample as a whole. Clearly, more evidence is needed to establish the reasons for the high level of interest at L.S.E. It is possible that it is in part a function of age, but other factors, including the student's field of study and his parents' attitudes to politics, are also likely to be important.

Table 3.4 Membership of political parties

Home Students

Percentage

	Political parties						Total	N
	Conservative	Liberal	Labour	Communist	Nationalist and others	None		
Undergraduates	7	4	7	0*	1	81	100	1260
Postgraduates	3	2	14	0*	2	79	100	400
All	6	3	9	0*	2	80	100	1606

* Proportion less than $\frac{1}{2}$%.

Party membership is likely to provide more substantial evidence of involvement in politics, particularly when, as here, individual membership rather than collective membership is measured. In all, one-fifth of home students claimed to belong to a political party. Again, no comparative data are available for other British colleges or universities, but L.S.E. students were more likely to be individual members than people in the country as a whole. Thus, while nationally between one in four and one in five Conservative supporters belong to the Conservative Party, about one in ten Liberals belong to the Liberal Party and one in thirteen or fourteen Labour supporters are individual members of the Labour Party,[5] the proportions at L.S.E. were one in three Conservative, one in four Liberal, and one in five Labour supporters.

It is necessary to interpret replies which add up to this rather high level of involvement with some caution. In this case it is quite possible that some students regarded membership of a political society within the School as the equivalent of membership of a national party or group (25% of all home undergraduates and 9% of home postgraduates said they belonged to party political societies at L.S.E.). But, whether the claims to party membership are accepted at face value or not, they were related to certain differences in political attitudes and background characteristics.[6]

Most of the party members belonged to one of the three main parties. The separate tables for undergraduates and postgraduates show that a significantly higher proportion of Conservative and Liberal than Labour undergraduates were members, party membership representing a third of the total supporting the former compared with about a sixth of those supporting the latter. A possible explanation of this finding could be that the proportionately larger membership of the the parties of right and centre reflected a heightened sense of political consciousness springing from the feeling of being a beleagured minority in a dominantly left-wing institution. But if this explanation accounted for differences in undergraduate replies it could not also have applied to the postgraduates, for amongst them Labour and Conservative party members formed almost equal proportions of all party supporters—25% and 23% respectively—while membership was only 13% of those giving allegiance to the Liberal Party.

Political issues

So far we have presented evidence which has shown that the balance of party support amongst home students was tipped quite heavily to the left, that substantial minorities amongst the students claimed a high level of interest in politics and implied a degree of commitment through party membership. But how important were the differences in outlook of the supporters of different political parties? It has been well established in national opinion polls that attitudes on many issues, particularly those concerned with foreign affairs, cut across party lines.[7] Some observers claim that since the Second World War there has been a tendency to convergence in views in Britain on all political issues and an increasing willingness on the part of supporters of different political parties to concede the merits of rival positions where attitudes do remain distinct.[8] To examine the meaning of differences in party allegiance amongst students, questions on five current political issues were included in the survey and related to party choice. These questions were chosen on the basis of a preliminary enquiry made to establish which current political problems the students themselves considered to be the most important. The international problems most mentioned were concerned with Vietnam, Rhodesia and aid to under-developed countries. Inside Britain the two issues regarded as most important were those of legislation against racial discrimination and comprehensive schools.[9]

In the following pages the over-all response of home students to questions on these issues is described, and the manner in which attitude was related to party allegiance is considered. We also attempt to measure the consistency of attitude of supporters of the different political parties.

The form of the questions used was as follows. Students were asked if they supported or opposed American involvement in Vietnam, when (if ever) there should be majority rule in Rhodesia, whether they felt legislation against racial discrimination in Britain was adequate, whether they favoured comprehensive education or the existing system of selective secondary education, and whether everyone in Britain should accept a reduction in their standard of living to enable aid to underdeveloped countries to be increased. Replies to the questions are summarised in Table 3.5. (The full wording of the questions is given in Appendix A and detailed tables are given in Appendix C, Tables 3.1A to 3.5A.)

A substantial majority of home students held radical views on four of the five questions, and on every issue a higher proportion of postgraduates than undergraduates expressed radical attitudes. Two-thirds of all home students opposed American involvement in Vietnam, over three-quarters wanted to see majority rule in Rhodesia within ten years, nearly as many thought that legislation against racial discrimination in Britain should be extended, and more than two-thirds were in favour of replacing selective secondary education by comprehensive schools. Only on the issue of reducing the domestic standard of living to extend overseas aid were the radicals in a minority. Just under a third favoured extending aid under these conditions, compared with nearly a half who op-

c*

Table 3.5 Summary of replies to five questions on political issues

Home Students

Percentages

Political issue	Undergraduates	Postgraduates	All
American involvement in Vietnam			
Support/strongly support	27	13	24
Oppose/strongly oppose	64	76	66
Majority rule in Rhodesia			
Now or within ten years	75	84	78
More than ten years	22	14	19
Legislation against racial discrimination			
Should be extended	70	76	72
Adequate or excessive	24	17	22
Comprehensive secondary education			
Favour/strongly favour	65	78	68
Oppose/strongly oppose	24	13	22
Extending overseas aid by reduction in home standard of living			
Favour	28	40	31
Oppose	49	39	46

posed the idea. However, almost a fifth of the students were undecided on this issue, which was a relatively large proportion
compared with the proportions undecided on the other questions.
This fact, taken together with the comments that many students
wrote against the question on their questionnaires, suggested that the
alternatives posed were felt to be too indiscriminate. The burden
of most of the comments was that it was unreasonable to ask *everyone* in Britain to accept a lower standard of living to help underdeveloped countries, when substantial numbers were living in
poverty in this country. If those sections of the population had
been excluded in the wording of the question, the proportion of
those in favour would certainly have been larger.

Party allegiance and attitudes on political issues

A generally consistent relationship between political allegiance and degree of radicalism-conservatism was suggested when replies were broken down by party. This is illustrated in Table 3.6, which shows the proportion of the supporters of different parties taking a radical position on each of the five issues. (Tables 3.6A to 3.10A in Appendix C give detailed breakdowns by party of the replies to each question.)

Table 3.6 Party allegiance: by radical attitudes on five political issues
Home Students

Percentages

Political issue	Conservative	Liberal	Labour	Left-wing groups	All
Vietnam: oppose/strongly oppose American involvement	26	65	78	93	66
Rhodesia: favour majority rule now or within ten years	52	77	87	96	78
Law against racial discrimination: should be extended	49	67	80	86	72
Comprehensive education: favour/ strongly favour	21	60	86	93	68
Extending overseas aid: favour	12	36	35	48	31

On every issue the Conservatives included the lowest proportion of radicals and the Left-wing Groups the highest. On every issue, except the ambiguously worded question on aid, there was a progressive increase in the proportion of those holding radical views as one moved leftwards through the party spectrum, and a marked difference between each party. The average holding radical views on the questions on Vietnam, Rhodesia, aid and comprehensive education increased from 37% of the Conservatives to 67% of the Liberals, 83% of Labour supporters and 92% of the Left-wing Groups. Furthermore, where the form of the question allowed a degree of opinion to be expressed, the proportion choosing the more radical reply also increased progressively from right to left.

The tendency already noted for postgraduates to be more radical than undergraduates was generally maintained amongst the sup-

porters of each party. The only exception was in the case of the
attitude of Conservative supporters to the Rhodesia issue, where
the proportion of postgraduates with radical views was smaller than
that of undergraduates.

It is interesting to note that the proportions of Conservatives
holding radical views on the different issues varied more than those
of the supporters of other parties. Whereas on the issues of Vietnam
and comprehensive education about a quarter or less held radical
views, on the issues of Rhodesia and legislation against racial discrimination about one-half were classified as radicals. Attitudes to
communism and competition, it would seem, separated the right
from the centre and left far more clearly than attitudes to race.

The proportion of individual students holding consistently radical
or conservative views on a number of political issues was also related to party allegiance.

Table 3.7 Attitude to three political issues[10] : by party allegiance

Home Students

Party allegiance	Attitude			Perecentage	
	Conservative reply to all three	Radical reply to all three	Other	Total	N
Undergraduates					
Conservative	25	4	71	100	243
Liberal	2	35	63	100	194
Labour	1	60	39	100	507
Left-wing Groups	—	85	15	100	103
Postgraduates					
Conservative	19	2	79	100	47
Liberal	—	43	57	100	56
Labour	—	70	30	100	213
Left-wing Groups	—	94	6	100	36

Table 3.7 compares the replies to questions on three issues:
Vietnam, Rhodesia and comprehensive schools. It clearly illustrates
that amongst both undergraduates and postgraduates the propor-

tions holding consistently radical attitudes on all three issues increased from a minority of Liberals to a substantial majority of all Labour supporters and a very large majority of Left-wing Groups supporters. Conversely, the large majority of those holding consistently conservative views were concentrated amongst supporters of the Conservative Party. But it should be noted that the hard core of Conservative supporters was much smaller than the hard core of radicals among the supporters of the parties of the centre and left.

Comparative data on attitude in the community as a whole were available on the issues of Vietnam and comprehensive education, the two questions which discriminated most effectively between Conservative supporters and the supporters of other parties amongst the students. In a survey carried out four months earlier by National Opinion Polls,[11] a sample of the electorate was asked 'On the whole do you think Britain should support the Americans in Vietnam or not?' Although this question is not identical to the one used in the L.S.E. survey the meaning is close enough to make comparison worthwhile. Conservative voters on the national sample were divided equally between those who favoured British support of America and those who opposed it. Liberal and Labour voters were divided about five to three against supporting America. Thus while, like the students, the Conservatives were more likely to back the Americans than the Liberals or Labour supporters the gap between the parties was much smaller in the national sample.

Replies to a question on comprehensive education used in a National Opinion Polls survey a month after the L.S.E. questionnaire had been sent out showed that in the country as a whole the relationship between party allegiance and attitude was of a similar kind although the difference between parties was less clear cut. Asked 'Are you in favour of comprehensive schools, or do you think it is better to have separate grammar and secondary schools?' 55% of the Conservatives preferred separate schools, compared with 36% in favour of comprehensives; while 54% of Labour supporters and 53% of the Liberals wanted comprehensives, compared with 33% and 34% respectively who opted for separate schools.[12]

In sum, the relationship of attitude and party indicated here does not appear to support the hypothesis of convergence, at least as far as L.S.E. students are concerned. Indeed, the limited comparison made with party and attitude relationships in the electorate suggests that opinion was divided much more deeply and clearly along party lines in the School than was the case nationally.

Party allegiance and background characteristics

The evidence discussed in the preceding sections suggests that there are still widely differing views on central political issues amongst students and that party allegiance is quite closely associated with distinct attitude constellations. But what evidence is there on the formation of these allegiances themselves? In what way are they related to the background of the student? This section examines the relationship of party allegiance to the background factors of sex, age, father's occupation, parents' voting, religion, secondary schooling, experience of full-time employment, year of course and department at L.S.E.

Sex

Most studies of political opinion, whether restricted to university students or of national samples, have found that women are usually rather more inclined to support the Conservative Party and less likely to support the Labour Party than men.[13]

Table 3.8 Party allegiance: by sex

Home students

Percentages

| Sex | Party allegiance | | | | | | N |
	Conservative	Liberal	Labour	Left-wing groups	Don't know No answer	Total	
Undergraduates							
Male	21	16	42	9	12	100	919
Female	18	17	41	7	17	100	283
All	20	16	42	9	13	100	1202*
Postgraduates							
Male	14	12	51	10	13	100	231
Female	9	17	56	9	9	100	168
All	12	14	53	9	12	100	399*

* Four undergraduates and one postgraduate did not reply to the question on sex and are excluded from the table.

L.S.E. women, however, did not conform to this pattern. Table 3.8 shows that they were at least as left wing as their male colleagues. Amongst undergraduates there was little difference in the proportions supporting any of the four parties, but postgraduate women were proportionately less strongly represented than men amongst the Conservatives and more strongly represented amongst supporters of the Liberals and left. Some light is thrown on this finding when we examine the sex composition of students in different subjects. It is shown (pp. 55-6) in the section on party allegiance and field of study that in certain subjects students of both sexes were much more likely to support parties of the left than in other subjects. The sex breakdown shows that women were over-represented in most of these subjects.

Table 3.9 Party allegiance: by age

Home Students

Percentages

Age	Conseravtive	Liberal	Labour	Left-wing groups	Don't know no answer	Total	N
Undergraduates							
19 and under	23	21	36	7	13	100	401
20/1	21	14	42	9	14	100	585
22/5	16	11	50	12	11	100	124
26 and over	7	15	57	3	18	100	93
All	20	16	42	9	13	100	1203*
Postgraduates							
20/1	(14)	(21)	(57)	(4)	(4)	100	28
22/5	12	10	56	9	13	100	263
26 and over	11	22	46	10	11	100	109
All	12	14	53	9	12	100	400*

* Three undergraduates did not reply to the question on age and are excluded from the table.

Age and party allegiance were related in the undergraduate replies; the older the student the more likely he was to state a preference for Labour and the less likely to support the Conservatives. Up to the age of twenty-five a similar trend is evident towards the Left-wing Groups, but in the twenty-six and over age-group this support fell away steeply. However, it cannot necessarily be assumed from this evidence that there is a steady movement to the left amongst L.S.E. students as they grow older. Students start and complete their courses at different ages, and it is quite possible that much or all of the increased support for the left amongst higher age-categories was due to a tendency for a larger proportion of older students joining the School to have left-wing views, an explanation we examine further in the conclusion to this section.

Most of the postgraduates fell into a single age-group, the 22-5 category. In this group they were slightly more inclined to take a left-wing position than undergraduates, but this difference may also have been related to age, since a larger proportion of graduates than undergraduates were likely to be at the upper end of the four years spanned. The postgraduates in the oldest age-group were less left wing and more Liberal than those in the 22-5 age-group.

Father's occupation

The father's occupation is usually a fairly good guide to the party allegiance of the child. For example, surveys at Bradford[14] and Manchester University[15] showed that of the students with fathers in middle-class occupations more said they would vote for the Conservative Party than for any other party.

In strong contrast to such findings the L.S.E. data (see Appendix C, Table 3.11A) show that no matter what the occupational category of the father support for the Labour Party amongst both undergraduates and postgraduates was almost always greater than that for any other. Further, support for Labour and Left-wing Groups taken together was always more than that for the Conservatives and Liberals combined. In the undergraduate table, however, some of the expected variations related to father's occupation are evident in the fluctuations in the size of the majorities of the parties of the left. Thus support for Labour and Left-wing Groups was substantially lower amongst the students whose fathers were in non-manual occupations compared with those whose fathers were manual workers. Specifically, support for the Conservatives was highest amongst the students who described their fathers as managers or as running their own business, while the greatest proportion of supporters for left-wing parties was found amongst students who said their fathers were skilled or semi-skilled manual workers.

Postgraduate distributions differed markedly from undergraduate. The non-manual category as a whole gave as much support to the left wing as the manual. Support for the left came in particular from postgraduate students whose parents were in professional or clerical occupations, 65% and 72% respectively giving allegiance to Labour or Left-wing Groups, compared with 42% and 50% of the undergraduates in these categories.

Parents' voting

Studies of voting-behaviour have tended to regard the family as the chief agent of political socialisation and have shown that children usually support the same party as their parents.[16] Opinion surveys of university students in this country and America have confirmed that an important proportion of students do in fact give allegiance to their parents' party.[17] Nevertheless, there is also evidence in the surveys of some movement away from parents' views. Most of the available studies of British university students, which were carried out in the late fifties and the first half of the sixties, showed that the largest defections were from the Con-

Table 3.10 Parents' voting and students' voting: summary

Home Students

Percentages

Parents' voting	Party supported								
	Conservative	Liberal	Labour	Communist	Other	Parent dead	Don't know no answer	Total	N
Undergraduates									
Fathers' voting	33	8	32	–	1	8	18	100	1206
Mothers' voting	39	10	30	1	1	3	16	100	1206
Students' voting	20	12	45	3	12	–	8	100	1206
Postgraduates									
Fathers' voting	31	8	27	1	1	17	15	100	400
Mother's voting	35	11	30	1	–	6	17	100	400
Students' voting	13	10	56	5	9	–	7	100	400

servative-voting parents and the most consistent gains were registered by the Liberals.

We have seen that L.S.E. parents were more left wing in their
sympathies than their social-class distribution would lead one to
expect and more so than the parents of students at other universities. Even so, the data in Table 3.10 show that a considerable number of students voted to the left of their parents and that the largest
gains were made not by the Liberals but by Labour.

**Table 3.11 Students' voting-intention: by fathers' vote in last General
Election**

Home Students

Percentages

	Students' voting-intention						
Father's vote in last general election	Conservative	Liberal	Labour	Communist	Other don't know	Total	No
Undergraduates							
Conservative	33	12	35	2	18	100	402
Liberal	20	31	32	2	15	100	98
Labour	4	6	66	5	19	100	381
Communist	—	—	—	(67)	(33)	100	3
Dead	26	13	44	4	13	100	101
Didn't vote	24	9	34	2	27	100	58
Other/don't know, no answer	21	12	34	1	32	100	163
All	20	12	45	3	20	100	1206
Postgraduates							
Conservative	18	13	53	1	15	100	122
Liberal	10	17	47	3	23	100	30
Labour	3	5	73	6	13	100	109
Communist	—	—	(100)	—	—	100	2
Dead	15	6	55	5	19	100	67
Didn't vote	(10)	(10)	(42)	(22)	(16)	100	19
Other/Don't know no answer	23	12	35	4	26	100	51
All	13	10	56	5	16	100	400

Table 3.11 shows one side of the movement of party allegiances in more detail, relating students' voting to that of their fathers. The movement away from fathers' party is substantial in the case of the children of both Conservative and Liberal supporters. Only in the case of Labour supporters did a majority share their parents' party preference. It will be seen that the largest proportion of children of Conservative and Liberal fathers to change their views became Labour supporters and that the movement to Labour was particularly marked amongst the children of Conservative fathers. The relationship of mothers' vote to students' vote was of a very similar pattern.

Taking the analysis one stage further, it is interesting to consider the effect of agreement and disagreement between parents in which party they support on the student's party allegiance. The findings are similar to those of the earlier American study by Campbell.[18] Students were only likely to vote as their father or mother when the other parent had also voted the same way. Where there was disagreement between the parents there was no obvious tendency for the children to prefer the politics of the father to the mother, or vice versa, or of either to those of a third political party. The only exception was when one of the parents was Labour. In this case, whether the other parent was Liberal or Conservative, mother or father, the student was more likely to say he would vote Labour.

Religion

Religion was found to be related to party allegiance amongst L.S.E. students in much the same way as has been indicated in previous studies of political opinion.[19] A majority of students with centre and right-wing sympathies adhered to a religion whereas most students supporting parties of the left were agnostics or atheists. Closer examination of the data shows that there was a continuum of belief/non-belief running parallel to the political continuum. Thus, amongst undergraduates, those claiming no religious belief increased from 31% of the Conservatives to 40% of the Liberals, 57% of Labour supporters and 84% of those in the Left-wing Groups. The same relationship between party and belief was found in the postgraduate replies, although the proportion with no religion was generally higher.

Looked at in terms of the political composition of the different denominations, Anglicans and Roman Catholics emerge as the re-

Table 3.12   Party allegiance : by religious beliefs

Home students

Percentages

Party allegiance

Religious beliefs	Conservative	Liberal	Labour	Left-wing groups	Don't know No answer	Total	N
Undergraduates							
None	12	13	46	14	15	100	631
Anglican	39	20	30	2	9	100	242
Roman Catholic	36	17	38	4	5	100	76
Non-conformist	17	24	45	2	12	100	132
Jewish	25	17	49	1	8	100	77
Other/no answer	10	17	36	12	25	100	48
All	20	16	42	9	13	100	1206
Postgraduates							
None	8	11	57	11	13	100	235
Anglican	21	25	35	7	12	100	71
Roman Catholic	(29)	(14)	(52)	(5)	–	100	21
Non-conformist	16	14	57	–	13	100	44
Jewish	–	(16)	(74)	(5)	(5)	100	19
Other/no answer	–	(1)	(3)	(3)	(3)	100	10
All	12	14	53	9	12	100	400

ligions with the highest proportion of Conservative voters, while the Non-conformists and Jews had larger proportions of Labour supporters. These relationships held for both undergraduates and postgraduates, although the latter tended to be more left wing in all religious denominations. A substantial majority of atheists and agnostics adhered to the left amongst both undergraduates and postgraduates.

Last secondary school

Amongst the undergraduates only students from independent schools showed a majority in support of the Conservative and Liberal parties. Students in the other maintained category were the most left wing, almost three-quarters supporting Labour or the Left-wing Groups. The students from grammar and direct-grant schools were more closely divided, about half supported a left-

Table 3.13 Party allegiance : by last secondary school

Home students

Percentages

Party allegiance

Last secondary school	Conservative	Liberal	Labour	Left-wing groups	Don't know No answer Other	Total	N
Undergraduates							
Grammar	20	17	43	8	12	100	793
Other maintained	10	12	57	16	5	100	105
Direct grant	21	11	41	9	18	100	117
Independent	31	20	26	6	17	100	153
Other/no answer	13	18	40	5	24	100	38
All	20	16	42	9	13	100	1206
Postgraduates							
Grammar	12	7	56	9	16	100	189
Other maintained	(17)	(13)	(45)	(21)	(4)	100	23
Direct grant	10	16	58	10	6	100	67
Independent	11	22	51	7	9	100	107
Other/no answer	(14)	(36)	(29)	(7)	(14)	100	14
All	12	14	53	9	12	100	400

wing party and two-fifths either the Liberals or Conservatives.

Postgraduate figures show that the majority of the students from all types of school were left wing with the exception of the other maintained, where there was a slight swing to the right. However, as the number of postgraduates in this category was very small this may be a chance difference. The party allegiances of undergraduates and postgraduates differed most strikingly in the case of those from independent schools. Whereas only a quarter of the undergraduates from these schools supported the Labour Party, compared to about a third who favoured the Conservatives, amongst postgraduates half were Labour supporters while the proportion of Conservatives dropped to only 11%.

Full-time employment

It seemed possible that a student's attitude to politics might be influenced by experience of employment between leaving school and coming to university. Comparison of data on employment and party allegiance appeared to bear out this hypothesis, showing that both undergraduates and postgraduates who had worked for six months or more before becoming university students were more likely to support parties of the left than those who had not. However, the pattern of relationships between periods of employment and party allegiance quite closely resembled that which was found to exist between party and age. When the three factors were compared, with age held constant, it was found that the relationship between employment and party allegiance was very weak. Within the 19 and 20-1 age-categories there was little difference in the political allegiances of students with and without experience of full-time employment. In the 22-5 age-group a rather higher proportion of those with two years or more full-time employment supported a party of the left, but it seems probable that much of this difference can be attributed to age differences within the group itself.

Year of course

Some studies of the political attitudes of students have suggested that there is a shift of attitudes to the left during the student's time at university.[20] The comparison of data for year of course and party allegiance at L.S.E. would at first seem to show some evidence of the same trend.

Table 3.14 shows that amongst undergraduates 6% fewer third-year students than first-year students supported parties of the centre and right, while those of the left made up 5% more of the third year than the first year. Amongst postgraduates there was a rather bigger swing to the left between first- and second-year students. Nevertheless, the differences in party allegiance by year of course were very much smaller than those associated with age, and it seemed possible that they simply reflected the higher average age of students in the successive years. A comparison of the three factors showed that when age was held constant the year of course made little difference to party allegiance. The difference between age-groups, on the other hand, was pronounced. For example, support for parties of the left amongst second-year undergraduates increased from about 40% of 19-year-olds to 50% of 20- and 21-year-olds and to 60% of the 22-5-year-olds.

Field of study

Earlier British student surveys have shown that support for

Table 3.14 Party allegiance: by year of course
Home students

Percentages

	Party allegiance						
Year of course	Conservative	Liberal	Labour	Left-wing groups	Don't know no answer	Total	N
Undergraduates							
1st year	21	19	41	7	12	100	416
2nd year	20	16	42	8	14	100	408
3rd year	20	14	42	11	13	100	310
Other/no answer	18	7	56	8	11	100	72
All	20	16	42	9	13	100	1606
Postgraduates							
1st year	12	14	54	9	11	100	306
2nd year	6	14	54	12	14	100	71
Other/no answer	(26)	(18)	(26)	(4)	(26)	100	23
All	12	14	53	9	12	100	400

political parties varied significantly between students studying different subjects. Typically, those in engineering, science, medical and law faculties tended to support the Conservative Party. Social-science students were more usually Labour voters, whilst arts students were likely to be divided more equally between the two main parties (see below, pp. 57-8). Where social class of parent has been taken into account it has been found that it was not related to the faculty differences in political allegiance.

Our data, summarised in Appendix C, Table 3.12A, show that differences in political allegiance between different departments existed at L.S.E. which paralleled faculty differences reported from other universities. The fields of study in which the undergraduates most strongly favoured the left were government, and sociology and anthropology. In both of these over 60% supported the Labour Party or Left-wing Groups. In most of the other fields a majority supported the left. Only in geography, law and the combined fields of industry and trade, statistics, accounting and computing, did the proportion of Conservative and Liberal supporters taken together outweigh that of Labour and Left-wing Groups students.

All postgraduate fields of study shown in the table had a majority of students supporting the left. The relative position of departments resembled the undergraduate pattern in so far as comparisons could be made. Of the five larger departmental groups with thirty or more students, the field of study combining anthropology, social psychology and sociology was the most inclined to the left, 72% expressing allegiance to Labour or Left-wing Groups. The smallest left-wing majorities were registered in economics and geography.

Discussion

Perhaps the most striking feature of the survey data on political attitudes is the extent of the support for the parties of the left which it reveals amongst home students and the prevalence of radical political attitudes with which this support was associated. Although the hoary popular image of the School as a communist stronghold can hardly be sustained in the face of findings which show that only 4% gave their allegiance to the Communist Party, nevertheless a clear majority of all home students supported Labour or the Left-wing Groups. Further, the comparative data available suggest that the strong preference of L.S.E. students for the left is not shared by other colleges or universities in the country.[21]

In considering possible explanations for the dominance of the left amongst home students it is important to bear in mind some of the details of the findings. It was established that postgraduates were more likely to support the left than undergraduates but that postgraduates of all parties were more likely to adopt radical attitudes on political issues than their undergraduate counterparts. The proportion of older students giving allegiance to Labour or Left-wing Groups were considerably higher than that of the younger students. Amongst both undergraduates and postgraduates support for the left was markedly stronger in some fields of study than others. Finally, although a majority of middle-class parents voted Conservative or Liberal, the proportion of Labour voters amongst them was substantially higher than amongst the middle-classes in the country as a whole.

In trying to discover reasons for this leftward orientation, the first point to be made is that, although the L.S.E. probably had an unusually high proportion of Labour and Left-wing Groups students compared with other British universities and colleges, in the context of the major subjects studied at the School the balance of political views was in no way remarkable. The large majority of the students at L.S.E. study the social sciences and the remainder take arts subjects such as history, geography, and philosophy. As we have already pointed out, these faculties at other universities, and particularly the social-science faculties, have been shown in several previous surveys to contain a division of political sympathies of much the same character as we found at L.S.E. The overall figures for political attitudes at other universities usually show a preponderance of right-wing students because of the popularity of Conservatism amongst students in the natural sciences, engineering and medicine, none of which are represented at L.S.E. For example, a survey of three universities conducted in 1964 found that while 41% of the students in social-studies departments would vote Labour the corresponding percentages of those in the departments of physics and engineering were 27 and 20. Conservative preferences were high in engineering and physics, and low in social studies.[22] Earlier studies at Manchester[23] and Bradford[24] reported similar findings.

Although the connection between the study of the social sciences and left-wing views has been known for some time, there seems to have been no systematic enquiry into the nature of the relationship. Most of those who have commented on the matter have seemed to prefer what might be called the 'conversion' explanation: exposure to the social sciences in the context of the university has a liberalising effect on students' attitudes and convinces them of the need for socialist solutions to social problems.[25] An alternative hypothesis, which stresses the importance of socialisation within the college or university, can be derived from Newcomb's studies of studies in the United States.[26] This would postulate that acceptance by the college community involves acceptance of its norms and that in the case of social-science departments, under the influence of radical teachers, such norms would emphasise socialist values. However, neither of these explanations are compatible with the L.S.E. survey data. Both imply that the processes concerned would be progressive and that the proportion of left-wing students would increase as the course went on. But, as we have seen, when the year of course was controlled for age there was very little difference between the proportion of Labour and

Left-wing Groups' students in the different years. It would seem that the major factors determining the social-science student's political views were operative before the student arrived at university.

It is possible that political views determined the choice of subject. A radical orientation could lead to an interest in understanding society in order to change it. But the evidence of intense commitment to politics on a widespread scale, which such an orientation would imply, is missing. It seems probable that the connection between political attitudes and field of study was less direct and less conscious. A more far-reaching and more convincing basis for understanding the relationship can be found in certain studies which have looked at the links between subject preference, performance and personality characteristics. Liam Hudson's work[27] is particularly relevant. He suggests that students can be divided into two broad categories or ideal types—'convergers' and 'divergers'. The converger is typically the science specialist. He prefers problems with one right answer. He is a high performer on conventional I.Q. tests but is unimaginative and does badly at open-ended tests. The diverger is typically the arts specialist at school. He is imaginative but relatively poor at formal reasoning, scores less well on I.Q. tests but highly on open-ended tests. More important for our argument is Hudson's observation that, while the converger tends to be authoritarian, the diverger is likely to have views which are liberal and non-authoritarian. If it can be shown that the diverger's more liberal outlook leads to left-wing views, while the converger's political attitude is usually conservative, and that most social-science subjects are more attractive to the diverger than the converger, we may have the basis for a comprehensive explanation of the differences in political attitudes of social scientists and students in other faculties.

We did not include questions in the survey to measure convergence-divergence but, nevertheless, some of our data are suggestive. The majority of social-science subjects, subjects such as sociology, government, psychology, and anthropology, share the 'open-ended' character of arts students. We found that most students studying these subjects had ' A ' levels in arts subjects, the subjects in which Hudson found the divergers excelled, but few had maths or science ' A ' levels; and that the supporters of the left predominated amongst them. A minority of subjects, such as statistics and demography, more closely resembled the natural sciences. Students in these fields all had 'A' levels in maths and many had 'A' levels in science subjects. As we have seen, a far smaller proportion of students specialising in these subjects supported the left.

The suggested explanation of the relationship between subject of study and political views in terms of divergence-convergence may also throw light on other aspects of the relation between the politics and background characteristics of L.S.E. students. The increase in the proportion of left wingers amongst older students can be explained in terms of the improved opportunities that the older student has to choose a subject of study that is compatible with his own inclinations. The younger student, coming to university straight from school, is likely to be more influenced in his choice of subject by teacher or parent and will have had less chance both to get to know himself and the full range of alternatives open to him.

The divergence-convergence thesis might also help explain the relationship between parents' and students' politics. The divergence of the student with Labour-voting parents would reinforce the factors which tend to influence the child to adopt the political views of his parents, hence the high proportion of students who were loyal to the politics of their parents when the parents were Labour voters. The divergence of the student with Conservative or Liberal parents would be likely to lead to the development of values which would conflict with theirs, and results in deflection to the left. The proportion of students with views to the left of their Conservative or Liberal parents may have been higher amongst postgraduates than undergraduates because, for reasons already suggested in the discussion of the age factor, the proportion of divergers amongst such students was higher.

The reason why Conservative and Liberal postgraduates were more radical than Conservative and Liberal undergraduates may have been much the same. The Conservative and Liberal postgraduates exercised a more independent choice in subject and institution than the younger and less experienced undergraduates, and a match between subject and personality would be achieved more frequently. The divergent element in these students would therefore be stronger and, even though it was insufficient to lead to formal allegiance to parties of the left, it could be expected to result in the formation of more radical attitudes on political issues .

Overseas students

In this section we examine the political attitudes of overseas students and compare them with those of home students. To correspond to the division of political orientation by 'party allegiance' used for home students, we employ the classification of 'party views'. The general political categories of 'conservative', 'liberal', 'socialist' and 'communist' were adopted to enable students from many countries, adhering between them to a multitude of parties, to locate their political views on a single continuum. We are able to show that these categories have some international validity in that they were chosen by students from different nations who held broadly similar political attitudes on a number of issues.

The section is divided into two parts. The first, after presenting data on the distribution of political views amongst overseas students as a whole and within their separate national groups, examines the attitude of the students to four of the five political issues used in the section on home students: Vietnam, Rhodesia, aid, and race. The purely domestic issue of comprehensive education was omitted from the overseas-students' questionnaire. The questions used for home students on party membership and interest in national politics were also omitted owing to the diversity of national background of the overseas students and the varying periods they had been away from home. The response of overseas and home students is compared both in terms of the over-all distribution of replies and in terms of the corresponding categories of political allegiance and political views. Where numbers are sufficient, we also examine the relationship of nationality to attitude within the separate categories of political views. In the second part of the section, the relationship of political views and background factors is considered and compared with the findings for home students.

Political views and political issues

The large majority of overseas students felt able to classify their views under one of the four labels presented in the question. Thirty-nine per cent said they were liberals, 29% said they were socialists, and only 8% that they were conservatives. Views to the left of the socialists received only small support: Two per cent checked 'communist' and a further 1% entered 'anarchist' or provo' in the 'other political views' column. Since the extreme left was so small it has been combined with the socialists in all the tables, bringing the total in this category to 32%. A wide variety of other political views were expressed by a further 6% of the overseas students, and the remaining 15% had no political views, didn't know what their views were or failed to reply to the question at all.

Table 3.15 Political views

			Political views				
All overseas students	conservative	liberal	socialist	Other	None no answer	Total	N
Undergraduates	9	35	36	3	17	100	207
Postgraduates	7	42	31	7	13	100	426
All	8	39	32	6	15	100	633

Table 3.15 shows that taken separately the undergraduate liberals and socialists were almost exactly balanced in strength while the postgraduate liberals outnumbered postgraduate socialists by about four to three.

Nationality and political views

When political views are broken down by the six national groups it becomes evident that the rough balance between liberal and socialist views in the over-all figures for overseas students conceals important differences between them. Only amongst European students was the representation of liberal and socialist students in much the same proportions as those shown in Table 3.16 for all overseas students. In the Asian, African and South American categories, socialist views were considerably more common than liberal views. In the Australasian/Canadian and the American national groups the reverse was true. Liberals formed a particularly high proportion of American students, outnumbering socialists by about five to one.

Taking undergraduate and postgraduate data separately there were no major differences in the proportions holding different political views within the same national groups. Liberals are shown to have formed a larger proportion of postgraduates than socialists

Table 3.16   Political views: by nationality

Overseas students

Percentages

Political views

Nationality	conservative	liberal	socialist	Other don't know no answer	Total	N
Canadian						
Australasian	10	44	34	12	100	93
Asian	9	27	44	20	100	132
African	6	22	48	24	100	98
United States	7	57	12	24	100	190
European	10	38	33	19	100	78
South American						
West Indian	3	34	46	17	100	35
All	8	39	32	21	100	626*

*Seven overseas students did not give their nationality and are excluded from the table: two socialists, three liberals, one conservative and one other.

because of the substantially larger representation of two of the more liberal national groups, the Americans and Australasians/ Canadians, at this level. Whereas amongst overseas undergraduates these two groups made up only 23% of all students, amongst post-graduates they constituted 55%.

Political issues

The overall distribution of opinion amongst overseas students on the four political issues was very similar to that found amongst home students. Table 3.17 summarises their attitudes. It will be noted that a substantial majority held radical views on all the issues except that of British aid to underdeveloped countries. About two-thirds opposed American involvement in Vietnam, four out of five wanted majority rule in Rhodesia within ten years, and seven in ten wanted to see legislation against racial discrimination extended. Although many overseas students came from countries which would benefit from increased British aid, they were not more favourable to extending it at the expense of the standard of living in Britain than were home students. It must be emphasised, however, that the over-all resemblance of attitudes between home and overseas students was largely a matter of chance. Attitudes on political issues were related to political views, as we show below, but the distribution of political views varied between national groups. If there had been a substantially larger proportion of overseas students from countries where either liberal or socialist views predominated, then the resemblance of attitude distributions between home and overseas students would have diminished correspondingly.

Table 3.17 **Summary of replies to four questions on political issues**

Overseas students

Political issue	Under graduates	Post graduates	Percentages All
American involvement in Vietnam			
Support/strongly support	21	22	21
Oppose/strongly oppose	65	69	68
Majority rule in Rhodesia			
Now or within ten years	84	83	83
More than ten years	13	9	11
Legislation against racial discrimination			
Should be extended	69	71	71
Adequate or excessive	13	12	12
Extending overseas aid by reduction in home standard of living			
Favour	32	28	29
Oppose	39	46	44

Turning to the breakdown of attitudes on political issues by political views, the over-all pattern of replies again resembles that found amongst home students. On most issues no more than a few percentage points separated the attitudes of overseas conservatives from home Conservative Party supporters, and overseas liberals from home Liberal Party supporters. Overseas socialists, who combined all views on the left, were usually found between Labour and Left-wing Groups. The relationship of political views to political attitudes is illustrated in Table 3.18, which shows the proportion of those holding different views who took a radical position on each of the four issues. (Tables 3.13A to 3.16A in Appendix C give detailed breakdowns by political view of the replies to each question.)

Table 3.18 Political view: by radical attitudes on four political issues

Overseas students

	Political views			Percentages
Political issue	conservative	liberal	socialist	All
Vietnam: oppose/strongly oppose American involvement	24	63	87	68
Rhodesia: favour majority rule now or within ten years	66	83	93	84
Law against racial discrimination: should be extended	46	74	80	70
Extending overseas aid: favour	12	27	40	29

The conservatives differed most markedly from the centre and left, as with home students, on the issue of Vietnam. Overseas conservatives and liberals, however, were more radical than the equivalent categories of home students on the issue of Rhodesia, and overseas liberals were also more radical than home Liberals on the question of legislation against racial discrimination.

The marked differences in attitude of students holding different political views, shown in the over-all distribution for overseas students, implied that the political labels used had some common meaning across national frontiers. When the data were broken down by nationality, this was confirmed. Conservatives, liberals and socialists of any one nationality had more in common with other students of corresponding views amongst other nationalities than with fellow nationals with different political views. Nevertheless, considerable variations in attitude existed between students of different nationalities who used the same political label. This is illustrated in Table 3.19, which compares the percentage of liberals and socialists in each group of countries who gave the most radical and most conservative replies to the four questions on political issues. (Conservative students were too few in number for a comparison of this kind to be meaningful.) American socialists were markedly more radical than socialists in any other national group. Differences in attitude between socialists from other countries were smaller but Asian socialists were next in order of radicalness, followed by the Australasian/Canadian group, the Africans and, lastly, the Europeans. Amongst overseas liberals the differences were less clear cut. Americans were the most radical on race and aid, but Europeans were more radical on Vietnam and Asians on Rhodesia. In general, however, the Europeans and Australasians/Canadians were the least radical of the liberals.

One can only speculate on the reasons for these variations. A possible explanation for the most striking of them, the radicalness

Table 3.19 Attitude to political issues: by political view and nationality

Overseas students

Percentages

Nationality	Vietnam U.S. involvement — Strongly support	Vietnam U.S. involvement — Strongly oppose	Rhodesia Majority rule — Postpone indefinitely	Rhodesia Majority rule — Now	Aid — Yes	Aid — No	Race Legislation — Repeal	Race Legislation — Extend	N
liberals									
Australasian/ Canadian	2	17	–	7	24	24	2	76	41
Asian	9	34	–	43	37	34	9	74	35
African	(9)	(27)	–	(32)	(14)	(32)	(9)	(73)	22
United States	3	37	–	22	53	19	1	80	107
European	–	(41)	–	17	24	48	10	45	29
socialists									
Australasian/ Canadian	–	(75)	–	(38)	(31)	(45)	–	(79)	29
Asian	–	59	–	61	33	37	–	89	54
African	–	67	–	63	30	39	–	67	46
United States	–	(86)	–	(91)	(41)	(18)	–	(95)	22
European	–	(58)	–	(50)	(38)	(46)	–	(63)	24

D

of the small contingent of American socialists, can be made in terms of the dominance of non-socialist parties in the political life of the country, and the tendency of many Americans to regard socialism as synonymous with communism. In this case, moderate left wingers might well support the Democratic Party and describe their views as liberal, leaving the more extreme left winger to monopolise the socialist label. This could also explain why American liberals were more radical than liberals in national groups where there was a larger proportion of socialists, such as the European group. In Europe a wide variety of parties are described as 'socialist', including many which are no more left wing than sections of the Democratic Party in the United States. Consequently, it is likely that some students with a more radical outlook, who would call themselves 'liberals' in America, classify themselves as 'socialists' in Europe, in this way reducing the proportion of radicals in the 'liberal' category.

Political views and background characteristics

In this section we examine the relationship between the political views of overseas students and the major background characteristics of sex, age, year of course, religion, parents' occupation, and field of study. The questions put to home students on education and parents' voting were omitted owing to the problems of comparing different national educational and political systems. On the whole, numbers were too small to permit a study of the relationship of political views and background factors within national groups, although in a few instances a general indication of the nature of such relationships can be given.

Sex

Unlike home students, amongst whom there was little difference in the proportion of men and women supporting the different parties, the political views of overseas students differed quite markedly by sex.

Table 3.20 shows that, while men were divided in roughly equal proportions between socialists and liberals, women favoured the liberal over the socialist view in the ratio of about two to one. This marked preference amongst overseas women students for liberal views can be traced mainly to the strong representation of American women at L.S.E. Forty-three per cent of the overseas women were from the United States, and 70% of them were liberals, compared with 11% who were socialists. In the other

Table 3.20 Political views: by sex

Overseas students

Percentages

	Political views					
Sex	conservative	liberal	socialist	Don't know no answer other	Total	N
Male	8	35	34	23	100	499
Female	6	51	27	16	100	127
All	8	39	32	21	100	626*

* Seven students did not reply to the question on sex and are excluded from this table: three were socialists, two liberals, one a conservative, and the other two fell in the residual category.

national groups the proportion of women socialists was not very different from the proportion of men socialists.

Age

The relationship of political views and age found amongst home students, showing a steady trend to the left up to twenty-five and a slight trend from left to centre amongst students over twenty-six, was not evident amongst overseas students.

Table 3.21 Political views: by age

Overseas students

Percentages

	Political views					
Age	conservative	liberal	socialist	Don't know no answer other	Total	N
—19	(5)	(40)	(32)	(23)	100	22
20/1	10	41	30	19	100	96
22/5	8	46	25	21	100	252
26 over	8	32	39	21	100	258
All	8	39	32	21	100	628*

* Five students did not reply to the question on age and are excluded from this table: three socialists, one liberal, one 'don't know'.

Table 3.21 shows that in the first age-group with any substantial numbers of students, the 20-1 group, there were more liberals than socialists. In the 22-5 age-group, liberal support increased further, but amongst those over 26 positions were switched and socialist views were held by a larger proportion. Nationality was again associated with the variations shown. American students were concentrated mainly in the two younger age-groups, making up two-fifths of the total in both and contributing substantially to the dominance of the liberals. In the 26-and-over age-group they represented only 17% of the total while the national groups with more socialist supporters were in greater strength.

Numbers were too small to allow meaningful analysis of the relationship between age and political views within individual national groups.

Religion

Amongst overseas students religion was related to political views in much the same way as amongst home students. As table 3.22 shows, those with no religion were more likely to hold left-wing views than those who had a religion. Anglicans were the most inclined to support the right and the least likely to support the left. A minor difference from home students was that overseas non-

Table 3.22 Political views by religion

Overseas students

Percentages

Religion	conservative	liberal	socialist	Don't know no answer	Total	N
			Political views			
None	5	35	38	22	100	238
Anglican	18	52	15	15	100	55
Roman Catholic	10	42	25	23	100	71
Nonconformist	12	35	30	23	100	73
Jewish	8	50	24	18	100	63
Other established religions	5	35	45	15	100	94
Other religious beliefs	—	(43)	(21)	(36)	100	14
No answer	(8)	(46)	(19)	(27)	100	25
All	8	39	32	21	100	633

conformists were rather more likely to hold socialist views than overseas Jews. But a more important difference was in the 'other established religions' category. This was only a small category amongst home students but was the second-largest grouping for the overseas students (consisting mainly of Moslems and Hindus) and had a higher proportion of socialists than even the 'no religion' category. Breakdown by nationality showed that 80% of the students in the other established religions were drawn from Asia and Africa, and that 95% of the socialists in this category were from these countries. Nationality was also related to differences in political views within other religious categories. In the African, Asian and South American national groups, socialists were more strongly represented in the various religions than in the other three national groups, although in all cases except that of the 'other established religions' category they remained a small minority.

Year of course

Most postgraduate overseas students were taking one-year courses at L.S.E., and the relation between year of study and political views can only be usefully examined amongst overseas

Table 3.23 Political views: year of course

Overseas undergraduates

Percentages

Year of course	Political views				Total	N
	conservative	liberal	socialist	Don't know no answer other		
1st year	9	29	43	19	100	58
2nd year	7	24	49	20	100	41
3rd year	8	50	24	18	100	66
no answer	16	28	28	28	100	39
All	9	35	36	20	100	207

undergraduates. Table 3.23 indicates that amongst these students the proportion holding conservative views was stable throughout the three years, the proportion with liberal views declined in the second year but increased steeply in the third, while the proportion of socialists moved in the opposite direction, increasing in the second year and dropping sharply in the third. There is no obvious explanation for the marked difference between second- and third-year views. Unfortunately, the numbers involved are too small to establish whether it is related to differences in the age structure of the different years, as appeared to be the case with home undergraduates.

Father's occupation

The tendency noted amongst home students for support for the left to be higher amongst students with manual-working and clerical fathers than amongst those from professional or managerial

Table 3.24 Political views: by father's occupation

Overseas students

Percentages

			Political views				
Occupation	conservative	liberal	socialist	Other	Don't know no answer	Total	N
Professional	9	45	31	6	9	100	179
Managerial	13	47	8	8	24	100	178
Own business	9	39	33	7	12	100	127
Clerical	(6)	(17)	(56)	(6)	(15)	100	18
Manual	3	35	32	9	21	100	34
Dead/retired	4	36	40	3	17	100	157
Don't know/ no answer	10	27	44	5	14	100	40
All	8	39	32	6	15	100	633

backgrounds was only partly repeated amongst overseas students. The proportion of socialists was considerably higher amongst students whose father held a clerical job than amongst those whose father was of higher occupational status, but students from manual-working backgrounds were no more likely to be socialists than those with parents who owned their own business or were in a profession. Students from a managerial background, however, were markedly antipathetic to socialism. Differences in the national composition of the different occupational groups go some way to account for these variations in political views. United States and Commonwealth students together constituted a majority of the managerial category and half of the manual category. Liberal views were dominant in both national groupings, while socialist views found very little support amongst the Americans and only limited backing amongst Commonwealth students. On the other hand, the small clerical category had a larger proportion of Asian and African students, all of whom held socialist views.

Field of study

Undergraduate numbers were too small amongst the overseas students to show the character of the relationship between special subject and political views, and consequently Table 3.25 is confined to data for postgraduates.

Table 3.25 Political views: by field of study

Overseas postgraduates

Percentages

Field of study	conservative	liberal	socialist	Other don't know no answer	Total	N
Government	11	45	24	20	100	38
Sociology, social psychology, anthropology	4	38	42	16	100	55
Social administration	3	15	69	13	100	39
Industrial relations, philosophy, other	(9)	(50)	(14)	(27)	100	22
International history, international relations, economic history	6	62	16	16	100	61
Economics	7	40	32	21	100	85
Geography	(8)	(39)	(23)	(30)	100	13
Law	8	42	16	34	100	38
Statistics, accounting, demography	10	39	36	15	100	36
No answer	8	40	25	27	100	39
All	8	39	32	21	100	426

Political views

As with home students, social administration and sociology were the fields of study with the most left-wing students. However, the proportion of overseas sociologists with socialist views was much lower than the proportion supporting the left amongst home students. In some other fields of study the balance of opinion was quite different from that found with the home students. In particular, government and law were both low in their support for the left but statistics included a relatively high proportion of socialists.

Again, the different national composition of the categories was significant. The social administrators were drawn in roughly equal proportions from the Australasian/Canadian, American, Asian and African national groups. Of those expressing a political attitude, students from the first two were divided almost equally between socialist and non-socialist views, while all the Asians and Africans were socialists. The views of sociology students were related to nationality in much the same way, but in this field the Americans formed a substantially larger proportion of the total and pushed up the proportion of liberals. In both cases, however, a higher proportion of students in each national group held socialist views than in the groups as a whole, suggesting a possible link between subject and political views of the kind noted amongst home students. But there was no evidence of a similar relationship in government, the other field which had a high proportion of left-wing support amongst home students. American and Australasian/Canadian students dominated the field, contributing thirty of the thirty-eight who were studying the subject and furnishing most of the liberal strength.

Discussion

Sex, religion, and perhaps some fields of study were apparently related to political views amongst overseas students of all national groups much as amongst home students. Numbers were too small, however, to show the nature of these relationships in detail, and, the nature of relationships between other background character-istics and political views within national groups. Consequently, there was insufficient evidence to develop any hypotheses on the possible origin of political attitudes which might be compared and contrasted with those developed in the study of the politics of home students.

Summary

The political attitudes of students were examined and their relationship to certain background characteristics considered. More than half all home students were found to support Labour or parties to the left of Labour whilst about one-third gave allegiance to Conservative or Liberal parties. Interest in national politics and membership of political parties were both high compared with the population as a whole. Evidence for convergence in the views of supporters of the different political parties, which some observers believe has taken place within the electorate as a whole, was not found at L.S.E. On the contrary, party allegiance was shown to be quite closely related to attitude on a number of political issues, students supporting the Conservatives tending to have conservative views, while the proportion with radical views increased progressively through Liberal and Labour party supporters to the Left-wing Groups. Postgraduate supporters of each party were more radical than undergraduates supporting the same party. The study of the relationship between political attitudes and background characteristics showed that women at L.S.E. were as likely to hold left-wing views as men, and that support for the left increased with age. The students' preference for the left in politics was almost as strong amongst the majority who came from middle-class backgrounds as the minority from working-class homes. However, the proportion of Labour voters was substantially higher amongst L.S.E. parents in middle-class occupations than in these occupations in the country as a whole. Religion and schooling were related to political sympathies in much the same way as indicated in previous studies: those with no religion were more likely to support a party of the left than those who were religious. The students with a state education similarly were more left wing than those from independent schools. Neither experience of full-time work between school and university nor the number of years the student had been at L.S.E. appeared to be related to political views. Party support did vary, however, with the different fields of study. Some fields such as sociology and government had a high proportion of students on the left, others such as statistics had a low proportion. An interpretation of the data is tentatively advanced which relates the predominance of the left amongst social-science students to the probable preference of 'divergers' as opposed to 'convergers' for many of the specialisms within the field.

D*

Overseas students were found to be divided mainly between liberals and socialists. Less than one in ten were conservatives. The proportion of liberals and socialists varied considerably between the different nationalities: amongst Asians, Africans and South Americans, socialists were the stronger, in the other national groupings liberals formed the larger proportion. Political views and attitudes to political issues were related much as we found with the home students: conservative views predominated on the right, radical views on the left. The relationships between background factors and political views could not be traced in detail because of the small numbers within the different national groups.

Chapter 4

Student life

There are many contrasting views of the typical student at the School. Some have seen the L.S.E. student as a politically aware, politically active young person, involved in the issues of the day, chiefly in the wider sense of world and national politics, but partly in the narrower sense of participation in university life. Those who hold this view would tend to see him as an individual who expresses his dissent, voices his criticism and discusses intellectual problems in organised groups. The manifestation of such group activity varies from demonstrations to discussion groups, both perhaps absorbing a good deal of the L.S.E. student's time. All this would lead to the expectation that L.S.E. student life is marked by high involvement in the Union and other kinds of student association. However, there is an alternative view which is a picture not just of L.S.E. but of the University of London as a whole. This is that there is little or no student life in the University, that it runs from 9 a.m. to 6 p.m., reminiscent of the offices of a large firm. The causes of this are thought to be, first, the lack of a university campus round which students live, and the consequent scattering of students over a wide area; and, second, the pull of alternative activities and entertainment in the metropolis. It is possible that both views may be valid. Many students may be uninvolved in pursuits at L.S.E., other than their academic work, because of the School's site in central London. But there may be a group of active students, who are not typical, but whose intense involvement is the source of the first image. This chapter discusses the levels of participation in various aspects of student life at the School, and throws some light on the validity of these images.[1]

Information was obtained both on participation in student activities and attitudes towards certain aspects of it. The latter is confined to a limited number of questions, most of which concern the nature of facilities, and in particular accommodation, provided by the School for student activities. All the formally constituted student organisations at the School fall under the auspices of

either the Students' Union, the Athletic Union or the Graduate
Students' Association. All undergraduates and postgraduates are
automatically members of the Students' Union and entitled to use
the facilities it provides. The Union's constitution states that ' the
objects of the Union shall be to promote the welfare and the corporate life of the students, and through the Union Council, to represent the students on all matters relevant thereto except those relating to Athletics '. Thus, student societies wishing to use the name
of the School or to use any of the facilities provided by the
Students' Union must be recognised by the Union. The constitution
of the Union states that they may fall into one of two categories:
' Union societies shall be societies which may receive grants from
the Union provided that these societies maintain accounts on a
system prescribed by Union Council and submit summary accounts
in the prescribed form to the Senior Treasurer at the end of every
term; Associated Societies which receive no Union grant.' Political,
religious and national societies fall into the second category.[2]
Appendix D lists all student societies in existence in 1967. Questions 28-32 of the questionnaire dealt with participation in student
organisations.[3]

The information on participation can be roughly divided between participation in student societies and participation in the
Union. Since all societies are affiliated to the Union, this division is
somewhat arbitrary. However, the distinction seems worth making,
since involvement in societies does not indicate the kind of commitment to the Union necessary to serve on a union committee,
for example, and may even be accompanied by negative attitudes
towards the Union in spite of the societies' formal affiliation to it.
Union participation indicates political consciousness in student
affairs as opposed to the non-political interests of those active in
most student societies.

Question 31 asked whether or not students had ever been on
union council[4] or held any other union office such as a post on the
students' newspaper or membership of a union committee. Question 32 asked students how frequently they attended union meetings. These meetings are held approximately once a fortnight
during term, and every full member of the Union is entitled to
attend and vote. Discussion at the meetings may be on private
matters, that is, issues concerning the Union and its policies, or
on public matters, that is, anything else.

Finally, questions 33-5 were concerned with students' opinions on various issues. Since gross overcrowding at L.S.E. has been suggested as a contributory factor to student unrest, question 33 asked whether or not accommodation for various activities was adequate. It also asked whether examples of the Union's welfare facilities, such as its housing bureau, the social activities it laid on, and its representation of student opinion were adequate. The latter was asked in the light of considerable criticism that has been made of the Union on this issue. Students and others have contended that a system whereby policy-making is the responsibility of regular union meetings has led to abuses, and, although in principle democratic, in practice it is not.[5] It is argued that such meetings can be dominated by a small well-organised minority who force through decisions which would not receive the support of most students. Question 34 asked whether or not Presidents of the Students' Union should be given a sabbatical year. For some years the Union had requested this, citing its practice in many other universities. At the time of the disturbances at L.S.E., the President and his predecessor had been granted sabbatical years, but the School had not accepted that all Presidents should be allowed this as of right. Question 35 on whether or not it is important or unimportant for the Union to have complete control over the premises it uses was asked for two reasons. First, the events of 31 January arose partly as a result of the fact that the Union does not own premises free from any restrictions the School might wish to impose, nor did it have the unconditional use of a room suitable for holding mass meetings; and, second, because the issue of its premises was closely related to the Union's lack of financial autonomy.[6]

The data on attitudes and participation have been related first to each other; second, with information on the background characteristics of the students; and, third, with the political attitudes of the students. Unfortunately, there is little information about other universities suitable for comparative purposes for any of these sections. This is a pity, since it is difficult to judge what constitutes high or low participation without comparative data and it would be interesting to know whether the relationship between political attitudes, for example, and involvement in the Student Union is unique to L.S.E. or a characteristic of universities in general.

Table 4.1 **Participation in student societies: by type of student**

Percentages

Participation in societies	HUG	OUG	HPG	OPG	All UGs	All PGs
			Type of student			
Attended at least one society meeting						
Yes	85	73	62	53	83	57
No	15	27	38	45	16	42
No answer	0	0	0	2	1	1
Total	100	100	100	100	100	100
Membership						
None	18	31	47	58	20	53
One	23	25	30	24	23	27
Two	26	19	15	11	25	13
Three	18	15	6	5	17	6
Four or more	15	10	2	1	15	1
No answer	0	0	0	1	0	0
Total	100	100	100	100	100	100
Types						
Academic	40	22	26	12	38	19
National	2	30	2	13	6	8
Religious	11	7	6	3	11	4
Cultural	41	23	18	13	38	16
Athletic	34	21	15	13	32	14
Political party	25	13	9	2	23	6
Other political*	7	10	4	3	8	3
Membership of Committees	36	26	17	8	34	12
Union officials	19	10	7	4	17	5
Attend union meetings						
Very frequently	14	12	4	4	14	4
Fairly frequently	33	30	14	14	32	14
Occasionally	32	38	29	25	32	27
Rarely	16	15	25	27	17	26
Never	5	5	28	28	5	28
No answer	0	0	0	2	0	1
Total	100	100	100	100	100	100
No	1206	207	400	426	1413	826

* Includes United Nations Association, Campaign for Nuclear Disarmament, Society against Racial Discrimination, War on Want.

Participation in student organisations
Before relating data on participation and attitudes to other information, it is necessary to look at actual levels of participation and
their interrelationships. Similarly, in the next section, the nature
of students' attitudes will be described before considering their
relationship with other variables.

Table 4.1 shows that undergraduates were more involved in
every respect than postgraduates, and British students participated
more than those from overseas. The only exception to this was
the higher proportion of overseas students who were members of
national societies. Otherwise the differences between British and
foreign students were less marked than those between undergraduates and postgraduates. Sixteen per cent of undergraduates had not
attended any society meeting during the academic year, compared
to 42% of the postgraduates. Most students were members of at
least one society, but the difference between undergraduates and
postgraduates is particularly marked with reference to society
membership, a fifth of the undergraduates belonging to no society[7]
compared with over half of the postgraduates. A third of the undergraduates belonged to three or more societies, whereas only 7%
of postgraduates do so. The proportion of undergraduates seems
high and indicates that the spread of membership is considerable,
at least amongst students taking first degrees. This provides some
support for the image of the L.S.E. student being highly involved in
student organisations, although membership itself does not necessarily imply active participation. However, committee membership
is a better measure of activism, and as many as one-third of all
undergraduates had been on committees. The type of society which
most attracted students is also interesting. The academic group
had the highest membership, 38% of undergraduates and 19% of
postgraduates belonging to one of these societies. This was followed
closely by the cultural societies, then the athletic, with the political
group taking only fourth place with a membership of 28% of
undergraduates and 8% of postgraduates.[8] Given the image of the
political awareness of L.S.E. students, it was not expected that both
cultural and athletic societies would prove more attractive than
the political organisations at the L.S.E., although probably few will
be surprised by the lack of popularity of the religious societies,
to which only 11% of undergraduates and 4% of postgraduates
belong.

Half as many undergraduates (17%) had held a post in the Union as had served on society committees (34%). However, the fact that *as many as* one in six undergraduates claim to have played an active part in the Union rather than *as few* as this perhaps deserves comment. The proportion of members of most trade unions who actually hold office is very low, but it would be useful to have precise comparative data about unions at other universities. Attendance at union meetings is another index of interest in the Union and involvement in student life. Only 5% of undergraduates said that they never attended, compared with 28% of postgraduates, whereas 46% of undergraduates and 19% of postgraduates claim to have attended frequently.[9] The special circumstances of the academic year 1966-7, in which the union meeting was the major forum for discussion, no doubt inflated the attendance at these meetings, and generalisation about other years should not be made from this evidence. It is very doubtful whether as many as nearly half the undergraduates and a fifth of the postgraduates attend frequently in a quieter year.

It seemed likely that high participation in one activity would be related to high participation in another. The results do indicate an association between one form of participation in student life and another in *every case*. However, the relationships between attendance at union meetings and membership of societies (see Table 4.2A), between membership of societies and office-holding in the Union, and between office-holding in the Union and sitting on society committees were all quite strong. There appears to be therefore a tendency for students, particularly postgraduates, who were highly involved in one aspect of student life, to be involved in other aspects of it, one kind of activity acting as a complement to, rather than a substitute for, other kinds of activity.

Attitudes towards aspects of student life
Turning from participation to attitudes towards aspects of student life shown in Table 4.2, one of the most obvious differences between the various groups of students was that those from overseas were far less likely to express an opinion than their British contemporaries. They also tended to be more satisfied with most aspects of student life, including both accommodation provided by the School and facilities which the Union was directly responsible for providing. Possibly the reason for this is that the refer-

Table 4.2 Attitudes towards aspects of student life by type of student

Percentages

% of students saying:	HUG	OUG	HPG	OPG	All UGs	All PGs
Union Social activities						
Very adequate	3	6	2	5	4	4
Fairly adequate	25	29	20	16	26	18
Rather inadequate	33	27	17	17	32	17
Very inadequate	19	10	15	7	18	11
Don't know or no answer	20	28	46	55	20	50
Total	100	100	100	100	100	100
Representation of student opinion in union						
Very adequate	3	2	2	7	3	4
Fairly adequate	29	35	29	28	30	28
Rather inadequate	35	29	27	20	34	24
Very inadequate	27	16	15	10	25	13
Don't know or no answer	6	18	27	35	8	31
Total	100	100	100	100	100	100
Sabbatical year for President						
On principle	74	60	60	37	72	48
At School's discretion	16	20	20	18	16	19
Not at all	6	7	12	21	6	17
No opinion	4	13	8	24	6	16
Total	100	100	100	100	100	100
Control over Premises						
Important	68	55	64	49	66	56
Unimportant	20	25	23	25	21	24
No opinion	12	20	13	26	13	20
Total	100	100	100	100	100	100
N	1206	207	400	426	1413	826

ence group from whom they derive their expectations consists of fellow students in their own countries, where the
standard of such facilities is probably often worse than at
L.S.E. On the other hand the home students tend to compare
themselves with those at other British universities, which are usually
better provided for in this respect. To continue by discussing the
individual facilities, the proportion of undergraduates and postgraduates who thought that the accommodation for the union
offices, union meetings and 'other activities including common
rooms' was inadequate is higher than the proportion who thought
it was adequate. In some cases a very large majority of students
was dissatisfied; for example, 81% of undergraduates believed that
common-room accommodation was inadequate, and only 11%
were satisfied with the present situation. Some students pointed out
that the accommodation for routine union meetings was adequate
but that for important meetings where motions such as a strike
resolution were discussed it was very unsatisfactory. Similarly, the
majority of students believed that the President of the Union should
have a sabbatical year as a general principle and that it is important that the Union should have complete control over its own
premises. Both these questions evoked written comments from
students on their questionnaires. A number of students pointed out
that the events of 31 January (when the Director banned the meeting to discuss direct action against the appointment of Dr Adams)
and their repercussions need never have taken place had the
students had their own premises where such meetings might be
held. The only exception to the dissatisfaction with facilities provided by the School for non-academic activities is accommodation for society meetings, which most students regarded as adequate. On the question of a sabbatical year for the President many
comments were made, revealing a wide range of attitudes. At
one extreme one student wrote, 'A Union President is most certainly not entitled to a sabbatical year. If he finds satisfaction in
this political training, well and good—I happen to find satisfaction
in other pursuits, yet no-one is offering me a sabbatical if I am
unable to do justice both to my studies and my other interests'. At
the other extreme, a student argued that 'The Union's executive
body as a whole should all have extra years, or at least automatic
vacation grants', partly because this would 'do away with one
all-powerful president'. Another student argued that the sabbatical

year should be at the School's discretion, since 'their granting as a matter of course creates a precedent for extending the privilege to other union officers'.

The majority of students were dissatisfied with the operation of the Union: 33% of undergraduates and 32% of postgraduates thought that representation of student opinion by the Union was adequate, whereas 59% of undergraduates and 37% of postgraduates thought it was inadequate.[10] The large difference of 22% between undergraduates and postgraduates was the result of the high proportion of the latter group who either did not answer or did not know whether the Union was representative or not (31%). A high proportion of students having no opinion is a feature of the replies to most of these questions and reveals lack of interest on their part. Several students said that the Union was dominated by a few vocal extremists, one commenting, 'The Union tends to represent extremist viewpoints because I suppose the majority of moderates are apathetic or just want to get on with their work'. But the following quotation represents a rather different attitude expressed by several of the respondents: 'Union only represents the views of those people who attended Union meetings, and is not representative of the student body as a whole but only of those sufficiently interested to take part. However, this is not necessarily a bad thing for if someone has not sufficient interest to attend then he must accept the decisions of the Union, even though strictly speaking the Union does not accurately represent the views of the whole student body'.

A high percentage of postgraduates did not know whether or not the social activities arranged by the Union were adequate (46%), presumably because they did not attend such activities. This was also true of as many as 17% of the undergraduates. Of those who did express a view, more were dissatisfied than satisfied. One student questioned the role of the Students' Union in arranging social activities, stating that 'I did not come to University to have my social life organised by yet another bunch of would-be bureaucrats'. There are many other aspects of students' opinions on the operation of the Union which need to be investigated before generalisations can be made. Yet the aspects of the Union we have reviewed here were the only ones which it seemed feasible to ask the students to assess on the questionnaire. Most students would be likely to have an opinion on them, whereas few of them could be expected to have enough knowledge to rate the administrative structure of the Union, or the ability of its executive, or the fairness of the allocation of funds by the Union to different organisations and activities. This is corroborated by the attempt to discover students' attitudes towards one of the welfare activities of the Union, the Union Housing Bureau: 57% of undergraduates and 71% of postgraduates did not know whether this was adequate or not.

Although dissatisfaction with various aspects of formally organised student life at L.S.E. was extensive, it was by no means universal. An average of 28% of undergraduates and 25% of postgraduates thought that accommodation provided by the School for the four activities listed above was adequate. The number of students who were satisfied with the *status quo* with reference to the union premises and a sabbatical year for the President is slightly lower, being, respectively, 21% and 16% for undergraduates, and 24% and 19% for postgraduates. Thus, between a quarter and a sixth of the students thought these facilities adequate. Nearly

Table 4.3 Sabbatical year for President: by union representation*

Percentages

| Representation | Sabbatical year | | | | | |
	On principle	At School's discretion	Not at all	Don't know	Total	N
Undergraduates						
Adequate	82	11	4	3	100	465
Inadequate	70	19	2	9	100	834
Don't know	50	21	9	20	100	89
No answer	(52)	(16)	(12)	(20)	(100)	25
Total	72	17	6	5	100	1413
Postgraduates						
Adequate	61	17	11	11	100	269
Inadequate	52	20	19	9	100	298
Don't know	33	18	24	25	100	218
No answer	34	22	10	34	100	41
Total	48	19	17	16	100	826

Table 4.4 Control over union premises: by union representation*

Percentages

| Representation | Control over premises | | | | |
	Important	Unimportant	Don't know no answer	Total	N
Undergraduates					
Adequate	79	12	9	100	452
Inadequate	63	25	12	100	834
Don't know	45	23	32	100	89
Total	66	21	13	100	1413
Postgraduates					
Adequate	72	17	11	100	269
Inadequate	53	31	16	100	298
Don't know	46	23	31	100	218
Total	56	24	20	100	826

* Union representation means the representation of student opinion by the Union.

a third believed social activities provided by the Union and the representation of student opinion by the Union was adequate. Some might contend that the greater maturity of postgraduates would lead them to be less critical of the School and more critical of the Union, but such a contention is not valid according to this evidence. Students doing higher degrees who express an opinion of these matters—many do not—do accept more readily what the School offers in terms of resources for student activities, but they are also less critical of the Union than the undergraduates. The differences between undergraduates and postgraduates, and British and foreign students are far less marked for attitudes towards student life than for participation in student life.

Nevertheless, the large differences between undergraduates and postgraduates in the extent of their participation in student life, and in the degree to which they express opinions about the adequacy of certain aspects of student life suggest the need for a separate analysis of the two groups, when investigating the relationships between involvement in student life and other variables.

These interrelationships have been examined in order to discover whether the students who are active in student life differ in other ways from those who are not. A greater emphasis will be placed on the undergraduates, since their involvement was so much higher and therefore it is easier to discern strong relationships between participation and other variables. The only exceptions[11] to this separate treatment are the associations between certain background characteristics, such as marital status, religion, sex and nationality, with aspects of student life, where the two groups have been combined.

Turning from the frequency-distributions considered so far to the associations between variables, Tables 4.3 and 4.4 show that students who were satisfied with the operation of the Union were rather more dissatisfied with the status of the President and the Union's premises than those who were dissatisfied with the Union. Yet many students who thought union representation was inadequate may have laid some of the blame on the School for its policies on these issues. Possibly they identified its shortcomings with the lack of a full-time leader, and inadequate premises, over which the Union had insufficient control. Although a higher proportion of students who were satisfied with the Union expressed dissatisfaction with the School, in terms of the accommodation and other facilities it provided, the difference is quite small.

Similarly, although there is a slight tendency for students with a high opinion of one aspect of the Union to have had a high opinion of another aspect of it, no such thing as a blind loyalty appears to have existed. As many as half the undergraduates who thought that representation was adequate believed that the social life provided by the Union was inadequate. However, the postgraduates tended to be more consistently uncritical.

Interrelationships of attitudes and participation in student life
By comparison with low participants, high participants in the activities about which information was collected tended to have more unfavourable attitudes towards school provision for student activities and more favourable attitudes towards the Union. The extent of the difference varied a great deal from one activity to another; for example, it was larger when union officers were compared with non-office-holders than when society members were compared with non-members, and there were cases where it did not hold at all.

For example, whether a student had attended a meeting during the year or not, and whether he had sat on a society committee or not was unrelated to his attitudes. The number of societies to which the undergraduate belonged was unrelated to his attitudes towards the Union, but was related to his attitudes towards facilities provided by the School.

For example, 70% of those who belonged to no societies were dissatisfied with accommodation for common rooms, compared with 84% of those belonging to five or more societies; and 63% of those who belonged to no societies thought that the President should have a sabbatical year on principle, compared with 83% of those belonging to five or more societies. The association between society membership and attitudes was negligible, with one exception: a higher proportion of postgraduates who were members of several societies regarded complete control of union premises as important than did those who were not society members.

These associations between attitudes and participation were strongest for measures of participation such as holding a union post, which indicate a higher level of involvement.[12] Seventy-five per cent of undergraduates who had served on union bodies thought that accommodation for union offices was inadequate, compared with 42% of the other students; and 92% of the former group thought that common-room accommodation was inadequate, compared with 78% of the latter. Similarly, 87% of those who had worked on the Union, compared with 63% of other undergraduates, believed that the president should have a sabbatical year on principle; and 80% thought that complete control over the Union was important, compared with 63% of other undergraduates. There is, however, a tendency for those involved in the Union to be just as critical of it as those who have held no union posts. On the face of it this seems surprising, but it may be the result of a greater awareness of some of the deficiencies of the Union resulting from greater familiarity with it. A very diverse group of union positions was covered by question 31 ranging from those who were most deeply involved, such as past and present members of the Union Council, to those in more peripheral positions, such as members of the staff of *Beaver* or committee members of the Graduate School Association. The latter group may be more self-critical and less defensive about the Union than the former group. Nevertheless, the degree of criticism expressed is high.

On the other hand, those who attended union meetings frequently were less critical of the adequacy of union representation than those who attended rarely. Table 4.5 shows this.

Table 4.5 Adequacy of union representation by attendance at union meetings

Percentages

Attendance at Meetings	Adequacy of union representation					
	Adequate	Inadequate	Don't know	No answer	Total	N
Undergraduates						
Frequently	46	50	34	1	100	650
Occasionally	26	66	6	2	100	458
Very rarely or never	15	68	15	2	100	304
Total	33	59	6	2	100	1413
Postgraduates						
Frequently	53	41	3	3	100	148
Occasionally	40	45	13	2	100	224
Very rarely or never	22	31	42	5	100	445
Total	33	36	26	5	100	826

Amongst postgraduates, this was the only form of participation which was associated closely with attitudes. Table 4.5 shows that 53% of those who attended frequently thought that representation by the Union was adequate whereas 22% of those who attended rarely or never believed this. The association between attendance and attitudes towards a sabbatical year for the President was even stronger: 66% of those who attended frequently were in favour on principle, compared with 39% of those who attended rarely or never. Among undergraduates, frequent attenders were also more critical of the accommodation for union meetings. It is interesting that 52% of those who never attended expressed a view about the accommodation, and 56% of this group expressed a view about representation of student opinion by the Union. Since in practice the union meeting was the only obvious way in which student opinion could be represented, those who never attended can have assessed the efficacy of representation only at second-hand. However, in general, low participants tended to have no firm attitudes.

Personal characteristics

The likelihood that certain background characteristics, such as age, sex and marital status, as well as other variables such as year of course, field of study and type of living accommodation, would be related to participation in student life was investigated.

Society membership amongst men was slightly higher than amongst women. This pattern was repeated for all the measures of participation. The most marked difference between men and women was in membership of the party political societies, where almost twice as high a proportion of men belonged (16%) as women (9%). But 14% of women had held a union post compared with 13% of men. In general the differences are small and, when compared with the contribution of women to political or quasi-political organisations in general, female students at L.S.E. are actively involved. The small differences in participation were only reflected in the attitudes in so far as a slightly higher proportion of women had no opinion about the issues on which they were questioned. There was no difference between men and women in the levels of satisfaction expressed.

The differences in participation between married and unmarried students were considerably larger than between men and women. Seventy-nine per cent of single students had been to a society meeting, compared with 50% of the married; 29% of single students were committee members, compared with only 12% of married students. There were large differences in society membership, and nearly half the married students had no opinion about the quality of social life, compared with 23% of those who were single, which is a further indication of lower participation.

The evidence on nationality indicates that British students occupied an intermediate position in terms of involvement in student life, some groups from overseas having been more involved and some less. It is interesting that American students are not always the highest participants amongst those from abroad according to this evidence.

Tables 4.6 and 4.7 show that for undergraduates society membership and attendance at union meetings were highest among Euro-

pean students and lowest amongst students from Africa in the
first case and from America in the second case. Among postgraduates, more British students belonged to societies than those
of any other nationality, but the Americans were the most regular
attenders at union meetings. Students from the dominions, that is,
Australasia and Canada, were the least active on both measures.
This pattern applied for other measures of participation, but the
differences were only partially reflected in the attitudes of the
students. The British were the least sympathetic towards the
Union, but a high proportion of American students also thought
representation of student opinion inadequate. Table 4.8 illustrates
this.

Any suggestion that American students are more highly involved in student life at L.S.E. than students from other countries,
that they provide a great deal of support for the Union and that
they run student life, is only partly true according to the above

Table 4.6 Society membership: by nationality

Percentages

| Nationality | Society membership | | | | | |
	0	1	2	3 or more	Total	N
Undergraduates						
British	20	23	25	32	100	1206
European	9	25	25	41	100	32
Asian	26	20	21	33	100	66
African	21	26	28	25	100	47
U.S.	18	21	28	33	100	43
Australasian/Canadian	(14)	(29)	(29)	(28)	(100)	7
All	20	23	25	32	100	1413
Postgraduates						
British	47	30	15	8	100	400
European	59	22	11	8	100	46
Asian	61	27	11	1	100	46
African	57	23	10	10	100	51
U.S.	55	28	11	6	100	147
Australasian/Canadian	65	18	11	6	100	86
All	53	27	13	7	100	826

Table 4.7 Attendance at union meetings: by nationality

Percentages

Nationality	Attendance at Union Meetings					
	Frequently	Occasionally	Very rarely or never	No answer	Total	N
Undergraduates						
British	45	33	22	0	100	1206
European	66	28	6	0	100	32
Asian	49	33	18	0	100	66
African	47	22	21	0	100	47
U.S.	42	30	28	0	100	43
Australasian/Canadian	(43)	(43)	(14)	(0)	(100)	7
All	46	32	22	0	100	1413
Postgraduates						
British	17	29	54	0	100	400
European	22	26	52	0	100	46
Asian	12	21	65	2	100	66
African	16	35	45	4	100	51
U.S.	26	25	47	2	100	147
Australasian/Canadian	7	24	66	2	100	86
All	18	27	54	1	100	826

evidence. American undergraduates tended to be rather inactive; indeed a lower proportion of American students (6%) than of any other national group were society committee-members. American postgraduates were the most frequent attenders at union meetings, but were otherwise not especially active in formal student organisations at L.S.E.

Accommodation, year of course and age
The distance of a student's living accommodation from L.S.E. does not seem to have such a marked effect on participation in student life as might be expected. Although the extreme group who spent more than one hour travelling to L.S.E. participated less than the rest, there is little difference amongst those taking less than one hour, and, where there are differences, these are not consistent in direc-

Table 4.8 Union representation: by nationality

Percentages

Nationality	Union representation				Total	N
	Adequate	Inadequate	Don't know	No answer		
Undergraduates						
British	32	62	5	1	100	1206
European	22	42	16	0	100	32
Asian	38	43	15	4	100	66
African	28	36	28	8	100	47
U.S.	46	47	5	2	100	43
Australasian/Canadian	(32)	(62)	(5)	(1)	(100)	7
All	33	59	6	2	100	1413
Postgraduates						
British	31	42	24	3	100	400
European	41	30	22	7	100	46
Asian	32	30	29	9	100	66
African	43	21	26	10	100	51
U.S.	33	35	27	5	100	147
Australasian/Canadian	26	31	38	5	100	86
All	33	36	26	5	100	826

tion. For example, a higher proportion of those taking forty-five minutes to one hour were on committees than of those taking less than this.[13] This is consistent with Rudd and Hatch's evidence from Exeter, Nottingham and University College, London. They found that distance from the universities had little effect on use of the campus or upon the level of participation. Perhaps this suggests that a certain amount of travelling is now accepted as an intrinsic part of the individual's day, and it therefore does not act as a deterrent to his pursuing various activities in addition to his work.

It seemed likely that those living in hostels or flats would participate more for several reasons, not all of them directly concerned with the nature of the accommodation. First, these types of accommodation are closest to L.S.E.; second, they are free of certain characteristics of the other types of accommodation which might limit the amount of time students spend at L.S.E. Students living in their parents' homes may have developed a social life based on their homes which acts as a counter-attraction to student life at L.S.E. This also applies to students living in their own homes, who in any case are an unusual group of older students. Those living in accommodation with board are subject to the constraints of having to return for an evening meal. However, the initial hypothesis proved to be incorrect (perhaps partly because distance proved to be unimportant), in that the highest participation was by those living in accommodation with board, followed by those in flats and hostels, with those living in their parents' homes or their own home participating least. A partial explanation of the high participation by those living in lodgings may well be the converse of the postulated cause of the low participation of those living at

Table 4.9 Participation in student life: by year of course
Undergraduates

					Percentages
Participation	1st year	2nd year	3rd year	No answer	All
Attending a society meeting	88	83	80	76	83
Belonging to:					
0 societies	13	18	25	34	20
1 society	18	25	27	22	23
2 societies	26	28	25	16	25
3 or more societies	43	29	23	28	32
Total	100	100	100	100	100
Sitting on a society committee	23	39	46	27	34
Holding union post	14	22	18	13	17
Attending union meetings:					
Frequently	53	52	33	41	46
Occasionally	32	29	37	32	32
Very rarely/never	15	19	30	26	22
Total	100	100	100	100	100
N	474	449	376	103	1413

home, that is, it has the fewest counter-attractions in terms of social activities of all the types considered. It is possible that part of the explanation also lies in the fact that more students live in lodgings during their first year at the School than later in their undergraduate career, and as is shown below there is a strong association between participation and year of course amongst undergraduates.[14]

Table 4.9 shows that a higher proportion of first- and second-year than of third-year students attended union and society meetings and were members of several different societies. This is probably due to the pressure of final examinations, which forces third-year students to concentrate on their academic work. The second-year group had the highest proportion holding a union post, where-

Table 4.10 Participation in student life: by age

Undergraduates

Percentages

| Participation | Age | | | | |
	19 or under	20/1	22/5	26 or over	All
Attending a society meeting	88	85	77	65	83
Belonging to:					
0 societies	14	19	21	39	20
1 society	18	24	28	28	23
2 societies	25	28	26	17	25
3 or more societies	43	29	15	16	32
Total	100	100	100	100	100
Sitting on a society committee	27	41	40	15	34
Holding union post	16	20	19	7	17
Attending union meetings:					
Frequently	53	46	42	28	46
Occasionally	32	33	31	34	32
Very rarely/never	15	21	27	38	22
Total	100	100	100	100	100
N	474	449	376	103	1413

as committee members were drawn more frequently from third-year than second-year students. The differences in attitudes between students in different years were small.

The results for age reflect the results for year of course. The younger the student, the more likely it is that he had attended at least one society meeting, that he was a member of several societies and that he attended union meetings frequently. On the other hand, the age-groups with the highest proportion of students holding union posts and sitting on society committees were the ' 20-1s ' and the ' 22-5s '.

There were similar differences for postgraduates: the younger students were more involved in every case, including committee membership. This can be explained perhaps by the fact that the younger postgraduates were less likely to be married and therefore more likely to be free to participate in student activities. There was no difference in attitudes between the older and younger students with the exception of the fact that a higher number of the latter group had a more favourable view of a sabbatical year for the president.

The variation with year of course was more difficult to gauge for postgraduates, since 75% of the respondents were in their first year. The small number of respondents in their third year means that only comparisons between students in their first and second years are meaningful. The differences were similar to those for undergraduates. There was higher participation by first year students with the exception of committee membership, which was greater amongst those in their second year. Differences in attitude were small.

Field of Study

Table 4.11 shows for undergraduates the association between field of study and participation in student life. Membership of societies was highest amongst students studying geography or law, followed by the sociologists and the statisticians. Those studying economics and government tended to join fewer societies. However, membership was lowest in the ' other ' category, which was a mixed group consisting primarily of general-course students. The participation of this group was lower than any other in every way. The large number of foreign students, in particular Americans, in this group was probably a contributory factor.

There were considerable variations between subjects in the pro-

Table 4.11   Participation in student life field of study
Undergraduates

Percentages

Participation	Economics	Statistics, indy. and trade computing	Government	Sociology, anthropology	Geography	History, economic history	Law	International relations, International history	General and others	All
Belonging to:										
0 societies	25	17	21	18	10	18	13	19	39	20
1 society	22	24	24	26	13	22	18	26	26	23
2 societies	23	27	24	23	28	30	33	23	19	25
3 or more societies	30	32	31	33	49	30	36	32	16	32
Total	100	100	100	100	100	100	100	100	100	100
Member of academic society	19	29	28	37	71	63	63	28	18	38
Sitting on a society committee	33	35	32	35	47	43	36	35	15	34
Holding Union post	13	16	24	23	14	14	43	35	9	17
Attending Union meetings:										
Frequently	43	37	51	57	39	49	50	50	38	46
Occasionally	37	36	26	26	35	31	34	28	35	32
Very rarely/ Never	20	27	23	17	26	20	16	22	27	22
Total	100	100	100	100	100	100	100	100	100	100
N	220	212	109	249	124	125	160	95	108	1413

portion of undergraduates who were members of an academic society. This form of participation was least popular amongst the economists (19%) and most popular amongst the geographers (71%). Geographers also had the highest proportion of committee members (47%), followed by the historians (43%). There was little difference between the other specialists. The variation in the proportion having held union posts was greater and, in this case the geographers and historians occupied the lowest places, along with the economists, and the lawyers had the highest proportion (43%). Although the participation of sociology students was fairly high on all the measures so far considered, they only occupied the highest position for attendance at Union meetings, 57% attending frequently and 17% rarely or never, compared with figures of 37% and 27% respectively for the statisticians, who attended least often. The general pattern was one of low participation in all activities amongst the economists, especially high participation in societies but not the Union by the geographers, the converse of this for the sociologists, and high participation in both by the lawyers. It is not at all easy to interpret these results, although it is possible to speculate about them in one or two instances. The high proportion of geographers who belong to the Geography Society may be due in part to the fact that the activities of the latter merge with those of the course more clearly than those of other academic societies. In the 1968 Student Union Handbook it is stated that, ' The association has a strong academic bias. Speakers, often from other universities, give lectures intended both for the specialist and for general interest. Week-end field trips are held in many parts of England. An annual journal, *Horizon,* is published, for which students are encouraged to submit original work '. The high proportion of the lawyers holding union posts might be related to an interest in the operation of political organisations with a constitutional basis, or possibly to a desire to develop the ability to speak in public.

In the case of postgraduates only three measures of participation were investigated, since the numbers holding union posts and on society committees were very small. The numbers in some of the departments were also small and the results must be treated with caution. Participation in society activities was highest among students doing diplomas in social administration, and, unlike the undergraduates, lowest amongst lawyers and geographers. One of the explanations for the high participation of students in social administration may be that quite a high proportion of this group were not graduates and were experiencing university life for the first time. Consequently, they would have been more inclined to

E

join societies enthusiastically or attend union meetings than those who have done all this before. Attendance at union meetings was highest for sociologists and lowest among statisticians and geographers, as was the case for undergraduates.

Among the postgraduates, the sociologists and geographers were the most dissatisfied with accommodation for common rooms. The geographers, consistent with their low participation in union life, were also the most dissatisfied with union representation and the least in favour of a sabbatical year for the President, whereas the sociologists, consistent with their high attendance at the Union, were least dissatisfied with union representation and, along with students of social administration, most in favour of a sabbatical year.

Father's occupation, secondary schooling, past employment and 'A' level performance
The association between involvement in student life and father's occupation was investigated separately for all British and all foreign students. The number of students from overseas with fathers in manual or clerical occupations was so small that it was only possible to investigate differences between the professional, managerial and own-business groups. These were negligible, and the differences among British students were also very small. The information collected on type of secondary school attended was confined to British students. There were some small differences among the undergraduates, with a tendency for students from independent schools to be less involved than those from grammar or direct-grant schools. For example, 35% of students from independent schools attended union meetings frequently, compared with 40% and 46% of the latter groups. These small differences in participation were reflected in attitudes; for example, 64% of students from independent schools were in favour of a sabbatical year for the President of the Students' Union on principle, compared with 76% of those from grammar schools and 79% of those from direct-grant schools.

There was an over-all tendency for students from direct-grant schools to be slightly more involved than those from grammar schools, but the differences were in all cases small. Perhaps the lower participation and more negative attitudes of students from independent schools were due to wider social contacts outside

L.S.E. which compete with their interests in it. We have, of course no evidence on this, but it seems likely that the predominantly upper-middle-class students who attended such schools would have a wider network of acquaintances in London than lower-middle- or working-class students. It may also be due to their greater conservatism (see Chapter 3, Table 3.13, p. 53). The difference between direct-grant schools and grammar schools is more difficult to interpret, and amongst the postgraduates this situation was reversed, with ex-grammar-school pupils attending the Union most often and having the most positive attitudes towards it, but again the differences were small.

There are slight indications of a non-linear relationship between amount of time spent in past employment and society membership. Those who had no employment experience and those who had more than two years' experience belonged to fewer societies than those who had worked for six months to two years. The lower membership of the students who had worked longest is related to the fact that they were also the older students. It was not clear why students with no employment experience, that is, the group who came to L.S.E. straight from school, should be less involved than the middle groups. It is possible that the student who deliberately avoids going to university straight from school in order to broaden his experience is more enterprising and more interested in non-academic pursuits when he arrives there. And those who did spend some time in employment, not as a result of a deliberate decision, but because it was forced upon them, might arrive at university more interested in non-academic pursuits there as a result of this break. Among the postgraduates there was little difference between those who had never been employed and those who had worked.

Finally, the effect of 'A' level grades was investigated to compare the levels of participation of the more academically successful students with those who had been less successful. Unfortunately, 'A' level grades were the only measure of academic ability available for all British students and are not applicable to the majority of students from overseas. Among British students (undergraduates and postgraduates combined), grades achieved in 'A' level appeared to make little difference to the extent of participation in student life. However, those students with no 'A' levels were less involved than those who did have them. Again, this was probably due to the fact that a high proportion of this group was considerably older than those who had taken 'A' levels.

Political views: home students
Interests in politics

Chapter 3 indicated that there are striking differences in political attitudes and levels of interest in politics between students of different party allegiance. For this reason it seemed important to investigate the relationship between some of these attributes and involvement in student life. Among the undergraduates, interest in national politics was related to all the measures of participation in student life covered by this survey, but in most cases the relationship was fairly small; the largest association was with attendance at union meetings, shown in Table 4.12.

Table 4.12 Attendance at union meetings: by interest in national politics

Home students

Percentages

Interest in National Politics	Union attendance				
	Frequently	Occasionally	Rarely or never	Total	N
Undergraduates					
Very interested	57	28	15	100	510
Moderately interested	42	35	23	100	543
Slightly or not interested	26	31	43	100	148
No answer	(40)	(40)	(20)	(100)	5
All	47	31	22	100	1206
Postgraduates					
Very interested	27	30	43	100	161
Moderately interested	11	29	60	100	186
Slightly or not interested	8	24	68	100	50
No answer	(67)	(33)	(0)	(100)	3
All	17	29	54	100	400

In the case of society membership, 14% of those who were very interested in politics belonged to no societies compared with 26% of those who were slightly or not interested. Thirty-nine per cent of those who were very interested compared with 30% of those who were only slightly interested or not interested, served on committees. Similarly, the percentages having held Union posts were 22% and 14% respectively. Lastly, 39% of those who were very interested in politics belonged to party political societies, compared with 9% of those who were only slightly interested or not interested. Turning to attitudes towards the Union, although there was a tendency for the most politically aware students to have the most favourable opinions about the Union, the differences were neither consistent nor large. Among postgraduates the differences were even less marked than among undergraduates.

Party allegiance

Party allegiances appeared to have little effect on participation in student life, with the exception of membership of political societies and attendance at the Union. In the former case, a higher proportion of the students aligned to the Conservatives were members of a party political society than of those aligned to Labour. Thirty-six per cent of the Tory students belonged to this type of society, compared with 25% of the Liberals and 21% of the Labour students.[15] However, the highest participation was by the Left-wing Groups, of whom 37% belonged to a party political society. The reason for this is that they were probably more deeply interested than other political groups. An alternative explanation might be that those students with minority views about politics have a greater need to belong to formal groups where they can meet and associate with others having similar political views. At L.S.E. the Conservatives and the extreme left constituted 20% and 10% respectively of the student population, excluding those from overseas. Although the former group is relatively large, the Conservative Party and the views it embodies are anathema to many of the other students at L.S.E., partly because most students who align themselves with Labour at L.S.E., we suspect, are to the left of the Party in the country or in the House of Commons. To suggest that the Conservative student at L.S.E. is ostracised for his views would be highly exaggerated, but in certain departments his allegiances would not endear him to many of his contemporaries. Consequently, he may feel a greater need for solidarity with those holding his views via membership of a formal association. Another more simple explanation, and in our view a more likely one, is that Conservatives in general tend to be ' joiners' and the Young Conservative image affects the size of membership of the Conservative Society at L.S.E. Extreme left-wing individuals complying with the doctrines of the left tend to organise themselves into groups to discuss and plan political action. Yet another possibility is that, as a result of the policies of the present Government, those students who aligned themselves with Labour lacked the enthusiasm to join the Labour Society because of their general disillusionment with the Government.

However, although those aligned to Labour did not belong to political societies in such large numbers as other groups, Table 4.13 shows that they did attend union meetings more frequently than their right-wing contemporaries. Forty-nine per cent of Labour undergraduates attended very frequently, compared with 42% of Liberals and 34% of Conservatives, and as many as 74% of the Left-wing Groups attended very frequently. The suggestion made by some students that the Union is dominated by political extremists on the left was true in terms of the proportion of this group which regularly turned up for meetings, but if the question is examined in terms of numbers rather than proportions it is not true. However, there may be some extremists on the issue of student power who align themselves to Labour, which would

Table 4.13 Attendance at union meetings: by party allegiance

Home undergraduates

Percentages

Party allegiance	Attendance at union meetings				
	Frequently	Occasionally	Rarely or never	Total	N
Conservative	34	38	28	100	243
Liberal	42	33	25	100	194
Labour	49	31	20	100	507
Left-wing groups	74	18	8	100	103
Don't know or no answer	46	28	26	100	144
All	47	31	22	100	1206

inflate these numbers; and, secondly, although the number of students in the Left-wing Groups was fairly small, they may have been more vociferous and better organised than the more moderate groups.

Although party allegiance was not associated with participation in student life apart from the above exceptions, it was associated with attitudes towards it. Tables 4.14 and 4.15 show this.

The further left the student, the more dissatisfied he was with the resources provided by the School, and the more satisfied he was with the Union. This pattern was less marked for postgraduates, for whom tables have not always been included, owing to the high proportion who had no opinion on these issues. Table 4.14 shows that amongst undergraduates 48% of the Left-wing Groups thought that representation of student opinion by the Union was

Table 4.14   Union representation: by party allegiance

Home students

Percentages

Party allegiance	Adequate	Inadequate	Don't know no answer	Total	N
		Union representation			
Undergraduates					
Conservative	17	76	7	100	243
Liberal	28	66	6	100	194
Labour	41	54	5	100	507
Left-wing groups	48	48	4	100	103
Don't know or no answer	21	67	12	100	144
All	32	62	6	100	1206
Postgraduates					
Conservative	23	45	32	100	47
Liberal	27	41	32	100	56
Labour	33	42	25	100	213
Left-wing groups	30	42	28	100	36
Don't know or no answer	31	38	31	100	39
All	31	42	27	100	400

Table 4.15 Sabbatical year for president: by party allegiance
Home undergraduates

Percentages

Party allegiance	Sabbatical year				Total	N
	On principle	At school's discretion	Not at all	Don't know no answer		
Conservative	63	24	8	5	100	243
Liberal	74	19	5	2	100	194
Labour	81	13	3	3	100	507
Left-wing groups	80	7	8	5	100	103
Don't know or no answer	69	15	8	8	100	144
All	74	16	6	4	100	1206

adequate, compared with only 17% of the Conservative students. However, the differences for postgraduates were much smaller, although they were in the same direction. The only exception to the general principle outlined above was some reluctance on the part of the Left-wing Groups to grant a sabbatical year to the President of the Union: Table 4.15 shows that the same proportion of this group as of the Conservatives believed that there should be no sabbatical year. The explanation of this seeming anomaly is probably the opposition of some of the very left-wing students to the union hierarchy, which they tend to regard as a system designed for bureaucratic nonentities who refuse to take a militant line.[16] There is a growing disdain amongst this group for formal office-holding and the accolades that go with it; the socialist society at L.S.E. has no chairman; it has instead a coordinating committee. This may be the reason for the reluctance of some of them to favour a sabbatical year for the President of the Students' Union. On the issue of control over union premises, a considerably higher proportion of the Left-wing Groups believed this was important than of those aligned to the main political parties. (See Appendix C, Table 4.4A.)

Political views: overseas students
The relationship between overseas students' political views, and their involvement in student life was also investigated. Again, the only measure of participation to be associated with political views was attendance at the Union.

Table 4.16 **Attendance at union meetings: by political views**

All overseas students

Percentages

Political views	Frequently	Occasionally	Very rarely or never	No answer	Total	N
Undergraduates						
Conservative	(32)	(42)	(26)	(0)	(100)	19
Liberal	33	42	25	0	100	72
Socialist	53	36	11	0	100	74
Other	(62)	(15)	(23)	(0)	(100)	13
Don't know or no answer	(38)	(38)	(24)	(0)	(100)	29
All	42	38	20	0	100	207
Postgraduates						
Conservative	16	13	71	0	100	31
Liberal	16	24	59	1	100	176
Socialist	21	31	46	2	100	132
Other	22	26	50	2	100	46
Don't know or no answer	17	22	54	7	100	41
All	18	26	54	2	100	426

Although there are slight inconsistencies, Table 4.16 shows that socialists attend more frequently than liberals or conservatives. As among the British, the more left-wing students from abroad had only slightly more favourable attitudes towards representation by the Union than the conservatives and liberals (see Appendix C, Table 4.5A), but a much higher proportion of the socialists than of the conservatives or liberals considered that control of union premises was important. The socialist students' attitude to a

E*

sabbatical year was also much more positive than that of the conservatives or liberals.

Summary

The level of participation in student activities at L.S.E. is higher on all measures amongst undergraduates than amongst postgraduates, and British students tended to participate more than those from overseas. Amongst the various forms of participation, 34% of undergraduates had at some time served on society committees, and 17% had held a post in the Union. Nearly half the undergraduates and one-fifth of the postgraduates attended union meetings frequently. There were positive associations of varying size between each of the various measures, indicating that the various activities were complementary rather than alternatives. Turning to opinions, there was a great deal of criticism of the accommodation available for common rooms and for union meetings. There was also a good deal of criticism of the Union; the majority of the respondents felt that representation of student opinion by the Union was inadequate. Nevertheless, most students believed that the President of the Union should have a sabbatical year on principle and that it was important that the Union should have complete control over its premises.

Various personal characteristics of the students were associated with high or low participation. In particular, married students were far less active than single students. There were differences between students of different nationality, the Europeans emerging as particularly involved and the Australasians and Canadians as least involved. Students in the first or second year of their course tended to participate more than those in their third year, and the younger students were rather more likely to be involved than older students. With the exception of those studying law, students whose field of study was of a vocational kind, such as accounting, tended to be less involved than those studying non-vocational subjects, such as sociology or international relations. There were small differences in levels of participation according to the type of secondary school the student had attended: those who had been to independent schools were less involved than those who had been to maintained schools. There were also small differences between those who had worked for six months to two years and those who had been employed for longer periods or not at all, the first group being more involved in student life than the latter two. There were no consistent differences according to the 'A' level grades or social class of the students, and fairly small differences according to sex and type of accommodation.

Interest in national politics was related to participation in student life; the measure of participation for which the association was largest was attendance at union meetings: the more interested the student was in politics, the more likely he was to attend frequently. Party allegiance was not consistently related to activism, although it was associated with attendance at union meetings, left wing students attending more often than those on the right. Finally, the further to the left were the student's political views, the more likely he was to have favourable attitudes towards the Union and critical attitudes towards the resources available for student affairs.

Chapter 5

Dissatisfaction with the school

At the time of the 1967 protest demonstrations at the School several commentators suggested that students were acutely and legitimately dissatisfied with the increasingly overcrowded buildings, the impersonality of contacts with staff, the low priority given by the staff to their teaching-duties and the inadequacy of student life at a commuter university. Although this dissatisfaction was not necessarily seen as the primary cause of the student protest, it was said to have provided the fertile ground in which the seeds of rebellion could flourish. Because of this theory, which seemed more plausible before the numerous incidents and demonstrations at other universities in Britain had taken place, we included in our questionnaire two questions relating to student satisfaction. The findings from question 33, which was concerned, primarily, with attitudes towards the facilities and functioning of the Union, were discussed in Chapter 4. In the other question (26) the student was asked to rate his level of satisfaction with each of nine aspects of the School, ranging from teaching to its libraries and location. The results are presented in this chapter.

Our objective in asking question 26 was two-fold: firstly to investigate the relative extent of dissatisfaction with each of the aspects covered and secondly to examine variations in the level of satisfaction of different sub-groups of students, defined in terms of their educational and family background, their courses of study at the School, their political views and their involvement in the various protest actions in 1967. It is possible that answers to question 26 were influenced by the events which had taken place at the School in the six months prior to the survey and the public discussion of these events and their causes. On this we have no evidence. Nevertheless, discussion of the relative levels of student satisfaction on the different aspects covered, and the variations between the expressed satisfaction of different sub-groups is meaningful. In presenting the results comparative data for students of the School and students elsewhere are quoted whenever relevant data exist.

Some discussion of the areas covered by the question is necessary for the evaluation of the answers obtained. Undergraduate teaching at L.S.E. is by means of lectures, classes and tutorials. Attendance at lectures is optional, and the size of the audience varies from a maximum of about 400 in one first-year economics course to a mere handful of students taking some of the special subjects or newer degrees. Many lecture courses are supplemented by weekly or fortnightly classes usually ranging in size from eight to twelve students. The classes, attendance at which is formally compulsory, vary in form from the impromptu lecture to the solution of a set of mathematical problems, but usually involve students in work preparation and discussion. They are regarded as an important teaching-instrument and provide an opportunity for the student's progress in each subject to be evaluated and for individual guidance to be given where needed.

Some use is also made at the School of the system of tutorial teaching. Each undergraduate is allocated to a member of staff as his tutor throughout each year of his course, but there is no set pattern in regard to the frequency with which tutors are seen, whether they are met individually or in groups, or whether the tutor interprets his function as one of general supervision or personal tuition. Variations in the form and frequency of tutorials occur principally between departments and depend largely on the use made of class teaching, but within every department there are no doubt differences between members of staff in regard to their interpretation of their role as tutors.

The range and structure of the degrees available to students of the School at both the undergraduate and postgraduate levels have continuously evolved over the years. In general there has been a steady addition to the number of first degrees and possible subjects of specialisation within a first degree, together with a reduction in the number of compulsory subjects. At the postgraduate level, the one-year M.Sc. by examination was first introduced in 1964. For this group of postgraduates, for those taking the Ll.M. and for diploma students, the teaching-programme is similar in form to that provided for undergraduates, consisting of lectures, classes, seminars and tutorials. As for the undergraduates, there is considerable variation in the frequency of postgraduate tutorials.

Informal contacts with staff can also take place in the various bars and eating-places provided within the School, but many members of staff use only the staff dining-room to which students cannot be invited. There are no departmental coffee-rooms or lounges where staff and students can meet casually. Most departments give parties for students, but each student is likely to be invited only once each year. Sherry or tea parties may also be provided by tutors for their tutees once or twice yearly at the expense of the School.

Since 1896 the School has housed, in increasingly inadequate space, the British Library of Political and Economic Science. This is the largest library of its kind in Europe. It attracts many research workers and also serves as the main working library for students of the School. Because of the extent of student demand for text-books, there is in addition a teaching library which has a stock of roughly 20,000 volumes covering the more important books required by both undergraduates and postgraduates for course work. The two libraries together provide seating-space for approximately 1,000 readers. Although the School's library has in the past been considered one of its main advantages, in recent years students have increasingly voiced complaints concerning the inadequacy of the seating capacity and the stock of text-books. The teaching library was expanded and library hours extended in order to try to meet student needs, but the basic problems due to space limitation seem likely to persist as long as the School continues to be located on the Houghton Street site.

Both the disadvantages and the advantages of a university site in central London are well known. It seems unlikely that a majority of the School's staff would ever be in favour of a move to any specific suburban site: several possibilities have been considered and rejected. No information concerning student views on the School's location has ever been sought and this was therefore included in question 26, together with the related topic of student lodgings. The School has two halls of residence in central London which together provide accommodation for 306 students. There are in addition a number of intercollegiate halls, some of which are specifically for postgraduates, and a small number of flatlets available for letting to married postgraduates at the School. The Lodgings Bureau of the University of London assists students in their search for lodgings.

The levels of satisfaction expressed by students in answer to question 26 provide measures of the extent to which certain of their expectations and needs in regard to university life were being met at the time of the survey. Where sub-groups of students express different levels of satisfaction with any specific aspect this may be due either to differences in their expectations and needs or in the real value of what they have experienced. Some evidence concerning the nature of students' expectations and the extent to which they are realised was obtained by Peter Marris[1] in his survey in 1961-2 of samples of students from three universities and a college of advanced technology. However, neither in the Marris study nor elsewhere have we found any evidence concerning the relationship between prior knowledge and expectations and eventual dissatisfaction. In interpreting differences between the satisfaction expressed by sub-groups of students with different backgrounds or following different courses of study, the compound nature of the measure must be borne in mind.

The findings are reported in five sections. We first compare the expressed levels of satisfaction of the undergraduates with those of the postgraduates and look at the differences in the views of home and overseas students. Variations in satisfaction with other characteristics of the student's background, course of study and political views are then examined in four sections, the first of which covers teaching, staff contacts and degree structure, the second the libraries, the third location and the fourth accommodation. The relationship between dissatisfaction and participation in the boycott and sit-in is discussed in Chapter 9.

Comparative levels of satisfaction with the nine aspects

As Table 5.1 shows, both undergraduates and postgraduates expressed more satisfaction with their accommodation and with the location of the School than with any other of the nine aspects listed in the questionnaire. In fact, just over half of the postgraduates and nearly half of the undergraduates were very satisfied with their accommodation. In the case of both student categories the greatest dissatisfaction was with the school libraries. In a sample survey of postgraduates carried out in 1964,[2] 80% of full-time graduates in the sample said they found the main library inadequate. Our figure of 65% of graduates regarding it as very or fairly unsatisfactory thus provides some evidence of a diminution in graduate dissatisfaction with the main library between 1964 and 1967.

Table 5.1 Satisfaction with L.S.E.
Undergraduates and postgraduates

Percentages

Attitude	Lectures		Classes		Tutorials		Degree structure		Staff contacts		Main library		Teaching library		Location		Accommo- dation	
	UG	PG	UG	PG	UG	PG	UG	PG	UG	PG	UG	PG	UG	PG	UG	PG	UG	PG
Very satisfactory	11	19	10	21	26	37	11	21	15	29	4	5	4	5	38	40	48	52
Fairly satisfactory	57	49	51	49	33	29	42	41	33	40	33	26	38	31	38	33	38	35
Fairly unsatisfactory	22	17	27	18	19	13	24	16	27	17	33	39	31	29	10	11	7	6
Very unsatisfactory	8	4	10	8	19	10	15	9	22	10	28	26	21	22	10	10	4	4
Other	2	11	2	4	3	11	8	13	3	4	2	4	6	13	4	6	3	3
All	100	100	100	100	100	100	100	100	100	100	100	100	100	100	100	100	100	100

Postgraduates showed a higher level of satisfaction than undergraduates with all aspects of teaching, degree structure and staff contacts, the difference being greatest in regard to tutorials and staff contacts. Comparison with the 1964 survey is possible in the case of tutorials. In 1964 25% of full-time postgraduates in the sample reported that they were receiving too little supervision. Our survey shows approximately the same percentage of those who expressed an opinion, classifying their tutorials as very or fairly unsatisfactory. Lectures and classes appear to have evoked less strong feelings either of satisfaction or dissatisfaction than tutorials. Classes were regarded as marginally less satisfactory than lectures. Sixty-eight per cent of both undergraduates and postgraduates regarded their lectures as either very or fairly satisfactory. This result may be compared with data from the Marris[3] survey of third-year undergraduate non-scientists at Cambridge, Leeds, and Southampton in which 44%, 62% and 54% respectively, judged over half of their lectures good.

Differences in the satisfaction of home and overseas students were in most cases negligible. At the undergraduate level overseas students showed slightly more satisfaction with lectures and classes and slightly less satisfaction with staff contacts than home students. In the case of overseas postgraduates, satisfaction with staff contacts, tutorials, accommodation and location were slightly less than that of their British counterparts.

Each student was asked to indicate which aspects of the nine covered by the questionnaire he regarded as the most satisfactory and the most unsatisfactory. Analysis of the replies to this question confirmed the above findings based upon individual-aspect ratings. The three aspects rated most satisfactory and most unsatisfactory by the largest numbers of students are shown in Table 5.2 for the four principal sub-groups of students. Accommodation was clearly regarded by both home and overseas students as the most satisfactory of the nine aspects, the School's location and tutorials tying for second place. This was a surprising finding as London students are normally regarded as badly placed in regard to accommodation compared with those in smaller cities or on campus sites.

The situation in regard to tutorials is interesting in that they are included both as one of the three most satisfactory and the three most unsatisfactory aspects. This confirms what is shown in Table

Table 5.2   Most satisfactory and most unsatisfactory aspects

| | *Undergraduates* | | | |
	Home		*Overseas*	
		%		%
Three most satisfactory aspects	Accommodation	29	Accommodation	25
	Location	20	Tutorials	18
	Tutorials	14	Lectures	14
		%		%
Three most unsatisfactory aspects	Main library	24	Main library	27
	Degree structure	14	Staff contacts	15
	Staff contacts	14	Tutorials	13
	Postgraduates			
	Home		*Overseas*	
Three most satisfactory aspects	Accommodation	22	Accommodation	17
	Tutorials	18	Tutorials	17
	Location	14	Location	13
		%		%
Three most unsatisfactory aspects	Main library	42	Main library	40
	Teaching library	11	Tutorials	7
	Staff contacts and Degree structure	8	Location	6

5.1, that there is a much greater variation between students in their attitudes toward tutorials than to any other of the aspects of life at the School. Though a considerable percentage of students regard their tutorials as very satisfactory, another fairly large group are highly dissatisfied.

The dominance of dissatisfaction with the main library over other dissatisfaction, particularly among postgraduates, is very striking. However, among undergraduates roughly one in seven were most dissatisfied with staff contacts and one in eight with their tutorials and the structure of their degrees. The teaching library, though shown in Table 5.1 to be regarded as very unsatisfactory by a large percentage of students, was rated the single most unsatisfactory aspect of the School by only about 8% of all students. One postgraduate commented that in his view the most unsatisfactory aspect of the School was none of the nine listed, but was 'the depressing, pervading, feeling of overcrowding'.

Satisfaction with teaching, staff contacts and degree structure: Undergraduates

Course of study

Satisfaction with teaching, staff contacts and degree structure showed considerable variation according to the degrees or special subjects of the B.Sc.(Econ.) which the undergraduates were taking. The results are shown in full in Appendix C, Table 5.1A, and summarised below in Table 5.3 which shows the variation in satisfaction by course of study, by specifying the range of percentage satisfaction and the extreme groups on each aspect.

Table 5.3 Range of percentage satisfaction within degree groups

Undergraduates

Aspect	Range of satisfaction* among degree groups	Most satisfied group	Least satisfied group
	% to %		
Lectures	84 to 53	Industry and trade†	Government and B.A./B.Sc. (Sociology)
Classes	74 to 44	L1.B	Sociology†
Tutorials	87 to 42	B.A./B.Sc. (Geography)	Statistics†
Staff contacts	87 to 29	B.A./B.Sc. (Geography) and B.A. (History)	Sociology†
Degree structure	69 to 23	Statistics†	B.A. (History)

*Derived from Table 5.1A, Appendix C, excluding groups of size thirty or less.
†Special subject in B.Sc.(Econ.)

Satisfaction with staff contacts shows the widest variation, specialists in sociology within the B.Sc.(Econ.) expressing greatest dissatisfaction and those taking degrees in history and geography the greatest satisfaction. Satisfaction with tutorials showed little correlation with satisfaction with staff contacts. Although the geographers expressed the same high level of satisfaction with both staff contacts and tutorials, the statistics specialists were least satisfied with tutorials, although well above average in their satisfaction with staff-contacts. The variations in satisfaction with tutorials by course of study no doubt reflect the reliance placed by the different departments on tutorials as an integral part of their teaching-programme. Where class teaching has largely replaced tutorials, students are less likely to have expressed satisfaction with the role of their tutorials. On the other hand, satisfaction with tutorials does not imply satisfaction with staff contacts in general. Both groups of sociology specialists, whilst showing fairly high levels of satisfaction with tutorials, expressed much lower levels of satisfaction with staff contacts.

Satisfaction with lectures and classes showed roughly the same amount of variation among degree groups, although satisfaction with lectures was, in practically every case, higher than satisfaction with classes. In interpreting these results the optional nature of lecture attendance must be remembered. One student who expressed strong views on the irrelevancy of lectures, with which no doubt many would agree, attacked his classes from a different standpoint: 'The fact that lectures are often boring and bad is of little importance since lectures are comparatively irrelevant to a course of study. One ought to be able to get as much if not more out of a good text-book. Class arrangements are bad because the classes have too many people in them'.

Year of Course

For the undergraduates as a whole, satisfaction with lectures and classes was unrelated to years at the School. Among the B.Sc.(Econ) students, dissatisfaction with lectures and classes was greatest among first years, whereas among those taking the Ll.B or the B.A./B.Sc. Sociology dissatisfaction was usually least among the first-year students. This finding may be explained by the different degree-structures, the B.Sc.(Econ.) students being able to specialise only in their second and third years.

In the case of tutorials, dissatisfaction was highest among first years, 29% of whom found their tutorials very unsatisfactory and a further 20% fairly unsatisfactory. B.Sc.(Econ.) first years who had tutors from departments unrelated to their future field of specialisation were more dissatisfied than those taking other degrees, 59% reporting their tutorials to be unsatisfactory. These results are consistent with those obtained in an unpublished survey of B.Sc.(Econ.) second-year students at L.S.E. Ninety per cent of respondents to a questionnaire, sent out in 1966, said that their Part I tutors set no work relevant to Part I and 63% that 'other than in relation to such set work' their tutorials were of little help. The tutorial arrangements for Part I B.Sc.(Econ.) students were changed from September 1967, first-year tutors being from the department of intended specialisation.

Satisfaction with staff contacts was also related to years at the School, increasing steadily from a level of 38% of first year students to 58% of third years. One can only speculate on the extent to which this increased level of satisfaction was due to more opportunities for contact or a change in the extent to which contact was desired.

Sex, age and nationality

Satisfaction with lectures and classes was unrelated to the sex of the student, but the women appeared to be slightly more satisfied with their tutorials and staff contacts. There was a tendency for the youngest students in each year to be most dissatisfied with all aspects of teaching, but differences were slight.

The differences in satisfaction shown by home and overseas

Table 5.4 Satisfaction with lectures: by nationality

Undergraduates

Percentages

Nationality	Very satisfactory	Fairly satisfactory	Fairly unsatisfactory	Very unsatisfactory	Other	Total	N
			Lectures				
British	9	58	23	9	1	100	1206
Asian	17	55	18	6	4	100	66
African	23	51	11	6	9	100	47
American	40	37	9	12	2	100	43
European	25	47	25	3	0	100	32
Other	(5)	(79)	(11)	(5)	(0)	100	19
All	11	57	22	8	2	100	1413

undergraduates are interesting. Overseas students, and Americans in particular, expressed more satisfaction than the British with both lectures and classes. Table 5.4 shows satisfaction with lectures for the four main sub-groups of overseas undergraduates and for the British. The differences did not appear to be due to the courses of study of the overseas students as they were found to exist within course of study sub-groups where numbers were large enough for the comparison to be made.

In regard to tutorials each of the four categories of overseas students was only marginally more satisfied than the British and, as Table 5.5 shows, satisfaction with staff contacts appeared to be greatest among British students. Although the Asian students were less satisfied with staff contacts than either the British undergraduates or the other overseas students, they were only marginally more dissatisfied than other students following the same course of study.

Table 5.5   Satisfaction with staff contacts: by nationality

Undergraduates

Percentages

Nationality	Very satisfactory	Fairly satisfactory	Fairly unsatisfactory	Very unsatisfactory	Other	Total	N
British	16	33	27	22	2	100	1206
Asian	6	23	36	23	12	100	66
African	15	26	19	26	14	100	47
American	9	42	26	21	2	100	43
European	6	44	22	22	6	100	32
Other	(26)	(16)	(11)	(42)	(5)	100	19
All	15	33	27	22	3	100	1413

Father's occupation and income

The small group of forty-one students whose father's occupation was classified as unskilled manual were slightly less satisfied than other undergraduates with lectures, classes, tutorials and staff contacts, whereas the group who classified their father's occupation as managerial were most satisfied with these aspects of L.S.E.

The relationship between satisfaction with lectures and father's occupation appeared to hold within courses of study, though differences were slight. Father's income was unrelated to satisfaction with classes or tutorials but appeared to be slightly related to satisfaction with lectures and staff contacts, satisfaction with staff contacts increasing from 44% of the lowest income-group to 55% of the highest and lecture satisfaction from 62% to 77%. These relationships still existed within the course-of-study sub-groups.

Secondary school and 'A' levels

Although the small group of thirty undergraduates from comprehensive schools showed slightly higher levels of satisfaction with all aspects of teaching than those from other types of schools, those from secondary modern schools were somewhat less satisfied than the rest. These results did not appear to be due to the courses being taken at the School. Those from independent and direct-grant schools were more satisfied with lectures, classes and staff contacts than those from grammar schools, though less satisfied with tutorials. These relationships still held within degree courses, and may reflect the different expectations of those from different types of schools.

No relationship could be observed between 'A' level performance and satisfaction with lectures, classes, tutorials or staff contacts. The 1966 survey of B.Sc.(Econ.) students showed satisfaction with Part I teaching-arrangements to be similarly unrelated to 'A' level performance.

Political and religious views

The political views of British undergraduates were found to be related to satisfaction with teaching, Conservatives being more satisfied than any other group with lectures, classes and staff contacts, though not with tutorials.

Although, as Table 5.6 shows, Labour supporters were clearly less satisfied with lectures and classes than Conservatives, the differences were relatively small compared with the large differences between the levels of satisfaction of the Conservatives and supporters of the Left-wing Groups. Differences in satisfaction with staff contacts were smaller, and satisfaction with tutorials showed practically no relationship to party allegiance. The observed patterns appeared to hold within course-of-study sub-groups and cannot therefore be assumed to be due to the different courses of study being pursued.

Table 5.6 Percentage satisfaction with teaching: by party allegiance

Home undergraduates

Percentages

Aspects of teaching	Conservative	Liberal	Labour	Left-wing groups	No Opinion	No answer
Lectures	80	71	71	45	39	50
Classes	70	65	57	45	47	57
Tutorials	58	61	57	53	55	73
Staff contacts	55	53	47	41	43	59
N	243	194	507	103	100	44

Note: The table shows the percentage of each group who found each aspect very or fairly satisfactory.

A strong relationship between party allegiance and religious beliefs had been found. It was therefore not surprising to find satisfaction with teaching was also related to religious beliefs. As Table 5.7 shows, undergraduates with some religious beliefs were more satisfied with each aspect of teaching and with staff contacts than were those of no religion.

Table 5.7 Percentage satisfaction with teaching: by religion

Undergraduates

Percentages

Aspects of teaching	Some religion	No religion
Lectures	75	61
Classes	67	54
Tutorials	61	56
Staff contacts	53	42
N	715	698

Note: The table shows the percentage of each group who found each aspect very or fairly satisfactory.

The largest difference (14%) was in regard to lectures, and the smallest (5%) was on tutorials. These differences again persisted within sub-groups of students following the same degree courses. No consistent differences were found between students of different religions although Anglicans and Non-conformists usually showed the highest levels of satisfaction.

Satisfaction with teaching, staff contacts and degree structure: Postgraduates and diploma students

Course of Study

Satisfaction with most aspects of the School varied quite considerably according to the postgraduate degree-course the student was taking. Table 5.8 shows for various degree categories the percentage of those answering who were satisfied (very or fairly) with the various forms of teaching, staff contacts and the structure of their courses. We have omitted from the table degree categories containing fewer than thirty respondents. Subjects of specialisation have not been taken into account because numbers became too small.

Table 5.8 Percentage satisfaction with aspects of L.S.E.: by course of study

Postgraduates

Percentages

Aspect	Course of study					
	Ph.D.	M.Phil.	M.Sc.	Diploma	Research fee	Ll.M.
Lectures	82	76	66	84	87	72
Seminars	77	71	62	85	78	59
Tutorials	75	78	64	88	72	48
Staff contacts	60	69	65	84	78	70
Degree structure	85	70	60	75	—	75
N	137	65	324	204	41	32

Notes: 1. The table shows the percentage of each group who found each aspect very or fairly satisfactory.

2. The percentages are based upon those answering the question.

3. Three M.A.s, one M.Sc. (Econ.) and nineteen no answers have been excluded.

The 204 diploma students, the majority of whom were studying social administration, expressed the highest level of satisfaction with each aspect of teaching, whereas the 324 M.Sc. students showed the lowest levels of satisfaction both with teaching and the structure of their degrees. Ph.D. students were less satisfied with staff contacts than were any other group. The forty-one research-fee students were fairly well satisfied with most aspects of the School.

Sex, age and nationality

As in the case of undergraduates, the female postgraduates showed a slightly higher level of satisfaction than the males both with tutorials and staff contacts. There was a slight tendency for satisfaction to increase with age.

Over-all comparisons of the satisfaction of home and overseas postgraduates revealed only small differences. A comparison of the attitudes of the two groups within each course of study was next made to see whether any larger differences would be revealed. Overseas postgraduates in each postgraduate-degree category appeared to be more satisfied than the British students with lectures, but the relationship was reversed among the diploma students. In regard to tutorials and staff contacts, overseas students working for a Ph.D. or M.Sc. were slightly more satisfied than the home students, but

Table 5.9   Percentage satisfaction with teaching: by nationality

Postgraduates

Percentages

Aspects of teaching	British	Australasian/ Canadian	Asian	African	American	European
Lectures	73	86	88	86	65	82
Seminars	73	65	77	75	66	72
Tutorials	72	69	81	68	67	72
Staff contacts	73	66	78	63	56	86
N	400	86	66	51	147	46

Notes: 1. The table shows the percentage of each group who found each aspect very or fairly satisfactory.

2. Thirty of other or unknown nationalities have been excluded.

other overseas postgraduates and diploma students were marginally less satisfied than the British.

The variation in satisfaction by nationality was examined for all postgraduates and is shown in Table 5.9 for groups of size thirty or more.

As in Table 5.8, percentages in Table 5.9 were based upon the number expressing some level of satisfaction or dissatisfaction, as the size of the 'no answers' and 'no opinion' categories varied considerably, being particularly high in the case of lectures, where the question was inappropriate for many Ph.D. students who attend few lectures. American postgraduates showed lower levels of satisfaction than students of any other nationality with each form of teaching and with staff contacts. The Asian postgraduates were, on the whole, the most satisfied group.

Although it would be of interest to compare the levels of satisfaction of students of different nationalities taking the same degree, numbers were too small in most cases for comparisons to be meaningful. The variations in the satisfaction of M.Sc. students of different nationalities are, however, shown in Table 5.10 and are seen to be quite large.

Table 5.10 Percentage satisfaction of M.Sc. students: by nationality
Postgraduates

Percentages

Aspect	British	American	Asian and African
Lectures	57	59	85
Tutorials	56	67	72
Staff contacts	66	57	75
N	131	87	57

Notes: 1. The table shows the percentage of each group who found each aspect very or fairly satisfactory.

2. Five Australians, sixteen Canadians, eighteen Europeans, ten others have been excluded.

Within the M.Sc. degree British students expressed a lower level of satisfaction with both lectures and tutorials than Americans, but the Americans were less satisfied with staff contacts. Asian and African students were, however, very much more satisfied than either British or American.

Father's occupation and income

No regular relationship was found between father's occupation or income and satisfaction with any aspect of the School.

School and university background

Satisfaction with teaching showed no relationship either to the type of school attended or 'A' level results. There was a small difference, however, in the levels of satisfaction with staff contacts shown by students from grammar schools (67%), direct-grant schools (82%) and independent schools (77%). This relationship was similar to that found in the case of undergraduates. Class of first degree showed no relationship to satisfaction with teaching.

The relative satisfaction of postgraduates who had taken their first degrees at L.S.E., at other London colleges or at other universities was examined. Satisfaction with lectures was highest (82%) among those students whose undergraduate work was at the School, and least (60%) among those from Oxford and Cambridge. In regard to tutorials differences were negligible, but graduates of the School again showed the highest level of satisfaction (80%) with staff contacts, those from other London colleges showing the lowest (58%).

Political views and religion

The party allegiance of British students showed a small but regular relationship to their expressed satisfaction with each aspect of teaching and staff contacts. The left-wing group of thirty-six students were considerably more dissatisfied than any other students, but the difference between Labour and Conservative party supporters was fairly small. Within the group of M.Sc. students there were only twenty-three supporters of the Conservative and Liberal parties. These students showed higher levels of satisfaction with each form of teaching and with staff contacts than those expressed by the eighty-three Labour Party supporters, the difference being greatest in regard to staff contacts. Among the diploma students there appeared to be no relationship between satisfaction and party allegiance. No other degree groups were large enough for meaningful comparisons to be made.

The political views of foreign students showed no regular relationship to satisfaction with teaching and staff contacts. Thus, although the thirty-one conservatives appeared to be rather more satisfied than the rest with their lectures, the liberals showed the greatest satisfaction with tutorials and the socialists were more satisfied than either conservatives or liberals with staff contacts.

Even these small differences disappeared for groups of overseas students taking the same degree. For both M.Sc. and Ph.D. students. there were no observed differences in the expressed satisfaction of those of different political views. Differences in the expressed satisfaction of postgraduates with different religious views were very small but, as in the case of undergraduates, those with no religion showed a slightly higher level of dissatisfaction with both teaching and staff contacts than did those with religious beliefs.

Satisfaction with the libraries:

Undergraduates

Satisfaction with the main library varied considerably by undergraduate course of study, ranging from 50% of the geographers to 22% of the general-course students. A similar degree of variation was found in regard to satisfaction with the teaching library, the statistics specialists who make relatively little use of the library being most satisfied (60%) and the historians least satisfied (23%). First-year students expressed slightly more dissatisfaction with the main library than other undergraduates, but satisfaction with the teaching library appeared to be unrelated to year of course. There were only small differences in the expressed levels of satisfaction of those with different political views.

Postgraduates

There was some variation in the amount of dissatisfaction with the libraries expressed by postgraduates following different courses of study. Forty-seven per cent of Ph.D. students found the main library very unsatisfactory whereas only 30% of diploma students were in this category. The dissatisfaction of other groups fell between these extremes. In the case of the teaching library the corresponding range was from 28% of Ll.M. students to 16% of diploma students.

The variation in satisfaction with the main library by field of specialisation was also examined. Over half of those specialising in international relations, international history and economic history found the main library very unsatisfactory as compared with roughly one-quarter of specialists in accountancy statistics and demography. It seems probable that this variation reflects to some extent the dependency of students in different departments upon the library, those in fields of specialisation requiring the most extensive reference to books and papers expressing the strongest dissatisfaction.

Satisfaction with location
Students may well have found some difficulty in rating their satisfaction with the School's location. As one student expressed his feelings:

One tends to adopt a slightly ambivalent attitude to L.S.E.'s siting in central London. There are some obvious advantages like the social amenities, theatres, cinemas etc., all within close reach. There is certainly very little campus life—I don't know whether this is good or bad. On the other hand, sporting facilities are limited and necessitate much travelling. And if one is used to country life, one misses the sight of trees and fields.

Few undergraduates have experienced life at more than one university and they therefore have no direct knowledge of the benefits of campus life. Little is known of the criteria used by school-leavers in deciding to which universities to apply. However, there were few students who did not answer the question or registered an answer of 'no opinion', and the over-all level of satisfaction with the School's location was high. In the case of both undergraduates and postgraduates women were rather more satisfied than men, 83% of all women expressing some level of satisfaction, compared with 71% of men. Among undergraduates there was a slight tendency for the youngest students and those with the shortest travel-times to be most satisfied, but the differences were small and did not show among the postgraduates.

Nationality
The variation in satisfaction by nationality is shown separately for undergraduates and postgraduates in Table 5.11.

Among the undergraduates the very large differences between the Americans, 61% of whom were very satisfied with the School's location, and the Asians and Africans, of whom only 23% were very satisfied, lead one to speculate on the extent to which the American undergraduates, most of whom spend only one year in Britain, were motivated to come to the School specifically because of its location. A similar pattern was shown among the postgraduates, although among British students postgraduates were more satisfied than undergraduates, whereas among Americans the postgraduates were less satisfied.

Table 5.11 Satisfaction with location by: nationality

Percentages

Location of L.S.E.

Nationality	Very satisfactory	Fairly satisfactory	Fairly unsatisfactory	Very unsatisfactory	Other	Total	N
Undergraduates							
British	38	38	11	10	3	100	1206
Asian	23	33	9	26	9	100	66
African	23	45	4	19	9	100	47
American	61	28	2	7	2	100	43
European	44	41	6	9	–	100	32
Other	(48)	(42)	(5)	(5)	(0)	100	19
All	38	38	10	11	3	100	1413
Postgraduates							
British	44	32	11	8	5	100	400
Australasian/ Canadian	37	42	6	9	6	100	86
Asian	23	35	15	21	6	100	66
African	22	28	12	28	10	100	51
American	50	31	10	5	4	100	147
European	33	30	15	13	9	100	46
Other	(33)	(30)	(17)	(13)	(7)	100	30
All	40	33	11	10	6	100	826

Satisfaction with location varied slightly with type of accommodation, those in rented accommodation without board being most
satisfied. There was also, not surprisingly, a relationship between
satisfaction with location and with accommodation, 80% of those
very satisfied with their accommodation being satisfied with the
location, whereas only 53% of those who were very dissatisfied
with their accommodation were satisfied with the location.

Satisfaction with accommodation

A high level of satisfaction with their living accommodation was
expressed by the students as a whole, and this satisfaction was
found to be unrelated to age, marital status or travel time. There

was a slight difference between the sexes, 90% of women as compared with 85% of men expressing some degree of satisfaction.

Nationality

Table 5.12 shows differences in satisfaction by nationality.

Table 5.12   Satisfaction with accommodation: by nationality

Percentages

Nationality	Living accommodation						
	Very satisfactory	Fairly satisfactory	Fairly unsatisfactory	Very unsatisfactory	Other	Total	N
Undergraduates							
British	48	38	7	4	3	100	1206
Asian	47	41	3	9	0	100	66
African	23	53	9	11	4	100	47
American	56	35	7	2	0	100	43
European	63	22	9	3	3	100	32
Other	(42)	(53)	(5)	(0)	(0)	100	19
All	48	38	7	4	3	100	1413
Postgraduates							
British	60	29	4	3	4	100	400
Australasian/ Canadian	49	41	8	2	0	100	86
Asian	29	49	14	8	0	100	66
African	45	43	2	6	4	100	51
American	57	31	5	2	5	100	147
European	30	52	11	4	3	100	46
Other	(27)	(57)	(0)	(10)	(6)	100	30
All	52	35	6	4	3	100	826

Among undergraduates the Africans were least satisfied and the Europeans most satisfied, with British students in an intermediate position. In the case of postgraduates, British students expressed the highest level of satisfaction. Differences were, however, mainly in regard to degree of satisfaction, and the numbers of students of any nationality rating their accommodation as very unsatisfactory were small.

Type of Accommodation

About one in five undergraduates and one in fourteen post-graduates were living with their parents. Table 5.13 enables a comparison to be made of the expressed satisfaction of these students with that of those living away from home.

Table 5.13 Satisfaction with accommodation: by type

Percentages

Living accommodation

Type of accommodation	Very satisfactory	Fairly satisfactory	Fairly unsatisfactory	Very unsatisfactory	Other	Total	N
Undergraduates							
Parental home	60	25	6	2	7	100	277
Hall or hostel	52	40	4	4	0	100	303
Rent with board	51	36	7	4	2	100	154
Rent without board	38	46	10	5	1	100	616
Own house or flat	68	22	5	5	0	100	37
No answer	(42)	(35)	(11)	(0)	(12)	100	26
All	48	38	7	4	3	100	1413
Postgraduates							
Parental home	62	27	3	0	8	100	60
Hall or hostel	50	41	4	3	2	100	139
Rent with board	(52)	(24)	(7)	(10)	(7)	100	29
Rent without board	49	38	7	4	2	100	526
Own house or flat	82	8	6	0	4	100	49
No answer	(52)	(35)	(0)	(9)	(4)	100	23
All	52	35	6	4	3	100	826

Both in the case of undergraduates and postgraduates a higher percentage of those living at home than of any other subgroup except those living in their own houses or flats, found their accommodation very satisfactory. This finding, though interesting, may

F

merely reflect the extent to which those not wishing to live in their London homes had found places in other universities. The percentage of those expressing some degree of satisfaction varied only between a low of 76% for the 29 postgraduates in lodgings with board to a high of 92% for the 303 undergraduates in a hall or hostel. The results are interesting in the light of their policy implications. Whatever students' preferences may be, in regard to how and where they live, fairly high levels of satisfaction with very different types of accommodation were expressed by the different sub-groups, by no means all of whom can be assumed to have exercised a free choice.

Summary
The satisfaction of students with nine aspects of student life at the School was examined. Most satisfaction was expressed in regard to their living accommodation and most dissatisfaction with the main library of the School. Over half of the respondents expressed some degree of satisfaction with each aspect of the teaching-programme, with the structure of their degree and with staff contacts, but a sizeable minority were very dissatisfied both with tutorial arrangements and with staff contacts.

There were large variations in the satisfaction expressed with each aspect of teaching, staff contacts, degree structure and the libraries by students pursuing different courses of study, either at the undergraduate or postgraduate level. Differences between home and overseas students were, by comparison, slight.

Among undergraduates following the same course of study satisfaction showed only small variations with sex, age, father's occupation, school background and 'A' level achievement. Among the British undergraduates there were, however, large differences in the expressed satisfaction with lectures and classes of students of different political views following the same course of study. Supporters of the Conservative Party were considerably more satisfied, and supporters of Left-wing Groups considerably less satisfied, than supporters of the Liberal or Labour parties. The relationship between satisfaction with staff contacts and political views was in the same direction but smaller, and for other aspects covered by the question there was little or no difference in the satisfaction of those of different political views.

In the case of British postgraduates the relationships between satisfaction and political views were similar in nature but smaller in size than those found among undergraduates. The political views of foreign students appeared to be unrelated to satisfaction either among undergraduates or postgraduates.

Satisfaction with both accommodation and location showed considerable variation by nationality. In the case of accommodation, although some degree of satisfaction was expressed by the vast majority of students, irrespective of the type of accommodation they were in, satisfaction was greatest among those with their own house or flat and least for the largest group, those in rented accommodation without board.

Chapter 6

Student participation in school decision-making

At many of the universities in the United States and in Europe in which there has been serious student unrest in recent years, students have demanded a greater degree of involvement in university decision-making. Although this issue formed no part of the demands of those participating in the 1967 protest at the School, it was already being discussed by students before the protest, and later became one of the major areas of concern among student activists. Question 27 covered in some detail student views on participation in decision-making. As a background to the presentation of our results some recent developments in this area both in Britain as a whole, and at the School, are briefly reviewed.

A statement issued by the British National Union of Students in April 1967 emphasised the role of students as partners in the educative process and expressed the view that there should be student representatives on all university governing bodies and academic boards and upon all other committees playing an important role in the life of a university. The Union stressed that it was not asking for students to have more than a fair share in policy-making but merely that 'the student voice should be heard, among all other voices, when decisions are made and when planning is in progress'. The scale of representation envisaged by the NUS appears to have been moderate. Although the Union expressed the view that the degree of representation must be large enough to reflect the need for sound continuity and adequate presentation of views, attention was drawn to the heavy load of responsibility representation would place on the 'two or three' student representatives. Specific recommendations on disciplinary procedures formed a separate section in the 1967 statement. The NUS expressed the view that within each institution all disciplinary matters should be handled by a Court of Discipline containing student representatives.

The actual situation in regard to student representation or consultation in universities in Great Britain appears to be extremely varied. A survey of disciplinary procedures and student participation in university government in British universities was carried out by the *Guardian* in 1968. Questionnaires were sent to all vice-chancellors and student officials, and results were reported on 28 March and 21 June 1968. The survey showed a widespread demand on the part of student leaders for greater student participation in university government by means of representatives on senate and council. Only two universities (Queen's Belfast, and Bradford) and one college of London University (Birbeck) were found at that time to have student representatives on their executive governing bodies. Reporting on the results of the *Guardian*'s survey, David Gourlay comments on the discrepancy between the views of vice-chancellors and student leaders:

Vice-chancellors with a few exceptions, interpret student participation in university government as meaning the involvement of student representatives in a wide range of sub-committees of senate and council 'where student interests are affected'. This means student representation on committees dealing with university amenities, halls of residence, athletic grounds, libraries, refectories. The student interpretation embraces all this but goes beyond it to include direct representation on council and senate.[1]

In June 1968, following many student-power demonstrations at colleges and universities in Britain, the president of the NUS issued a strong statement[2] demanding that 'machinery should be put into action immediately to provide real equality in what is an undemocratically governed system of higher education'. Specific demands included effective student presence on all relevant college committees, staff–student control of discipline, student control of their own organisations and staff–student discussion of course-content and teaching-methods. These demands were backed by a threat of sanctions to be applied in any institutions not establishing satisfactory procedures within a six-month period. The NUS had for the first time expressed a readiness to abandon negotiations and instigate or sponsor protest action within institutions.

On 7 October 1968 a joint statement was issued by the Committee of Vice-Chancellors and the National Union of Students, following a series of discussions. The statement[3] outlined an agreed national plan for university reforms in the areas of student participation in university decision-making, the examination system and disciplinary procedures. Student participation in decision-making in the whole field of student welfare was recommended. It was also agreed that student views on curricula, courses, methods of teaching, major organisational matters and issues concerning the planning and development of universities should be ' properly taken into account ', although the ultimate decision should remain that of the statutorily responsible body. The exact nature of the process by which student views on these matters should be taken into account was left undefined, though both parties agreed that student membership of the relevant university committees should be extended. Various principles which should underly all disciplinary procedures were agreed, and it was recommended that there should be provision for student participation. Universities were asked to consider in what areas it would be appropriate to delegate responsibility for discipline to the student body and to review their existing arrangements accordingly.

At the London School of Economics in 1967 there were no student representatives on any of the major decision-making bodies. In February 1967 a joint committee of members of the Court of Governors and of the Academic Board was set up to make recommendations for changes in the machinery of government of the School. In June 1967, after the student demonstrations, five student members were added to this committee, which issued a report in February 1968. Among its many recommendations the report contained proposals for a small number of student members on all the major policy-making and executive bodies and their subsidiary commitees. Two of the student members in a Note of Reservation argued for a slightly larger number of student representatives: five rather than three on the proposed council of twenty-four members, and nine rather than five on a senate of approximately fifty members.

Much more radical proposals in regard to the level of student representation were contained in a lengthy Minority Report by a further two of the student members of the Machinery of Government Committee. They recommended a court of eighty members, twenty of whom would be students, a senate containing a hundred students and one-third of the academic staff, and a proportion of student representatives ranging from one-fifth to three-fifths on committees of the Senate. Although the main proposals of the Majority Report were not accepted by the academic staff of the School, the principle of student representation on most committees of the Academic Board was approved.

At the time of the student survey in 1967, although the student negotiating committee set up after the demonstrations, was expressing demands for strong student representation on committees, little was known of the views of the student body as a whole. We therefore included in our questionnaire a question (27) in which we sought to discover the extent to which representation or consultation was desired on a wide range of matters. Any question of this type may justifiably be criticised on the grounds that there is no means of evaluating the real extent of the interest or concern of respondents in what is offered. Although we accept the limitations of our results, they nevertheless provide interesting evidence of a type not elsewhere available on the order of priorities in regard to representation of one student body, and the extent to which a student's views on this question were related to his other characteristics and attitudes.

The results are presented in two sections. The first discusses the level of representation desired in each of the ten areas of decision-making by undergraduates and postgraduates. A comparison is also made of the views of home and overseas students. In the second section the relationship between a student's views on representation, his political views, the nature of his family and educational background, his course of study and his participation in student life is described.

The representation desired by students

Both undergraduates and postgraduates showed considerable discrimination in their answers to question 27, expressing a desire for a high level of representation on matters such as the library and discipline but with a majority opposed to any level of representation on the appointment of the Director, other administrative or academic appointments, and student admissions. The results are shown in Table 6.1.

A higher level of demand was expressed for representation on the library committee than on committees responsible for any of the other areas of decision-making covered by the question. This result was not surprising in view of the widespread dissatis-

Table 6.1 Representation desired in ten areas of decision-making
Undergraduates (UG) and postgraduates (PG)

Percentages

Area		Representation with student				No consultation or representation	No opinion or no answer	Total
		Majority	Equality	Minority	Only con-sultation			
Library	UG	14	55	24	5	1	1	100
	PG	11	46	32	7	1	3	100
Discipline	UG	12	42	29	9	6	2	100
	PG	12	41	29	9	6	3	100
Careers	UG	6	37	27	15	4	11	100
Service	PG	7	33	31	14	2	13	100
Teaching-arrangements								
	UG	2	41	37	16	2	2	100
	PG	1	25	39	24	6	5	100
Course-content	UG	3	32	38	21	5	1	100
	PG	1	21	40	28	7	3	100
Examina-tions	UG	2	24	30	27	13	4	100
	PG	1	17	28	28	31	5	100
Appointment of Director	UG	2	11	22	31	32	2	100
	PG	1	12	21	28	33	5	100
Academic appoint-ments	UG	1	8	20	27	42	2	100
	PG	1	6	20	24	43	6	100
Senior ad-ministra-tive appoint-ments	UG	1	8	19	26	42	4	100
	PG	1	9	18	24	41	7	100
Student ad-missions	UG	1	8	17	19	51	4	100
	PG	1	6	18	21	47	7	100

Note: The ten areas have been ordered according to the amount of representation desired in each.

faction with the library, reported in Chapter 5. Discipline came a close second to the library, roughly one in eight students expressing a desire for students to be in the majority on any disciplinary body and over one-half being in favour of at least equality. Although feelings on discipline were no doubt at an unusually high level due to the events of the previous term, the views expressed were not out of line with the demands made the following year by the National Union of Students.

Both undergraduates and postgraduates expressed the same relatively low level of demand for representation on the appointment of the director, senior administrative appointments, academic appointments and student admissions. It is interesting to note, however, that even in regard to academic appointments 28% of respondents expressed a desire for some student representation and a majority wanted a say of some kind. The greatest differences between the expressed views of undergraduates and postgraduates were on matters relating to teaching. Thus, 30% of postgraduates as compared with 18% of undergraduates were opposed to any student representation on committees concerned with teaching-arrangements, and whereas 56% of undergraduates wanted at least minority representation on committees concerned with examining-arrangements only 46% of postgraduates were in favour of any student representation on examining.

Differences between British and foreign students were in most cases very small. The detailed results are shown in Appendix C, Table 6.1A. A slightly larger percentage of foreign students, both at the undergraduate and postgraduate levels, expressed a desire for student representation on discipline, admissions and all appointments, whereas British students showed a greater interest in representation on teaching-arrangements, course-content and examinations.

Correlates of attitude towards representation
In looking for characteristics of the students associated with their views on representation, the analysis was largely confined to three of the ten areas covered by question 27; the library, discipline and the appointment of the Director. The library was selected because it had proved to be the aspect of the School regarding which student dissatisfaction was greatest. The other areas were included because the appointment of the new Director and the disciplinary

F*

action taken against student leaders in 1967 were important stages
in the sequence of events leading up to the sit-in and therefore of
particular interest.

In presenting the results student views are frequently summarised by showing the percentages of those in different sub-groups
wanting a specified level of student representation. In the case of
discipline and the library the percentages wanting at least equality
in the numbers of student representatives are shown, whereas for
the Director's appointment, on which the desire for representation
was considerably less, the summary measure used is the percentage
wanting at least a minority of student representatives, i.e. any level
of representation.

Nationality

Table 6.2 shows the variation in the desire for representation by
nationality in terms of the summary measures.

**Table 6.2 Percentage desiring specified levels of representation: by
nationality**

Percentages

Nationality	At least equality on Discipline	Library	At least minority on Director's appointment	N
Undergraduates				
British	53	69	33	1206
Asian	65	76	48	66
African	53	72	42	47
American	44	56	40	43
European	69	62	66	32
other	(42)	(58)	(50)	19
All	54	69	35	1413
Postgraduates				
British	53	58	33	400
Australasian/Canadian	41	44	29	86
Asian	39	55	18	66
African	61	74	59	51
American	61	56	35	147
European	54	56	39	46
other	60	60	43	30
All	53	57	34	826

Among the undergraduates Asians and Africans expressed the greatest demand for representation on the library, roughly one-third wanting to see students in the majority on the library committee. European undergraduates showed the greatest interest in representation on discipline and the Director's appointment. Twenty per cent of both the Europeans and Americans, compared with 11% of the British, wanted a student majority on any disciplinary body. In regard to the Director's appointment, only one in three British undergraduates wanted any student representation. A further third wanted consultation, and the remainder wanted neither consultation nor representation. Among the small group of European students very different views were expressed, one-third wanting at least equality of student representatives, one-third a student minority and one-third no representation.

One British undergraduate who was in favour of student consultation on the Director's appointment qualified his answer by adding the proviso that ' the number of academics should be equal to the number of Governors on the Appointments Committee '. Another student who wanted to see students' views taken into account in regard to the appointment of the Director, although he was not in favour of consultation on any other appointments, explained that this was because of the arbitrary power which he believed the Director to possess.

African postgraduates showed the highest level of demand for representation on both the library and the Director's appointment, though in the case of discipline their demand was exceeded by that of the Americans, 25% of whom wanted a student majority on disciplinary matters. Australian, Canadian and Asian postgraduates showed the least interest in representation. These groups were all considerably older than average.

Father's occupation

No regular relationship between desire for representation and father's occupation was found. Undergraduate demand for representation on discipline and the Director's appointment was greatest among those who classified their father's occupation as semi-skilled or unskilled manual and least among those with fathers in managerial positions. Thus, 63% of the former as compared with 49% of the latter and 56% of those with fathers in the professions were in favour of at least equality on discipline. In the case of the library, the percentage in favour of equality of student representation ranged only from 65% of the semi-skilled manual to 76% of the unskilled manual, other sub-groups lying between these extremes. Among postgraduates the findings were somewhat similar, the desire for representation on both discipline and the Director's appointment being greatest among the ninety-one students whose fathers were in clerical or skilled manual occupations and least among the 'managerial' and 'own-business' groups.

Year of course

Undergraduate demand for representation on the Director's appointment showed practically no variation with years at the School: 36% of first years, compared with 34% of third years, wanted some student representation; and 30% of first years, compared with 34% of third years, wanted neither representation nor consultation. In the case of discipline and the library the results are shown in Table 6.3.

Table 6.3 Representation desired: by year of course

Undergraduates

Percentages

Year of course	Student representation on discipline					Student representation on library					
	Majority	Equality	Minority	None	Total	Majority	Equality	Minority	None	Total	N
First	11	47	29	13	100	18	56	22	4	100	474
Second	12	41	29	18	100	13	57	24	6	100	449
Third or later	11	38	29	22	100	10	51	29	10	100	386
No year given	16	37	36	11	100	11	57	24	8	100	104
All	12	42	29	17	100	14	55	25	6	100	1413

Differences in the views of students in different years were small, the greatest being in regard to the library committee, on which 74% of first years, compared with 61% of third years, wanted at least equality of representation. The relationship is in the same direction in the case of discipline but slightly smaller. The similarity of the views of undergraduates in different years shows that there was no overriding tendency for greater experience of the way in which the School functioned to lead to either an increase or a decrease in the desire for participation in decision-making.

Postgraduate views on representation also showed only small variations with year of course, the 138 students in their second postgraduate year expressing the greatest desire for representation in all three areas, and the fifty-four in their third (or later) year, the least interest. The difference was greatest in the case of the Director's appointment, on which 38% of second years, compared with 22% of third years, wanted some degree of student representation. The largest group, comprising 600 students in their first postgraduate year, most of whom were taking the one-year M.Sc., expressed a slightly lower demand than the second years in each area.

Field of study

The demand for representation showed considerable variation by course of study. Results for combined-subject groups are shown in Table 6.4.

The undergraduate demand for representation was greatest for all three areas among the sociologists and least among those specialising in accounting or statistics. The rank orders of the level of demand of other sub-groups showed considerable variation over the three areas, the correlation between the rankings on discipline and the Director's appointment being highest (Spearman's $p=.75$). The desire for a student majority on the disciplinary body and on the library committee was strongest among the sociologists, one in five of whom expressed this preference. In the case of the Director's appointment, although the sociologists were still in the lead, only 6% of them (fifteen students) were in favour of a student majority.

Among postgraduates the sociologists and social psychologists are seen in Table 6.4 far to exceed other sub-groups in their desire for at least equality on disciplinary matters. As in the case of the undergraduates, roughly one in five postgraduate sociologists wanted a student majority on discipline, though their demand was exceeded by that of the government specialists one in three of whom wanted a student majority. The twenty-eight postgraduate geographers had least desire for student representation in all three areas.

Table 6.4 Percentage desiring specified levels of representation by field of study

Percentages

Field of study	At least equality on Discipline	Library	At least minority on Director's appointment	N
Undergraduates				
Sociology and anthropology	74	80	56	249
International relations and				
international history	60	71	36	129
General studies and others	55	59	41	127
Economic history and history	53	67	30	83
Law	53	73	28	160
Government	51	68	30	109
Geography	50	70	25	124
Economics	49	65	31	220
Industry and trade,				
accounting, statistics	35	59	25	212
All	54	69	35	1413
Postgraduates				
Sociology, anthropology,				
social psychology	71	66	48	119
Social administration	55	60	34	192
Government	55	55	45	56
Economic history, international				
history, international relations	51	50	30	94
Industrial relations,				
philosophy, other	50	68	45	38
Statistics, accountancy,				
demography	48	58	25	67
Economics	48	51	28	130
None given	46	59	28	54
Law	42	46	29	48
Geography	(32)	(39)	(18)	28
All	53	57	34	826

Postgraduate course

The views of postgraduates showed relatively little variation by course of study and no consistent rank order. Thus, in Table 6.5, the Ph.D. students show the lowest level of demand for representation on discipline and the library, but the highest level on the Director's appointment.

Table 6.5 Percentage desiring specified levels of representation by course of study

Postgraduates

Percentages

Degree or course	At least equality on Discipline	Library	At least minority on Director's appointment	N
Ph.D.	49	50	38	137
M.Phil.	55	54	35	65
M.Sc.	54	59	32	324
Ll.M.	50	53	28	32
Diploma	53	59	33	204
Research fee	56	51	37	41
All	53	57	34	826

Note: Three M.A., one M.Sc.(Econ.), nineteen no answer have been excluded.

Academic achievement

An attempt was made to discover whether there was any relationship between academic achievement and views on student representation. The only measure available for most undergraduates was 'A' level performance, but for all B.Sc.(Econ.) second-year students we were able, through an index-number link with the Part I survey referred to in Chapter 5, to use in addition the class of degree they obtained after the survey in 1968. Appendix C, Table 6.2A, shows the extent of the undergraduate desire for representation in each of the ten areas, by 'A' level results. No relationship appears to exist. An analysis of the relationship of attitudes towards representation on discipline with class of final degree, for the 262 B.Sc.(Econ.) students, showed a small association. Thus 54% of the firsts and upper seconds, 51% of the lower seconds and 41% of thirds, pass degrees and failures were in favour of at least equality.

In the case of the postgraduates with first degrees from British universities the views of those giving the class of their degree as a first, upper second or lower second are compared in Table 6.6. Undifferentiated seconds have been excluded.

The twenty-five students with first-class degrees show a consistently lower desire for student representation than other postgraduates. There appears, however, to be no consistency of direction in the difference between upper and lower seconds.

Table 6.6 Percentage demand for some student representation: by class of first degree

Postgraduates

Percentages

Area	First	Upper second	Lower second
Admissions	(16)	22	17
Teaching	(52)	68	62
Course-content	(56)	58	62
Examinations	(24)	46	35
Discipline	(76)	84	81
Library	(84)	88	92
Careers	(40)	36	52
Academic appointments	(16)	24	23
Director's appointment	(24)	34	27
Senior administrative appointments	(16)	31	25
N	25	94	48

Note: The table includes only those postgraduates with a first degree classified as a first, upper second or lower second from a British university.

Political views

Among British students, both at the undergraduate and post-graduate level, a strong relationship was found between demand for representation and party allegiance. The results are shown in Table 6.7.

This relationship, together with the variation in party allegiance by field of study, discussed in Chapter 3, accounts to a large extent for the variation in views on representation by field of study. In practically all cases, for students with a given party allegiance, the undergraduates' desire for representation exceeds that of the postgraduates, differences being least in the case of the Director's appointment and greatest in the case of the library. The high level of demand in all three areas expressed by supporters of Left-wing Groups is very noticeable. Roughly 40% of the 139 students in this category wanted a student majority on disciplinary matters and 46% wanted at least equality on the Director's appointment. When level of interest in national politics was taken into account together with party allegiance, the variations in views on representation were in predictable directions. Thus, the greater the interest in

**Table 6.7 Percentage desiring specified levels of representation:
by party allegiance**

Home students

Percentages

Party allegiance	At least equality on Discipline	Library	At least minority on Director's appointment	N
Undergraduates				
Conservative	28	55	12	243
Liberal	53	72	23	194
Labour	60	72	36	507
Left-wing groups	83	74	76	103
No opinion	52	78	39	100
Other	54	64	39	59
All	53	69	33	1206
Postgraduates				
Conservative	19	43	11	47
Liberal	38	57	13	56
Labour	58	56	35	213
Left-wing groups	83	86	69	36
No opinion	(61)	(56)	(43)	23
Other	(60)	(60)	(44)	25
All	53	58	33	400

politics of a supporter of the Conservative Party the less likely was he to be in favour of any student representation, whereas the reverse was true of a Labour Party supporter.

A strong relationship was also found beween the political views of overseas students and their views on student representation. This is shown in Table 6.8.

The self-classified socialists consistently desired a higher level of student representation than the liberals, and the conservatives wanted least.

Union attendance

Table 6.9 shows the relationship between demand for representation and frequency of attendance at union meetings. The greater the frequency of attendance at union meetings the more likely was a student to desire a high level of student representation. This result is no doubt largely due to the relationship between party allegiance and views on representation, together with the find-

**Table 6.8 Percentage desiring specified levels of representation:
by political views**

Overseas students

Percentages

Political views	At least equality on Discipline	Library	At least minority on Director's appointment	N
Undergraduates				
Conservative	(16)	(57)	(37)	19
Liberal	44	54	35	72
Socialist	72	76	65	74
None, no answer	66	80	37	35
Other	(86)	(71)	(57)	7
All	57	67	47	207
Postgraduates				
Conservative	19	19	16	31
Liberal	50	50	24	176
Socialist	66	69	53	132
None, no answer	47	56	32	59
Other	(61)	(61)	(43)	28
All	53	56	35	426

**Table 6.9 Percentage desiring specified levels of representation:
by union attendance**

Percentages

Union attendance	At least equality on Discipline	Library	At least minority on Director's appointment	N
Undergraduates				
Very frequent	78	78	57	195
Fairy frequent	65	76	44	455
Occasional	45	66	26	458
Very rare	34	52	21	237
Never	34	64	19	67
All	54	69	35	1413
Postgraduates				
Very frequent	76	67	64	33
Fairy frequent	83	69	58	115
Occasional	55	63	38	224
Very rare	45	53	25	214
Never	40	47	24	231
All	53	57	34	826

Note: Ten no answers on union attendance have been excluded.

ing reported in Chapter 4 that Labour and Left-wing Groups supporters attend union meetings more frequently than do Conservatives.

Satisfaction with teaching

The relationship between desire for student representation on teaching-arrangements, course-content and academic appointments, and expressed satisfaction with lectures is shown in Table 6.10.

Table 6.10 Percentage desiring specified levels of representation: by lecture satisfaction

Percentages

Satisfaction with lectures	At least equality on		At least minority on	
	Teaching arrangements	Course content	Academic appointments	N
Undergraduates				
Very satisfactory	31	23	16	154
Fairly satisfactory	39	31	25	811
Fairly unsatisfactory	55	46	37	308
Very unsatisfactory	60	51	45	119
No opinion or no answer	(24)	(30)	(14)	21
All	43	35	28	1413
Postgraduates				
Very satisfactory	18	15	21	146
Fairy satisfactory	30	25	29	423
Fairly unsatisfactory	30	26	31	143
Very unsatisfactory	39	30	46	46
No opinion or no answer	30	28	23	68
All	28	24	28	826

The greater desire for representation on matters related to teaching expressed by those dissatisfied with lectures is not surprising. The relationship was also found to exist within the party allegiance sub-groups, and Table 6.11 illustrates the joint dependency of a student's attitude towards representation on teaching-arrangements upon his party allegiance and satisfaction with lectures. Although Conservatives, at each level of satisfaction, have a lower desire for student representation than supporters of other parties, a dissatisfied Conservative has much the same view as a satisfied left winger.

Table 6.11   Representation on teaching-arrangements: by lecture satisfaction and party allegiance

Undergraduates

Percentages

Satisfaction with lectures	Percentage desiring at least equality on teaching			
	Conservative	Liberal	Labour	Left-wing groups
Very satisfactory	(22)	(25)	42	(33)
Fairly satisfactory	25	40	44	48
Fairly unsatisfactory	39	51	51	62
Very unsatisfactory	(43)	(40)	63	(67)
All	28	40	47	55

Summary

Considerable discrimination was shown by both undergraduates and postgraduates in the level of student representation they considered appropriate to the various areas of decision-making covered by question 27. Most representation was desired on the library and discipline, and least on appointments and student admissions. Over half the students, though rather more undergraduates than postgraduates, believed there should be at least a minority of student representatives on committees concerned with teaching-arrangements, examinations and course-content. Overseas students, as a whole, held very similar views to the British.

Among both British and overseas undergraduates and postgraduates, demand for student representation on discipline, the library and the Director's appointment was more strongly related to field of study, political views and frequency of union attendance than to any other variables. Among British students, the amount of representation desired on teaching-arrangements, course-content and academic appointments was found to be independently and equally strongly related to party allegiance and satisfaction with lectures. The very satisfied Conservatives wanted least representation and the very dissatisfied left wingers wanted most representation in all of these areas. There was little or no relationship between academic ability and views on representation.

Part 2

The 1967 student protest

Chapter 7

The boycott and sit-in
—an outline of events

In this chapter we outline the events leading up to the boycott and sit-in of March 1967, and describe the course of the strike and the subsequent settlement in April. Our principal concern is description rather than interpretation, but even as a factual outline this chapter has limitations. Although a considerable number of accounts of the boycott and sit-in have already been published, almost all have been written either by student participants or by outsiders. With the exception of the brief report made by the Director, we have no history of the matter from the point of view of the school authorities and little to guide us as to the nature of the decision-making processes of the key administrative bodies involved.[1]

The structure of the government of the School

To set the scene for those who are not familiar with the organisation of the School it is necessary to give a brief outline of the way in which it is governed. Legally, the governors are the School. The Court of Governors is a self-perpetuating body, choosing new governors itself, with the exception of a small number representing outside bodies and the academic staff (the professorial governors). Although it is the supreme governing body of the School, the Court is too large to act in an executive capacity (it had seventy-two members in 1967) and delegates most of its power to the Director and the Standing Committee. The Standing Committee consists of the chairman and vice-chairman of the Court, the Director and up to eleven other governors including the three most senior professorial governors. The other important part of the machinery of government is the Academic Board. This consists of all full-time members of the staff and certain administrators. The exact powers of the Board are nowhere clearly stated. All major policy items ' affecting the academic life of the School and its development '[2] are brought before it, but theoretically decisions of the Academic Board could

be overruled in the last resort by the Court of Governors. The
Board appoints committees to deal with such matters as the affairs
of the Graduate School, scholarships and accommodation. It also
appoints members to sit on committees jointly with members of
the Court.

In addition to this general structure, each of the sixteen academic
departments of the School has its own organisation headed by a
convener, who is a senior member of the teaching-staff. The convener consults the staff of the department through regular staff
meetings, but again decision-making powers as between the convener and other members of the staff are not clearly defined.

As far as the formal structure of the School is concerned, the
people with the most power or influence in the day-to-day running
of the institution are the Director and other senior members of the
administration, such as the Secretary and Registrar, the members
of the Standing Committee of the Court of Governors, the conveners, and the various members of the Academic Board sitting on
the principal committees.

At this period there was very little provision for student participation in the government of the School. Students had no representation on the major policy-making bodies—the Court of Governors, the Standing Committee and the Academic Board—nor on a
body which exclusively affected them, the Board of Discipline.
However, they did elect representatives to five administrative committees, the Refectory Advisory Committee, the London Lectures
Committee, the Committee on the Student Health Services, the sub-
committee of the hall of residence, and the Athletics Committee.

In addition there was a Staff–Student Committee. This was a
consultative body, but its exact purpose and method of functioning
were not clear and it seemed to play little part in the communications system of the School. There was a tradition of regular informal meetings between the Director and the President of the
Students' Union but, according to the Director of the day, Presidents of the Union had let the practice fall into disuse over the preceding two years.[3] Some departments had instituted staff–student
committees which met regularly, but there was no obligation for
the departments to set up such bodies. In fact there was no mention
of any kind in the conveners' terms of reference of the need for
contacts with students.[4] However, it had been recognised for some
some time that all was not well with staff–student relationships

and in March 1966, following a proposal from the students that the President of the Students' Union should be allowed a sabbatical year, the Academic Board set up a committee on the relationships between the School and its students. This was to examine not only the specific proposal for the extra year for the President, but also 'the increasing failure of communication between the School and its student body'. The committee was to consult student opinion and carried out interviews with a number of undergraduates during the summer term, 1966. However, it was still sitting when the first open conflict between the administration and students broke out and did not report back to the Academic Board until after the disturbances were over. Dissatisfaction with the governmental structure of the School had also been expressed for some time by members of the staff and administration, and following a paper by the Director recommending major changes in organisation[5], the Academic Board and Court of Governors set up a joint Committee on the Machinery of Government of the School. The Director's outline proposals did not mention the possibility of student representation on the governing bodies of the School nor at this stage were any student members included in the Committee.[6]

The appointment of the new Director

Ironically the appointment of the new Director to succeed Sir Sydney Caine at the beginning of the next academic year, October 1967, involved more consultation and participation than the appointment of any previous Director of the School. The selection committee included not only members of the Court of Governors but also several senior members of the teaching-staff elected by secret postal ballot by the Academic Board. These representatives were specifically asked to consult amongst the academic staff as a whole on the choice of the new Director. However, this consultation was to be informal, and there was no question of counting heads. More relevant to the particular subject of this study, there was no consultation of any kind with students.

The choice of Dr Walter Adams, then Principal of University College, Rhodesia, was announced in June 1966. The appointment was attacked in an article in *Private Eye* which attracted the attention of members of the Socialist Society at L.S.E. At the beginning of the Michaelmas term twenty members of this society published a pamphlet *LSE's New Director: A Report on Walter Adams*. The

750 copies produced were rapidly sold out and a second run of 250 copies was produced and sold. The pamphlet claimed to be based on three reports dealing with University College, Rhodesia: the Birley Report, a confidential report for Amnesty International by Louis Blom Cooper, and a report signed by fifty-five lecturers at U.C.R. The pamphlet was strongly critical of Dr Adams, alleging that: (*a*) he had been shown to be a poor administrator, and (*b*) he had been insufficiently strong in resisting pressures from the Smith Government for racialist policies in the organisation of U.C.R. Views of the pamphlet differed widely. The *Guardian* regarded the amalgam of the three reports as ' in the main accurate and fair ', although it was critical of the way in which Blom Cooper's comments were used.[7] Others felt the reports on which the pamphlet was based had been distorted, and both Birley and Blom Cooper complained that extracts of their reports had been used out of context.[8]

Before turning to student reactions to the Socialist Society pamphlet, it is worth noting the active interest that many students at L.S.E. had shown in the Rhodesian rebellion long before the appointment of Dr Adams was announced and the strong opposition demonstrated to the Smith régime. The declaration of U.D.I. in November 1965 led to three public protest demonstrations by L.S.E. students within a week, involving on each occasion between 250 and 350 students.[9] The Socialist Society pamphlet was received, therefore, by a student body including many who were actively critical of the Smith régime and impatient with their own Government's handling of the issue, and a substantial number of students took the allegations of the pamphlet seriously. On the day the pamphlet appeared the President of the Union wrote to the chairman of the governors, Lord Bridges, to ask if the charges laid against Dr Adams had any substance. Four days later a meeting of the Students' Union rejected a private motion condemning Dr Adams, but passed by 425 votes to 10, with 15 abstentions, a motion ' seriously questioning ' his appointment and committing the Union to opposing it, if Dr Adams did not reply satisfactorily to the accusations made in the pamphlet within eighteen days. A telegram was sent to Adams reporting this motion on the same day and a copy of the pamphlet was airmailed to him. However, the administration of the School reacted quickly and the Secretary, Mr Kidd, sent a telegram to Dr Adams on the following day on behalf of the

chairman of the governors and the Director, advising and request-
ing him not to reply to the Students' Union. This was followed later
by a similar request from the Standing Committee of the Court of
Governors. On 25 October a letter from the chairman of the governors, deploring the attacks on Dr Adams was published by *The
Times*:

Sir, as Chairman of the Governors of the London School of Economics
and chairman of the selection committee which recommended to the
Governors the appointment of Dr Walter Adams as director of the
School, I write to express the indignation which many of us feel at the
recent deliberate campaign against the character of a man whose help
before the war to refugees from racial tyranny in Europe, and whose
services over the last two decades to education in many lands, constitute a record of most honourable achievement, notable particularly
for the courage which he has shown in founding and fighting to maintain in most difficult circumstances a multi-racial college in Rhodesia.

The campaign against him is one to which I would think it neither
necessary nor indeed proper that any reply should be made by L.S.E.,
nor would it be right for us to comment on the internal affairs of
another university college, but I should not wish to run any risk that
silence might be misinterpreted. It is on this account that I write this
letter.

I am, Sir, your obedient servant,

BRIDGES

Officers of the Students' Union immediately drafted a reply to
this letter and submitted it to the Director in accordance with the
school regulation, which required his permission before a student
could use the address of the School in a letter to the Press. The
Director refused permission for the Students' Union to reply because he ' could not agree that it was within the competence of the
Students' Union to comment on the appointment of the Director '[10]
It was reported that the Director felt that if he had granted permission for the letter to be submitted for publication in the name
of the Union he would have appeared to be condoning an attack on
the chairman of the governors and his own successor.[11] However,
he did give permission to students to write as individuals, using the
address of the School.[12]

On 28 October the Students' Union met to discuss the issue. It
was advised by two members of the staff of the law department that
the Director's interpretation of the regulations was mistaken. The

Union decided that, although it had no formal standing in the process of choosing the Director, it should nevertheless be allowed to comment in public on the choice made, and consequently instructed its President to write to *The Times* in his official capacity.

The President accordingly submitted his letter to *The Times*, and it was published on 29 October.

Sir, Lord Bridges (25 October) states that the character of Dr Adams has been the subject of a deliberate campaign in respect to which it is thought neither necessary nor proper that any reply be made by L.S.E.

What concerns the students is that a number of adverse statements have been made about his administration of the University College of Rhodesia—not least important being those contained in a report by Dr Robert Birley, published in April, 1966—which suggest that he may not be the most appropriate choice for the post of Director. Those of us who have misgivings about his appointment regret no less than Lord Bridges that what was intended as reasoned criticism should appear as personal denigration.

It is significant in this regard that the Students' Union rejected a motion simply condemning Dr Adams' appointment in favour of one giving him the opportunity of making a full reply to the criticisms which have been made of him.

Lord Bridges suggests that it would not be right to comment on the internal affairs of another university college, but it is difficult to understand how one can avoid discussing a man's record as an administrator in one college when he is being considered for the post as Director in another.

Yours faithfully,
David Adelstein, President,
Students' Union.

At a meeting of the Academic Board four days later the staff also discussed the appointment of their new Director. The Board gave specific instructions that the course of the debate should not be disclosed, but did announce that a motion endorsing Dr Adams's appointment was passed by a substantial majority.

Meanwhile, the publication of the President's letter had produced an immediate response from the school authorities, and Adelstein was informed by the secretary that he would bring the matter before the Board of Discipline. The Board had only met once since 1945, and it took some time to set the machinery in motion. It was finally convened on 21 November.

The decision to hear the case against Adelstein and the manner in which the hearing was to be conducted provoked an increasingly strong reaction from many of the students in the weeks preceding it. A petition for the withdrawal of the charges signed by 1026 students was sent to the Board. The signatories accepted joint responsibility for *The Times* letter with their President. But the student body was not yet ready for direct action. At a meeting of the Union on 11 November a motion for a one-day boycott of lectures and classes was defeated.[13] However, in the following days student attitudes hardened. Their discontent focused particularly on the composition and procedure of the Board. The Board consisted of two governors, two professors and the Director. The Director was considered by the students as a party to the dispute. They also objected to what they understood to be a lack of provision for a record of the proceedings and the refusal to allow Adelstein to have legal representation. When by Friday, 18 November, the last teaching day before the Board was due to meet, it appeared that none of these criticisms had been met, the Union debated another motion deploring 'the threat of disciplinary action against its President for carrying out Union's instructions in writing to the press', and calling for a boycott of lectures and classes on the following Monday to coincide with the meeting of the Board of Discipline. This time the motion was approved by a large majority.[14]

On the day of the disciplinary hearing it was made known that the Board had made changes which met the main criticisms raised by Adelstein and his legal advisers. The Director had withdrawn from the Board of Discipline.[15] Adelstein was to be allowed advisers from the academic staff, and a verbatim record of the hearing would be taken. However, by the time these changes had been announced the boycott had been under way for an hour and a half and there was no question of abandoning it.

The boycott was organised thoroughly. Students carrying posters picketed all the entrances to the School and the length of Houghton Street, which runs between the main school buildings. A control room was set up from which students were sent out to lecture halls and classrooms to persuade their fellows to join the boycott, and an hourly count of the numbers attending lectures and classes was made. At the end of the day the student organisers announced that the boycott had been 78% successful. One group of about sixty students, acting on their own account, took more militant action.

They staged a sit-in the passage outside the room in which the Board of Discipline was meeting and sang protest songs. This action was taken without the sanction of the Union and was subsequently disowned by the official union leadership.

Late in the afternoon a report-back meeting was held by the Union to hear the decision of the Board. Adelstein himself announced their findings, that, while he had committed a breach of the relevant regulation, he had

acted in good faith and in the belief that he was not infringing a Regulation of the School. In accepting this belief under strong pressure and following incorrect advice, he committed an error of judgement. We have decided to impose no penalty . . . .

Staff–student dialogue

Some students saw the decision of the Board as a victory, interpreting its failure to impose a penalty on Adelstein after finding him guilty of breaking a regulation as a response to the threat of further student action implied in the boycott. A meeting of the Union later in the term called for the repeal of the regulations concerned, under which the Director was responsible for controlling communications to the Press by students wanting to use the name of the School.

Others saw the Board's decision as a 'victory for moderation and commonsense '[16] and as opening the way to closer staff–student contacts and to more active consideration by all concerned of the way students could participate more fully in the affairs of the School. The Director himself took a number of initiatives to bring the school authorities and students closer together. In December he attended a meeting of the Union and spoke on various student problems. He reported that the School had decided to set up an *ad hoc* committee with equal student representation to undertake a complete review of the regulations affecting students. However, at the same meeting his expression of strong reservations about student proposals for extending their representation and the autonomy of the Union suggested that the gap between the school authorities and at least the more radical students was still very wide. He said he could not accept student demands for representation on the committee considering relations between staff and students and on other school committees because students did not have a broad enough view of the situation and could not serve long enough on such committees to acquire it. He also questioned the Union's claim for full autonomy on the grounds that it was indirectly financed by public money and for the same reason justified the School's refusal to allow the Union to give financial grants to its political, religious and national societies.[17]

Another step taken by the Director to try to improve relations with the students was a circular sent to every student in the School at the beginning of the Lent term. This outlined the problems faced by the School at the time and described the ways in which attempts were being made to solve them. Accommodation difficulties were mentioned, as were financial limitations on any plans for improvement, but the most important sections of the circular outlined the current structure of the government of the School and described in general terms the nature of the various changes in its organisation which were then under consideration and which would be likely to affect the students. The questions referred to included student representation on school committees, the sabbatical year for the President, teaching-arrangements, and consultation with students at the departmental level. However, the specific character of the changes contemplated, and the manner in which they might affect students were not dealt with, and there was no promise of student involvement in the relevant discussion, with the exception of the proposed committee on regulations.

The 'stop Adams' meeting

When the Lent term opened, the issue of student rights, and in particular that of representation in the government of the School, was still very much alive. But the issue of Dr Adams's appointment which had sparked off the confrontation of the previous term appeared to be dead and buried. The January edition of *Beaver* carried articles for and against the appointment, but there was no evidence of widespread interest. Nevertheless, a number of students with the backing of the Students' Union decided to hold a teach-in on the appointment. A large lecture-room known as the 'Old Theatre' was booked for the meeting by Marshall Bloom, an American postgraduate student who was President of the Graduate Students' Association. The meeting, which was to take place at 4 p.m. on 31 January, was widely advertised in the School, several of the posters incorporating a xerox copy of a *New Statesman*

leader of June 1956 which was very critical of Adams's handling of
the segregation issue at U.C.R. On the day of the meeting itself a
duplicated notice of the meeting was distributed in the refectory
under the title ' Stop Adams '. This outlined earlier criticisms of the
appointment and suggested it was ' symbolic of a host of problems
including the place of the students in their college, and there is no
better place to begin work for a different L.S.E. than by opposing
the appointment of Adams '. It was, however, the last three sentences of the notice which seem to have been decisive in the developments which followed:

Although the selection committee itself is unlikely to reverse its
decision, given his own health, Adams might resign if it were clear that
enough students did not want him.

We must make it clear that we still don't want Adams and are
prepared to take direct action to prevent his becoming our Director.
Come to a meeting on Tuesday, at 4.0 p.m., in the Old Theatre, to
discuss what can be done to stop him.

This notice was brought to the attention of the Director
by the School Secretary, Mr Harry Kidd, and the Director
decided that the meeting must be cancelled. He felt that the notices
' made it plain that the meeting was being organised not simply
for discussion, but to organise what was described as direct action
to prevent Dr Adams taking up his appointment '.[18] He concluded
' that it was not proper that School premises should be used for a
meeting with such a purpose in mind ' and forthwith called in
Bloom to tell him that permission to hold the meeting was withdrawn. Bloom immediately sought out the Council of the Students'
Union and told them of the Director's decision. The subsequent
discussions of the Council seem to have been confused. The President of the Students' Union tried unsuccessfully to contact the
Director by telephone. There was a suggestion that the venue of
the meeting might be changed to the students' bar. It was clear that
' everyone present wanted the meeting to be held somehow and
none of them suggested the meeting should be called off ',[19] but no
formal resolution was moved and no line of action decided. During
the afternoon a further notice was prepared and circulated by
students who were never identified in the subsequent enquiries. This
announced the Director's decision to ban the meeting and urged
that the meeting should go ahead in the Old Theatre as planned:

'This meeting was sponsored by the Students' Union Council and the Graduate Students' Association. This is an attack on free speech. *It must be opposed*. This meeting shall take place. 4 p.m. In the Old Theatre.'

By about four o'clock a large crowd of perhaps five or six hundred students had gathered in the lobby and corridors outside the Old Theatre. The doors to the lecture hall were guarded by porters and, as a further precaution, the light fuses for the Old Theatre had been removed. Bloom tried to bring the crowd to order. He told them of the Director's ban on the meeting and also said that the students' bar had been fitted with microphones so the meeting could be held there instead. Then the Director came down to explain to the students why he had withdrawn his permission for the use of the Theatre. Adelstein had by now arrived on the scene, and both he and Bloom spoke to the students amidst mounting confusion. Finally at the suggestion of members of the crowd, Adelstein put to them three alternative lines of action: they should adjourn the meeting to the students' bar; they should stay where they were and hold the meeting there; or they should storm the Old Theatre. A considerable number apparently favoured the last course. Those nearest the Old Theatre pushed aside the porters guarding the doors and several of the students entered the lecture hall, a few producing candles to give some light. As the students forced their entry, the Director was asked by Adelstein if he would allow them to adjourn their meeting to the students' bar and, if they agreed to do so, if he would agree to take no action against those students who had already broken into the Old Theatre. The Director accepted this proposal and was himself in the Old Theatre trying to announce his decision to the students, when he received news that one of the porters guarding the doors had suffered a heart attack and died.

The shock of this tragedy completely transformed the situation and the students left the Old Theatre. Later it was learnt that the porter concerned suffered from a heart condition and had not been detailed by the administration to help guard the doors but had gone to join the other porters on his own initiative. There was not the slighest evidence that he had been physically assaulted by the students. That evening the School and Union issued a joint statement deeply regretting his death.

G

The Committee of Enquiry and Board of Discipline

The following day a special meeting of the Academic Board was called. Feelings against the students ran high amongst some of the staff, and there was a move to suspend all those involved immediately. However, more moderate counsels prevailed and the Board decided to set up a committee of enquiry ' to try to ascertain what responsibility attached to individual students for the events .'[20] The report was completed a week later but was never submitted to the Board as a whole. Some suggest that it inclined to the view that no proceedings should be instituted against any students. However this may be, after receiving the report the School Secretary, in consultation with the Director, decided to bring disciplinary charges against Adelstein, Bloom and four other members of the Students' Council on the grounds that they had promoted and encouraged the holding of a meeting in defiance of the Director's ruling. The Board of Discipline was convened for a second time within the academic year.

Meanwhile, within the School as a whole there was evidence of divisions of opinion both amongst staff and students. One hundred and twenty-four members of the staff signed a statement condemning the attacks made on Adams by some of the students and the violence to which they claimed the attacks had led ' as entirely contrary to the spirit in which the affairs of the School should be conducted and a potential threat to academic freedom '. A counter statement backing the rights of students to hold the meeting obtained the support of a smaller number of academics. The first reaction of many students had been hostile to those of their fellows who had been involved in the Old Theatre meeting. There were moves to censure Council and to remove Bloom from his post as President of the Graduate Students' Association.[21] But the announcement of the decision to prefer charges against the student leaders seems to have united student opinion again. A Union meeting asked the Board of Discipline to drop proceedings against the students and, when the Board did meet, the Union organised a silent vigil outside the hall where the hearings were being held.

The hearings, the subsequent deliberations of the Board and preparation of a detailed report of its findings extended over more than three weeks. Some students began to suspect the Board of deliberate delay and believed its decision would not be announced until the end of term in order to make it difficult for them to take any action in the event of an unpopular judgement. It was therefore in an atmosphere of mounting tension that the decisions of the Board were published; first, on 9 March, that the four council members had been acquitted; and, second, on 13 March, that Adelstein and Bloom had been found guilty of disobeying an instruction of the Director. Adelstein was also found guilty of encouraging the students to demand admission to the Old Theatre. The sentence on both students was suspension until the end of the summer term in July. The implication of this for Bloom, who was to sit his M.Sc. exams in September was considered by some as tantamount to expulsion.

The boycott and sit-in

The Board of Discipline was to announce its decision on the charges against Adelstein and Bloom during the afternoon of Monday, 13 March. The Union called a general meeting to hear the verdict and decide subsequently what action, if any, was called for. The Old Theatre was packed. According to one account eight hundred students were crammed into the hall, which has a maximum seating-capacity of five hundred. When the Board's decision was announced to the meeting the President-elect, Peter Watherston,[22] was moved into the chair. He proposed that the Union should organise a boycott of all lectures and classes until the sentences were lifted and also proposed a sit-in in the main foyer of the School. In the ensuing debate it appeared that, while support for the boycott was practically unanimous, some people were opposed to the sit-in. A number of students decided not to wait for the vote on the motion but took the matter into their own hands by leaving the Old Theatre and immediately sitting down in the lobby outside. Soon afterwards the meeting approved the motion for the boycott and sit-in by a large majority and by five o'clock the lobby and entrance to the School were blocked by students sitting on the floor.

The boycott and sit-in continued for the next eight days, until the end of term. During those eight days the School presented an extraordinary spectacle to people used to its normal ordered appearance. The lobby and corridors of the main building were filled with students sitting on the floors, holding seemingly endless discussions, listening to distinguished outsiders who thought they had the solution to the problems of L.S.E., reading, singing, eating or just sleeping. The blackboards normally displaying neatly written notices of school functions bore boldly drawn slogans, and banners were draped from the walls. In the Old Theatre the Union seemed to be in permanent session. Outside the main entrance TV teams rubbed shoulders with the pickets. No attempt was made to block the passage of staff or students who wanted to go about their business, but many classes and lectures were cancelled as a result of low attendance.

At the start of the boycott and sit-in the students declared that their primary aim was the revocation of the sentences on Adelstein and Bloom. Nothing occurred during the following eight days to suggest that this first aim had changed. Reasons for opposing the sentences were doubtless many, but three in particular emerge from student pronouncements made during the disturbances:

(a) it was unjust to single out the two student leaders and to make them responsible for the actions of a large number of their colleagues,
(b) the Board of Discipline, consisting of governors and senior academics, could not be regarded as impartial,
(c) the School's authority was arbitrary and actions by its own administrators and staff were not subject to any kind of judicial enquiry.[23]

Probably the simplest way of presenting the complex developments that followed during the eight days and nights of the sit-in is to give a chronological account of events, and this is the course we shall adopt here. However, first it is necessary to say something in general about the disposition of staff and students and the over-all impact of the sit-in and boycott on the life of the School. It was evident from early on that, although a very large number of students were actively supporting the boycott and sit-in, some were continuing their work, and at least a few were in open opposition to it, wearing a white badge as a sign of their views. Later we will present our own evidence on the numbers holding these different positions (see below, pp. 181-192). Within the body of students supporting the sit-in and boycott there were also differences in point of view. The students themselves distinguished those on the left from the 'moderates'. How many held each particular view at any one time cannot be known, nor is it possible to say with any certainty what part different student leaders played, although it is clear that from the beginning many informal leaders emerged, including several on the left, and that the official Union leaders were not always in control.

Divisions also emerged early in the affair amongst the staff. The administration represented by the Director, the Standing Committee and the Secretary had much support, particularly amongst the more senior academics. However, throughout the first five days a growing number of staff, referred to as the 'doves' by the Press, identified themselves with a conciliation movement and held frequent meetings to try to find a peace formula. Feelings ran high between those clearly identified with one group or the other, and not a few academic colleagues cut each other in the senior common room. But these divisions did not prevent frequent meetings between students and staff of all views from taking place. There were, besides the formal negotiating meetings between the school authorities and student leaders, several departmental meetings of staff and students, and innumerable individual contacts.

We have noted in the Introduction that the impact of the boycott and sit-in was the subject of dispute at the time they were taking place and has been so since. Some of the differing estimates of support for the strike are reviewed there (see above, pp. 2-3), and it is sufficient at this point to recall that at one extreme it was held that only a small minority of the students were involved, while at the other it was claimed that the large majority took part in one activity or another. Our own evidence on the extent and nature of student participation is presented in detail in Chapters 8 and 9.

A chronology of the sit-in and boycott
Monday, 13 March

The school authorities seem to have been caught unprepared by the speed and size of student reaction to the judgement of the Board of Discipline. When their first representative, an academic delegated with disciplinary powers by the Director, arrived at the scene of the sit-in, his behaviour suggested indecision. According to a student account he told all those sitting on the floor of the entrance lobby that if they did not leave within ten minutes he would use his powers to suspend them. At the end of ten minutes no one had moved but, whether because he had no means to enforce a suspension and remove the several hundred students involved, or whether because he had changed his mind, the Director's deputy took no further action.[24] He did, however, later suspend until the end of term two students who had refused to move from a stairway where they were sitting.

The authorities used other methods to try to shift the students during the evening. One tactic they adopted was locking the main doors connecting the entrance lobby with the street in an open position, apparently hoping to freeze out the students who now found themselves sitting in a chilling draught. Another tactic was to remove the light fuses. The students countered by up-ending tables against the open doorways and throwing themselves in front of the cupboard containing the fuse boxes. Later the Director himself came to address the sitters-in. He told them that as long as they allowed free passage to people who wanted to go about their business he would let them stay where they were that night. From the account in his annual report it is evident that the Director and the members of the Standing Committee had seriously considered the use of police in clearing the School and been assured of their willingness to help. Their reasons for finally deciding not to use them, except in the much more limited incident in Connaught House described below, was apparently due to tactical difficulties in clearing so many students from such a large area and the implication that subsequently the School would have had to be closed for several days or even longer.[25]

Meanwhile, the first meeting of a small group of staff unhappy with the decision of the Board of Discipline and with the administration's management of the whole affair was taking place. The meeting prepared a statement which was read out to the students later in the evening and issued to the Press. Signed by fifteen members of the staff, it read: ' We are shocked by the sentences handed down today by the Board of Discipline against two elected representatives and believe that their severity is deeply injurious to the interests of the School.'

Before the students settled down for their first night in the School some of them organised an impromptu revue in the Old Theatre. A highlight was the performance by a professor from the law department of ' They are digging up father's grave to build a sewer.' Several hundreds spent the night in the School, sleeping on the seats in the Old Theatre, in classrooms and on the floor of the entrance lobby.

Tuesday, 14 March

The sit-in continued throughout the day. Many students were

encouraged by the wide coverage their action was receiving in the Press and on radio and television, as well as by the messages of support which were beginning to pour in from students in other universities and colleges. They set up their own press office and started to produce duplicated handouts explaining their position.

In the afternoon the school authorities gave a press conference. Their official statement, after explaining why the Director had banned the original 'Stop Adams' meeting and outlining the disciplinary proceedings that had followed the students' defiance of the ban, went on:

The present agitations are, fundamentally, not against these penalties themselves but against any disciplinary procedures at all. They are being organised by a relatively small number of individuals. The School has three and a half thousand students. Few of the meetings concerned have been attended by more than two or three hundred students.

It was suggested at the conference that the trouble was due to a small number of left wingers. Professor Ben Roberts, a member of the Standing Committee, outlined his understanding of the philosophy of some of these activists:

Some of the hard core of the group in opposition to the School do hold views about the nature of society which make them rebels continuously against authority of all kinds . . . . They are opposed to the state, to the School as an institution. All they want is a completely free society where there are no constraints or restrictions and no discipline of any kind.[26]

Professor Roberts was also quoted as tracing some of the agitation to a number of American students: 'Some have taken up this agitation only weeks after arriving in this country. Some of them have been prominent in the United States in similar sorts of agitations.'[27]

Many students and staff felt this press conference, with its 'reds under the bed' arguments and its underestimate of the numbers involved, had only served to deepen the gap between the demonstrators and the School. A second meeting of staff seeking to find some way out of the confrontation attracted more than twice the numbers that had attended the meeting of the previous evening. It was decided to try to draw up a peace proposal and to send a delegation of senior academics to discuss it with the Director and Standing Committee.

Wednesday, 15 March

During Tuesday evening two new initiatives were planned by some of the students. A group of thirteen decided to start a hunger strike to 'dramatise' their commitment. A larger number decided to try to force the hand of the school authorities by invading the separate administrative section of the School, Connaught House, which had so far been unaffected by the sit-in. Early on Wednesday morning a small advance-party of students entered Connaught House with the cleaners and were rapidly followed by others. About eighty in all sat in the passages, on the stairs and blocked the doorways. Whether by design or oversight, they did not lock the entrance door behind them and a member of the staff, deputising for the Director, was later able to enter. He warned the students that they would be suspended if they did not leave at once. No one would budge, and the School Secretary arrived and, in his turn, asked them to leave the building immediately. This time the police had been requested to stand by. When the students still refused to leave of their own accord, they were told that they had been suspended for a period of three months and then were carried out one by one by the police and deposited in the street. On this occasion the administration had been prepared to act but, even so, it was doubtful if it could apply the suspension in full for, given the size of the School, most of the students involved were not known by name to the staff concerned and there was no certain way of identifying them. Initially it was thought that the school authorities intended to use press photographs of the incident but, apart from the obvious objection that only some of those taking part had been photographed, it seemed likely that identification by this method would be open to challenge in the courts. In any case most of the students ignored their suspension and rejoined their fellows in the main building.

A further and more peaceful initiative taken by the students during the day was the sending of a letter to all members of the staff, explaining their position and offering to meet any staff who wanted to discuss it in an effort to resolve the dispute. 'It is essential,' the letter said, if we are to act as civilised and educated men, that we try to find out what we have each been trying to say to each other. We feel sure that the suspension of 85 more students demonstrates how very far we are from this ideal. We would like to resurrect the dialogue that has died. We think we are right. If you think we are wrong, we would like to know why. We are prepared to listen. In simplest terms, some of us would like to prevent even more of a blow-up than has already occurred.

Several members of the staff took up this offer to hold discussions with the students, and while the talks were going on the staff group in favour of conciliation met again to approve the peace plan which had been drafted since its previous meeting and to choose a delegation to submit it to the Standing Committee. The plan included the revocation of all suspensions of students since the start of the sit-in, the end of physical obstruction of the school premises by students, permission for Adelstein and Bloom to use the library, whatever the outcome of their appeal, and the establishment of a staff-student committee to discuss the future and make the summer term 'a bridge to a more effective, democratic, controlled and harmonious functioning of the School'. The statement was duly presented to the Standing Committee, but the delegation returned to report that it had been received with little sympathy.

In the evening the Director addressed a crowded meeting of the Union and made what one newspaper called a 'mild gesture of conciliation'. He announced that the appeals against sentence by the student leaders would be heard as soon as possible, that representations by students suspended that morning who would now be unable to take exams would be carefully considered, and that the School would continue discussions on its affairs with students as soon as conditions returned to normal. However, the concessions fell far short of student demands and, when the Director ended with what appeared to be a threat to use police to clear the whole building that night, the final effect of his appearance seemed to have been to increase rather than diminish the militancy of the students. Police reinforcements were seen near the School, and several members of the staff who were sympathetic to the students' case decided to stay in the building overnight, fearing that a further crisis might develop. It was not until almost midnight that it became known that the Director did not intend to take any action to remove the students.

G*

Thursday, 16 March

The fourth day of the sit-in saw the first important initiative to conciliation by the administration when two members of the Standing Committee, together with the Director, offered to open discussions with student representatives. After a lengthy debate the Union decided to send some dozen of its members to meet them. Concurrently, the staff conciliation group, which had now expanded in numbers to almost ninety, met again and sent a further deputation to meet members of the Standing Committee. Once more the staff delegation reported back that it had made little progress. Some members of the delegation were disturbed by evidence of tiredness and strain which they detected in the members of the Committee whom they had met, and feared the consequences for the negotiations.

However, in the evening the student representatives were able to announce to a report-back meeting of the Union that the Director had agreed to make at least one concession and had replaced the sentence of suspension on the students involved in the Connaught House sit-in with £5 fines which were to be donated to charities chosen by the Union.[28] The School would also look favourably upon the student proposal for an independent enquiry into the whole situation. But it was clear from the reaction of the meeting that the students' attitudes would not be materially affected by these concessions alone. Everyone was waiting for the outcome of the appeal of Adelstein and Bloom against their sentences which was expected the following day.

Friday, 17 March

Support from outside students had increased during the week, and many were now arriving in person to help at the School. Clearly this kind of involvement could be seen as damaging to the L.S.E. students' case and, anticipating criticism, the Union published a special leaflet for students from other institutions asking them to keep to certain parts of the School and not to take part in union meetings. They were welcomed, however, on a mass protest march and rally organised on Friday, the seventeenth. Two thousand or more students from L.S.E. and all over the country took part in the procession through the City and attended a meeting in Lincolns Inn Fields.

On Friday evening the decision on the appeal by the student leaders was announced. The second charge against Adelstein, that of encouraging students to disobey the Director's decision banning their use of the Old Theatre, was dismissed but the first charge against both leaders, that they had been guilty of disobeying an instruction of the Director themselves, was upheld. Their sentences were somewhat modified in that they were to be allowed access to school facilities from the beginning of June if the Director was satisfied with their conduct in the interim. Most students seem to have expected the sentences would be put aside altogether, and reactions to the announcement were angry. Several of the staff who were present at the union meeting which heard the news also condemned the decision in strong terms. But the students' problem was what to do next. A majority felt that they were still far from gaining their objective, but the end of term was only a few days off. After a long debate the meeting recessed until the following day.

Saturday, 18 March—Sunday, 19 March

At the start of the resumed meeting of the Union the School Secretary read a statement to the students repeating the position of the administration that discussions on the future of the School, urgent as they were, could not take place under duress and would not be taken up until the sit-in was called off. As to the decisions of the Standing Committee on the suspension of Adelstein and Bloom, ' they have never been and will not be a matter for negotiation '. This statement was greeted with fury by some of the students who had been meeting with members of the Standing Committee. They claimed it was a complete misrepresentation of the facts, since the suspensions had been central to all their discussions with these members, and to all intents and purposes these discussions had been negotiations.

Nevertheless, some students felt they had come to the end of the road, either because they believed they had won genuine concessions from the School, or because they felt that the sit-in could not go on beyond the end of term. It was moved that the sit-in should be abandoned on the following Monday. After a protracted debate the motion was defeated (by 280 votes to 210) and a counter motion that it should be continued was passed (by 347 votes to 116). A committee of thirty-four students was then elected to organise the continuation of the sit-in. Over the week-end this committee prepared a lengthy letter to the staff. It explained once more why the students had acted, and reaffirmed their intention to continue the protest, but also noted that twelve of their number had been specifically appointed to further attempts at negotiation with the School. The letter ended by disclosing plans for setting up an 'open university' in the School during the vacation. This was to be a series of informal discussions, meetings and seminars, and members of the staff were invited to participate.

Monday, 20 March—Tuesday, 21 March

On Monday the Union met again. This time, with the end of term imminent, the 'moderates' were apparently the stronger party. A motion not to abandon the sit-in but to suspend it from 5 p.m. the following day until the beginning of the next term was passed by 232 votes to 177.[29] The demonstration ended peacefully at the appointed time, and already some of the students were actively preparing for their 'open university'.

Negotiation and settlement

The committee on the relationships between the School and its students set up a sub-committee to meet the student representatives, and negotiations began early in the vacation. The first item proposed for the agenda by the students was the suspension of Adelstein and Bloom. Although some of the staff side were unhappy about interfering over the suspensions, it was finally decided that, since the matter was more likely to affect the good relationships of the School and its students than anything else, the Committee would ask the Governors to give an audience to the President of the Students' Union to discuss it. The President appeared before the whole Court of Governors and made a plea that as an act of clemency the suspension of Adelstein and Bloom should not be enforced. After a lengthy discussion, followed by negotiations with Adelstein and Bloom, the governors decided to accept the President's plea. The document which sealed the act read as follows:

The Court of Governors of the London School of Economics and Political Science have heard a plea by the President of the Students' Union, Mr Peter Watherston, for the suspension of the penalties imposed on Mr Adelstein and Mr Bloom. The Court have also received the following statement from Mr Adelstein and Mr Bloom:

We sincerely regret that events have arisen which have led to conflict within the School and we hope that this conflict can now be ended.

We, for our part, take full responsibility for our share in these events. We are intent on working with the School authorities through constitutional processes. We hope to see the re-establishment of good relations in L.S.E., and we will use our best endeavours to bring this about on the basis of co-operation and mutual respect between all sections of the School.

(Signed) D. L. ADELSTEIN
M. I. BLOOM

In the light of the undertakings given, the Court of Governors have decided on an act of clemency, and have accordingly, during the good behaviour of Mr Adelstein and Mr Bloom, suspended the penalty imposed on them.

(Statement issued by the Court of Governors on 13 April 1967)

Adelstein and Bloom were immediately re-admitted to the School and, when the summer term began, the Union met and formally agreed to abandon the boycott and sit-in. The first major student strike in the history of British universities was over, but the conflicts which it symbolised and the consequences which flowed from it were only beginning to become apparent.

Chapter 8

The boycott and sit-in—student attitudes and participation

Chapter 7 described events which took place at the School from October 1966 to April 1967. This chapter is concerned with only part of that period, the eight days in March during which the Students' Union organised a sit-in in the School's buildings and a boycott of lectures and classes, and, using data from the student survey, it describes the degree of student involvement in these events. It begins by considering students' attitudes and opinions both at the time of the survey and at the time the events took place; this is followed by descriptions of the participation of students in the sit-in, the boycott, picketing, the march and Students' Union meetings. The chapter ends with an assessment of the extent to which the week's events disrupted students' academic work.

Opinions and attitudes
Retrospective opinions

During the term, students expressed their dissatisfaction with the actions and decisions taken by the School authorities and attempted to influence such actions and decisions in a variety of ways. Petitions were circulated, protest meetings held and staff lobbied, and the term culminated in an eight-day sit-in in the School buildings and a boycott of lectures and classes. In the survey, students were asked for their opinion on whether the use of the various methods of expressing student grievances had been justified or unjustified, and Table 8.1 shows the answers which they gave. In interpreting these data, it must be remembered that students were asked for their opinions specifically in relation to the events at L.S.E.

The various methods are listed in Table 8.1 in order of the proportions of students who thought their use wholly unjustified, and can be divided into three categories. The first comprises petitions, protest meetings and lobbying staff, none of which attracted any significant opposition. Protest marches might also be put in this category, although the proportion who thought their use wholly unjustified was slightly higher. The second comprises the main methods of protest which had been used the previous term—the sit-in[1] and boycott—and although these attracted more opposition most students thought their use at least partly justified. Thus, 22% thought that a sit-in was wholly unjustified, while 27% held a similar view of the boycott of lectures and classes and of the picketing which had taken place at entrances to the School and lecture halls. The third category—a sit-in immobilising the School —attracted far more opposition than any other, and over half the students considered that such tactics would have been wholly unjustified.

Table 8.1   Retrospective opinions on the use of various ways of expressing student grievances

All students

Percentages

The use made of this method of expressing student grievances was

	Wholly unjustified	Partly justified	Wholly justified	Undecided	No opinion	No answer	Total
Petitions	3	12	80	1	1	2	100
Protest meetings	5	22	70	1	1	1	100
Lobbying staff	6	20	69	2	2	1	100
Protest marches	14	24	54	4	2	2	100
Sit-in without immobilising School	22	26	44	4	2	2	100
Picketing	27	24	42	3	1	3	100
Boycott of lectures, etc.	27	23	44	3	1	2	100
Sit-in, immobilising School	53	18	22	5	11	2	100

Note: The question asked was: 'Which of these ways of expressing student grievances do you now think were justified and which unjustified at L.S.E. last term?'

During the last few years, there have been radical changes in the ways students at British universities have conducted disputes with university authorities, and these changes are reflected in the three categories referred to in the previous paragraph. Petitions, meetings and discussions with academic staff were acceptable to almost all the student body, and this is not very surprising since these were the methods which students had generally used in the past. Thus, if negotiations between students and university authorities were deadlocked, with neither side appreciating the other's point of view, these were the kind of actions which administrators might expect students to take.

At universities abroad—for example at Berkeley, Berlin and Tokyo—students had begun in the early 1960s to use quite different methods of protest. But it was not until March 1967 that a large-scale student sit-in and boycott took place at a British university. The unexpectedness of such tactics must have contributed to the L.S.E. administration's difficulties in understanding and handling the situation, and to the belief that no more than a small proportion of students could be supporting such relatively extreme action. In fact, as has been shown, only a quarter of the students thought that such actions were unjustifiable.

The 1967 L.S.E. sit-in was a relatively mild form of protest compared with more recent student action, and did not completely disrupt the academic life of the School. The more extreme form of sit-in with the object of effectively bringing the work of the School to a halt was known to have some adherents among the students but was never seriously attempted. (An attempt was made to occupy the administrative buildings on one night, but was not subsequently repeated.) Since then, of course, such sit-ins or 'occupations' have taken place, with students taking control of university or college premises as, for example, at Bristol, Birmingham, two London art colleges and the L.S.E. itself. But in March 1967 the type of sit-in which took place was itself a radical departure from past practice, and it was a reasonable hypothesis that few students would support more extreme action which would close the School. In fact, a very substantial minority (40%) retrospectively considered that a 'sit-in immobilising the School' would have been at least partly justifiable under the circumstances, illustrating both the degree to which these new tactics had already been found acceptable by students, and also the lengths to which many students were prepared to go in opposing the administration.

The rank ordering of the various methods listed in Table 8.1

is also interesting from another viewpoint, for it seems to be related to the extent to which a given method inconveniences those students not directly involved. As is apparent from their comments, many students' opinions were determined by this factor. Thus one student wrote:

I think that the sit-in and boycott, as far as they went, were justifiable, since they did not interfere with students' rights to attend lectures and go to the library if they wished. I cannot accept a sit-in immobilising the School as this would have effectively abrogated those rights.

The data have shown that only a minority of students considered the sit-in and boycott wholly unjustifiable, but it could reasonably be supposed that the degree of opposition might differ between the main groups of students.[2] In particular, that postgraduates and overseas students who are known to play a less active part in the general life of the School, would be less interested in the student demonstrations. But this does not seem to be the case, for there was little difference between the opinions of different groups of students with regard to the sit-in or the boycott,[3] and support for the Students' Union's action was spread evenly over the whole student body.

As was seen in Table 8.1, there were, on average, only slight differences between students' opinions of the sit-in and the boycott. However, many students did not hold the same opinions of both forms of protest, and the extent of the difference can be seen in Table 8.2. Almost two-thirds of students held the same opinion of both forms of protests, with many more considering both wholly justified than thought both wholly unjustified. Thus one-third held different opinions of the two methods, with the emphasis on the greater acceptability of the sit-in rather than the boycott; but very few held diametrically opposed views.

Thus, among those who thought that some protest had been justified, there would appear to have been some difference of opinion as to the appropriate way to make the protest. It is therefore useful to look at the proportion of students who held different combinations of opinions and in this way obtain variously defined measures of support for actions going beyond petitions and meetings. In the first place, 16% of students thought that both sit-in

**Table 8.2   Retrospective opinions of the sit-in, in relation to
opinions of the boycott**

All students

Percentages

	The sit-in was						
The boycott was	Wholly unjustified	Partly justified	Wholly justified	Undecided	Other answers	All	N
Wholly unjustified	16	7	2	1	(–)	27	612
Partly justified	3	12	6	1	1	23	519
Wholly justified	1	6	34	1	1	44	976
Undecided	(–)	1	1	1	(–)	3	69
Other	(–)	(–)	1	(–)	2	3	63
All	22	26	44	4	4	100	2239
N	483	590	986	89	91	2239	

Note: Each percentage is based on the total number of students.

and boycott were wholly unjustified, and at the opposite end of the
scale 34% thought both were wholly justified. These percentages
give some idea of the size of the extreme groups among the
students. A rather wider measure of the support for the Student
Union's actions is given by considering those who thought both
sit-in and boycott were partly or wholly justified, and 53% were
in this position. The widest measure is to take anyone who thought
that at least one out of the two methods was partly or wholly
justified, and the proportion is raised to 79%. Thus, taking this
final measure, almost four-fifths of students retrospectively thought
that some action of the kind which took place was at least partly
justified. Again, there was on the whole little difference between the
main groups of students. (See Appendix, C. Table 8.2A.)

Current attitudes

As has been described in Chapter 7, the eight days of sit-in and
boycott comprised a complex series of discussions, meetings, interview, statements and rumours, which took place under the glare
of press and television publicity. It was not possible to obtain a full
record of the attitudes of students to the sit-in and boycott or to

discuss in detail the changes in attitude which took place. However, it was thought worth while to ask students what their attitudes had been at two points—when the sit-in and boycott started on Monday, 13 March, and when they ended on 22 March, at the end of term. A number of problems still remain and should be borne in mind in interpreting the data—the complexity of the events, the fact that some students genuinely did not remember what their feelings had been and the possibility that their opinion at the time of the survey would influence their answers concerning their opinions at an earlier point in time.

Table 8.3 shows the net changes in students' attitudes between the start and the end of the sit-in and boycott. There is over all, a very strong similarity between the attitudes to the sit-in and to the boycott; the only difference being that marginally fewer students approved initially of the sit-in than boycott. More noticeable, perhaps, is the fact that there was little if any *net* change over the ten days, in approval or disapproval of either action. But there was a marked polarisation of attitudes, with much higher proportions of students indicating strong rather than mild attitudes at the end of term.

Table 8.3   Attitudes to the sit-in and to the boycott, when they started and at the end of term

All students

Percentages

	Strong disapproval	Mild disapproval	Mild approval	Strong approval	Undecided	No opinion	Don't remember	Total
Sit-in								
Start	20	20	26	22	8	2	2	100
End	25	14	20	36	3	1	1	100
Boycott								
Start	21	17	21	32	5	2	2	100
End	25	14	17	38	3	2	1	100

However, these data in Table 8.3 conceal the fact that a substantial number of students altered their attitudes to the sit-in and boycott over the week, and Table 8.4 shows these gross changes.

Looking first at the sit-in data, 29% disapproved at both its start
and end, and rather more (39%) approved at both times. Thus,
over all, two-thirds held consistent attitudes of approval or disapproval over the period, and the large majority of the remainder
changed their attitudes one way or another. As can be seen, rather
more moved to approval from some other initial attitude than to
disapproval, but it is interesting to note that much the same proportion crossed over the border from approval to disapproval as did
from disapproval to approval.

The data on the boycott, however, show a rather different picture. Again one finds that more approved at both points than
disapproved. But the absolute proportions are larger than for the
sit-in, and the large majority of students (81%), held the same
attitude at the start and the end of term. Thus, attitudes to the
boycott seem to have been much more clear cut and, once taken
up, were held.

**Table 8.4   Changes in attitudes to the sit-in and to the boycott, between
their start and the end of term**

All students

Percentages

	Disapproval at start and end of term	Approval at start, and end of term	Disapproval to approval	Other to approval	Approval to disapproval	Other to disapproval	Other movements	Total
					Changes of attitude between start, and end of term			
Sit-in	29	39	10	7	8	2	5	100
Boycott	33	48	5	3	5	1	5	100

Note: 'Other' includes those who were undecided, had no opinion, did
not answer.

The attitudes of the main groups of students at the start of the
sit-in and end of term are shown in Appendix C, Table 8.3A. Support for the sit-in increased over the week amongst each category
of students, and at both points in time was highest amongst overseas undergraduates. Support for the boycott was higher amongst
undergraduates than postgraduates at the start and end of term,

but there was little difference between home and overseas students. Unlike the sit-in, there was little change in support for the boycott over the week.

Participation
Sit-in

Students were asked on the survey to record the number of days they had sat in at any time during the day.[4] Over one-third of the students said they had participated in the sit-in on one or more days: 14% sat in on 1–3 days, 12% on 4–6 days and a further 10% on 7–9 days; 62% did not sit in on any occasion.

It was suggested earlier that both in terms of attitudes and participation there would be differences arising between the main groups of students. In practice it was seen that the attitudes of students to the sit-in were much the same regardless of the group to which they belonged. In terms of participation, however, there were differences as is shown in Table 8.5. Over all, 36% of students sat in on one or more days. As expected, undergraduates were more likely than postgraduates to sit in, and this was so among both home and overseas students. The table also show that more home students than overseas students participated; but this is rather misleading as these proportions are much the same when undergraduates and postgraduates are considered separately, and the over-all difference arises because the majority of home students are undergraduates while the majority of overseas students are postgraduates.

Table 8.5   Percentage of students who sat in on one or more days

			Percentages
	Undergraduates	Postgraduates	All
Home	41	31	39
Overseas	44	27	30
All	41	28	36

However, if the degree of participation is considered, a different picture emerges, and Table 8.6 shows the students who sat in on more than three days as a percentage of those who sat in on any occasion. Over all, 61% of these students sat in for three or more days, but there is a difference between home students (63%) and overseas students (51%) which persists for both undergraduates and postgraduates considered separately. The difference between undergraduates and postgraduates are more marginal, although the percentages are consistently a little higher for the latter.

Thus, in considering the over-all participation-rate for the sit-in, the major distinction is between undergraduates and postgraduates, but in considering the degree of participation this difference is relatively unimportant and the major distinction is between home and overseas students.

Table 8.6 Students who sat in on more than three days as percentage of those who sat in on at least one day

	Percentages		
	Undergraduates	Postgraduates	All
Home	62	67	63
Overseas	48	54	51
All	59	61	61

Agreement with a course of action is not always synonymous with participation, and some students who supported the sit-in did not themselves sit in. Also, some students did sit in but had either previously or subsequently opposed it. (See Appendix, C, Tables 8.4A and 8.5A.) Thus, two-thirds of students who had supported the sit-in at its start and at end of term had sat in on one or more days, as had two-thirds of those who retrospectively thought the sit-in wholly justified; in addition, a fifth of those who retrospectively thought that it had been only partly justified and a very small number of those who thought it wholly unjustified had sat in. In each case these proportions were higher among undergraduates than postgraduates.

Boycott of lectures and classes

Almost exactly a half of the students at the School actively participated in the boycott by deliberately staying away from at least some lectures and classes. The large majority of these students (76%) had in fact missed all their lectures and classes, while 18% had missed over a half and 6% less than a half.

Thus, the participation-rate in the boycott was much higher than in the sit-in, and as can be seen from Table 8.7 this was true for each of the main groups of students. The pattern of differences between groups in the percentages who boycotted is the same as for those who sat in. As before, participation among undergraduates is much higher than among postgraduates, and this is so for home and overseas students separately; again there is no difference between home and overseas students.

Table 8.7   Percentage of students who missed at least some lectures and classes in order to support the boycott

		Percentages	
	Undergraduates	Postgraduates	All
Home	56	40	52
Overseas	56	38	45
All	56	40	49

The degree of participation in the boycott was greater than that in the sit-in and, as shown in Table 8.8, three-quarters of all students who had missed some lectures had missed them all. As for the sit-in, this proportion was higher among home students than overseas students, but unlike the sit-in was also higher among undergraduates than postgraduates.

Table 8.8 Students who missed all their lectures and classes, as percentage of those who missed any, in order to support the boycott

		Percentages	
	Undergraduates	Postgraduates	All
Home	81	75	80
Overseas	70	61	65
All	80	68	76

Compared with the sit-in, supporters of the boycott were more likely to participate themselves. (See Appendix C, Tables 8.6A and 8.7A.) Thus, over four-fifths of those who consistently approved of the boycott over the week did boycott at least some lectures and classes, as did over four-fifths of those who retrospectively thought it wholly justified; in addition over two-fifths of those who retrospectively thought it partly justified and a small number of those who thought it wholly unjustified had missed at least some lectures in order to support the boycott.

In terms of attitudes, it was shown earlier that the sit-in generally commanded rather more support than did the boycott. In terms of participation, however, it has been found that the reverse was true, with 49% of students boycotting some lectures and 36% sitting in on at least one day. This difference is perhaps to be expected if the nature of these methods of protest is taken into account. The boycott can be looked on as a negative form of action, which simply involves staying away from lectures and classes, while the sit-in would require more positive action by would-be participants in having to appear at a particular spot and be openly identified with the protestors. Thus, it is found that almost all those who sat in at any time also boycotted lectures, but quite a large proportion of those who boycotted did not sit-in.

Finally, considering the combined figures for participation in the sit-in and boycott, 32% of students sat in and boycotted, 17% boycotted lectures, but did not sit in, and 4% sat in but did not boycott lectures. Thus, in all, 53% of students participated in one way or another.

Sit-in at night

As was described in Chapter 7, discussions and meetings went on late into most nights, and many students slept at the School. Since the School is officially closed at 10.30 p.m. and permission was not given by the School authorities for an extension of hours, students were asked whether they had stayed at the School after 10.30. The results are shown in Table 8.9.

Table 8.9 Students who stayed at the School after 10.30 p.m. for part or for the whole of the night

All students

Percentage

	Number of nights					
	None	1–3	4–6	7 or more	No answer	Total
Stayed at the School:						
Part of night only	67	17	12	3	1	100
Whole night	79	10	7	1	3	100

A third of students had stayed at the School part of the night only on at least one occasion and a sixth had stayed all night on at least one occasion. In each case the majority of those who stayed had stayed for between 1–3 nights, and the number of undergraduates involved was much larger than the number of postgraduates.

Picketing

Pickets, most of whom were organised by the Students' Union, stood outside the main lecture halls and at the School entrances. In all, 20% of students said that they had acted as pickets, 24% of undergraduates and 14% of postgraduates.

The protest march

As described in Chapter 7, a mass protest march and rally took place on Friday, 17 March, in which students from other universities as well as from L.S.E. took part.

In all, 28% of L.S.E. students took part in the march and attended the subsequent meeting in Lincolns Inn Fields. A further 2% took part in the march only and 9% attended the meeting. Sixty per cent did not participate in either march or meeting.

Action taken against the sit-in and boycott

As far as can be ascertained, there was little organised action against the sit-in and boycott involving more than a few students, even though quite substantial numbers of students did not support the Students' Union position.

The only organised action was taken by students at one of the halls of residence and consisted of wearing a white badge to show opposition to the boycott and sit-in. Four per cent of students reported wearing such a badge, 7% of undergraduates and 1% of postgraduates. All of these students subsequently considered both boycott and sit-in to have been wholly unjustified.

However, it was apparent at the time that some students were arguing against the Students' Union's position, and in the survey students were asked if they had at any time tried to dissuade others from supporting the sit-it and boycott. As one might expect, quite a large proportion of students had done so. (See Appendix C, Table 8.8A). In all, 16% had tried to dissuade others not to participate in the sit-in and 14% in the boycott, with 11% having done both and 18% either one or the other. Both among undergraduates and postgraduates, such action was much more likely to come from home than overseas students.

Attendance at union meetings

Since the Union had met almost continuously for the nine days, debating and voting on many different issues, questions were restricted to attendance and voting at the meeting on 13 March, at which the motion to begin the sit-in and boycott was passed, and the meeting on 20 March, at which a motion to suspend them was passed. Even with these restrictions, there are problems, however. The meeting on 13 March, being the first, was a fairly clear and discrete event, and, even though the question was asked two months later, it was thought the results would be reasonably reliable. As regards the meeting on 20 March, however, the Union had already been debating the suspension or ending of the sit-in and boycott for at least one or two days; also, at the particular meeting on 20 March, a number of motions were debated and voted on, and the question in the survey simply asked whether students had voted at the meeting. Thus, the data relating to 20 March were not expected to be as reliable as those of 13 March, and this was borne out, in part, by the fact that the numbers who claimed to have voted at the meeting were higher than the actual voting-figures on the motion to suspend the boycott. The data do, however, give an idea of the numbers of students who took part at some point during the final discussions to end or suspend the sit-in and boycott.

Table 8.10 shows the proportions of students who attended the two meetings. On 13 March, as many as 25% of students were not at the School and a further 9%, though they did not remember whether they had been at the School during that day, had certainly not attended the meeting. Forty-two per cent of students, in attending the meeting, were involved in the decisions which were taken, with 32% actually voting. Thus of the students who were in the School, two-thirds had attended the meeting.

The meeting, at which the sit-in was suspended, took place on 20 March, the day before the end of term, and it is possible that by this time many students had returned home for the vacation. Thus, as many as 45% of students were not at the School on that day, and a further 10%, while not remembering whether they had been at the School, had definitely not attended the meeting. The proportion of students attending and voting at this meeting was lower than that of 13 March, but 83% of students who were actually on the premises attended the meeting. As was to be expected, in view of the complex nature of the events of the last few days of the sit-in, the proportion voting at the meeting is higher than the proportion who, from the records, actually did vote on the specific motion to suspend the student action.

The table also gives comparable data for undergraduates and postgraduates. On 13 March very many more postgraduates (50%) than undergraduates (25%) were either definitely not at the School or could not remember, and many more undergraduates (53%) than postgraduates (22%) actually attended the meeting. Thus the first meeting was composed preponderantly (80%) of undergraduates.

On 20 March the situation was somewhat different in that the difference between the two groups of students had narrowed considerably. The balance at the meeting was still of undergraduates (62%), but this is very near the over-all proportion of undergraduates at the School. On both dates, there was little, if any difference between home undergraduates and overseas undergraduates, or between home postgraduates and overseas postgraduates.

Table 8.10 Attendance at union meetings on (a) 13 March, at which it was decided to begin the sit in and boycott, and (b) 20 March, at which it was decided to suspend them

Percentages

| Union meeting of | Not in School | Do not remember if at School | In School and | | | Oher answers | Total |
			Attended and vote	Attended only	Did not attend		
(a) 13 March							
Undergradutes	19	6	41	12	19	3	100
Postgraduates	35	15	16	6	25	3	100
All	25	9	32	10	21	3	100
(b) 20 March							
Undergraduates	44	8	32	6	8	2	100
Postgraduates	48	13	23	5	8	3	100
All	45	10	29	6	8	2	100

In Table 8.11, students' attitudes at the start and end of the sit-in are compared with their attendance at the relevant union meetings. Looking first at the Table 8.11 (*a*), attendance at the 13 March union meeting increases sharply with the degree of support for the sit-in. This is not, however, mainly a question of whether students were or were not at the School, but rather of whether students of varying attitudes who were at the School knew of the meeting or were interested enough to attend. Thus, of those who were at the School and strongly disapproved of the sit-in, a half attended the meeting and only just over a third actually voted; while, among those who strongly approved of the sit-in, almost nine out of ten attended the meeting and about eight out of ten actually voted. Thus, those who disapproved were less likely to attend, with the result that, of all students who attended the meeting, 32% dis-

Table 8.11 Attendance at union meetings on (a) 13 March and (b) 20 March: by attitudes to sit in when it started and at the end of term respectively

All students

Percentages

	Not in School or don't remember	In School and attended meeting	In School but did not attend meeting	Other answers	Total	N
(a) 13 March meeting						
Attitude to sit-in when it started:						
Strong disapproval	34	33	31	2	100	452
Mild disapproval	35	32	31	2	100	452
Mild approval	39	43	15	3	100	579
Strong approval	25	65	9	1	100	496
Other answers	48	25	20	7	100	260
(b) 20 March meeting						
Attitude to sit-in at end of term:						
Strong disapproval	64	22	12	2	100	557
Mild disapproval	65	22	9	4	100	316
Mild approval	59	30	8	3	100	452
Strong approval	42	52	4	2	100	797
Other answers	67	24	3	6	100	117

approved of the sit-in, 27% mildly approved and 35% strongly approved.

Table 8.11 (*b*) shows comparable data for the 20 March meeting and attitudes at the end of the sit-in; more or less the same pattern emerges. This time, however, not only were students who were at the School more likely to attend the meeting if they approved rather than disapproved, but also they were much more likely to be at the School. Thus, of those who attended the 20 March union meeting, 25% disapproved of the sit-in, 17% mildly approved and over a half (53%) strongly approved.

Effect on academic work

The actions taken by the students obviously affected their academic work. This was particularly true of the boycott, for many courses were badly attended and cancelled, and some students expecting their courses to be disrupted stayed at home.

It has already been shown that half the students missed at least some lectures in order to support the boycott. What effect did the boycott have on other students? Table 8.12 showed that of all students, 29% missed no lectures. A further 10% missed lectures because they were cancelled, and 7% for a variety of other reasons which included anticipating lectures being cancelled and being out of London; less than 1% said that they had missed some lectures because they had been persuaded to do so or otherwise impeded by pickets. Very few of these had missed all their lectures and the majority had missed less than a half.

More important, perhaps, than these general considerations is the effect of the boycott on those who were consistently opposed to it. Thus, considering those students who disapproved of the boycott both at the start and end, as many as 67% attended all their lectures and classes, 18% missed some lectures (in almost all cases less than a half) because lectures had been cancelled, 7% missed some lectures for other reasons. Thus, those students who wished to attend lectures were, in most cases, able to do so, and their studies do not seem to have been interrupted as much as was thought at the time.

Quite apart from lectures and classes, the sit-in and boycott affected the general pattern of study of students—certainly of those who participated and probably of those who did not. Thus, in the survey students were asked whether they had used the library and worked at home more or less than usual. The expectation would

Table 8.12 Attendance at lectures and classes during the boycott

Percentages

	Missed none	Missed some lectures and classes				Total
		To support the boycott	No lectures held	Other reasons	Other answers	
Undergraduates	25	56	8	8	3	100
Postgraduates	36	39	11	7	7	100
All	29	50	9	7	5	100

be that, of those who had done any work at all, more time would have been spent at home and less in the library. The results are shown in Table 8.13: almost a half had used the library more than, or the same as, usual; a third had used it less than usual, and the remainder had not used it at all. Almost two-thirds had stayed at home more than, or the same as, usual, a sixth less than usual and the remainder not at all.

Table 8.13 Use made of the Library, and work undertaken at home during the boycott

Percentages

	More than usual	Same	Less than usual	No work	Other answers	Total
Used the library						
Undergraduates	7	37	35	20	2	100
Postgraduates	6	44	26	18	2	100
All	7	39	32	19	2	100
Worked at home						
Undergraduates	18	44	21	17	2	100
Postgraduates	15	55	15	9	4	100
All	17	47	18	14	2	100

But it is the combination of these two sets of data which is more useful. Forty-one per cent had in fact used the library and worked at home more or the same as usual, implying that they had done more or the same amount of academic work as they normally did. Twenty-four per cent had worked more or the same as usual at home, but less in the library, and, as expected, only 5% had made more or the same use of the library, but spent less time at home. A further 10% had done less work than usual at home and in the library. But the most surprising figure is that only 8% of students said that they had neither used the library nor done any work at home. Thus it would appear that many students did their usual quota of academic work during the week, but the disturbances at the School led some to avoid using the library and to work at home.

Patterns of work were necessarily related to involvement in the events of the week, for those fully involved had no time for academic work. Table 8.14 shows the relationship of work-pattern to participation in the sit-in and the boycott. In terms of the sit-in, the students who were not involved at all seem to have taken the opportunity to do more academic work, as over a half had spent more time than usual working at home and in the library and a further quarter, though they had made less use of the library, had worked at home. As one would expect, the pattern is entirely different at the other extreme—among students who had sat in on four or more days. Here, 27% had effectively done no work and 43% had done less both at home and in the library. The same conclusions are drawn from the data on participation in the boycott, with 67% of those who missed no lectures and classes both using the library and working at home more than usual, and 29% using the library less but working at home more; and those who supported the boycott generally doing less work than others, but with still 52% of them either using the library and/or working at home the same or more than usual. Thus, the same conclusion can be drawn as from the data on lectures and classes; apparently the studies of those who were not involved were not affected as much as might have been expected.

Nevertheless, the academic work of many students was disrupted, particularly in the case of those who were actively involved in the sit-in and boycott. In addition, as might be appreciated from Chapter 7, the atmosphere in the School for most of the year had

Table 8.14 Use made of Library and work undertaken at home: by participation in (a) the sit-in and (b) the boycott

All students

Percentages

	No work at home or library	Less work at either or both home and library	Less work in library, same/or more at home	Less work at home, same or more in library	Same or more work both at home and library	Total	N
(a) Number of days on which student sat in							
None	2	8	26	4	56	100	1391
1–3	9	26	30	6	29	100	322
4 or more	27	43	15	5	7	100	488
(b) Boycott							
Missed no lectures (—)	4	20	5	67		100	670
Missed some:							
To support boycott	15	30	24	5	23	100	1106
No lectures given	1	7	34	5	50	100	215
Other reasons	7	23	22	6	35	100	194

Note: A small proportion of students, on average 3%, did not answer the question on patterns of work; for this reason the percentages do not in all cases add up to 100%.

Table 8.15 Degree results of full-time students at the School for 1965 to 1968

Year	*Final degree examinations* Percentage of entrants who gained a first or upper second	*Part I, B.Sc. (Econ.)* Percentage of failures
1968	35	7
1967	38	8
1966	35	8
1965	31	5

Notes : 1. Final degree examinations relate to all degrees taken by students at the School. Examinations are taken in the third year.
2. Part I of the B.Sc. (Econ.) examination is taken in the first year.

not been conducive to study. It was therefore feared by some that the events at the School would affect examination results. One cannot, of course, show that there was no effect, but the data in Table 8.15 do show that the results of the degree examinations and of Part I of the B.Sc. (Econ.) degree in 1967 were not out of line with results for previous years.

H

Chapter 9

Factors related to support for the boycott and sit-in

In looking for student characteristics associated with support for the boycott and sit-in, we restricted ourselves to five indicators of support. Attitudes at the time of the survey to whether or not the 'boycott of lectures' and 'sit-in without immobilising the School' had been justified (question 1) provided two measures. Several indicators of degree of participation in the sit-in were available from the questionnaire. We chose to use day-time participation (question 15) as the least ambiguous measure of support. Participation in the boycott was measured from answers to question 20 (*b*), which enabled the identification of those who said they had missed lectures in support of the boycott. Finally, one measure of active opposition, identifying those who had tried to dissuade others from supporting the sit-in, was used (question 4). Although many alternative measures of both attitudes and actions were available, the strong interrelationships between them suggested that the choice would have little influence on the findings concerning the correlates of support for the demonstrations. The results are discussed in three sections. In the first, the relationship of support to background characteristics of the students is examined. The second section describes its relationship to their political views, and the third its relationship with course of study, involvement in student societies and attitudes towards the Students' Union and the School.

Background characteristics
Age and sex

As older students had been found (see Chapter 4) to play a less active part than younger students, both in the Union and in other student societies, it was not surprising to find more support for the boycott and sit-in on the part of the younger students. Table 9.1 shows the attitudes of undergraduates and postgraduates in four age-groups.

Table 9.1 Attitudes to the boycott and sit-in: by age

Percentages

Age in years	Percentage saying wholly justified					
	Undergraduates			Postgraduates		
	Boycott	Sit-in	N	Boycott	Sit-in	N
Less than 19	50	47	423	—	—	0
20 or 21	46	44	668	51	46	41
22–25	43	43	182	44	48	457
26 and over	35	40	136	33	38	323
No answer	—	—	4	—	—	5
All	46	44	1413	40	44	826

Although there is a marked decrease in attitudinal support for the boycott with age among both undergraduates and postgraduates, the relationship is small in the case of the sit-in. An unexpected feature of the table is that postgraduates aged twenty to twenty-five supported both the boycott and sit-in rather more than undergraduates in the same age-range.

Table 9.2 shows that participation in the sit-in was more strongly related to age than was attitudinal support.

Table 9.2 Participation in the sit-in: by age

Percentages

Age in years	Number of days at participation in sit-in						
	None	1–3	4–6	7–9	Other	Total	N
Undergraduates							
Less than 19	51	18	17	11	3	100	423
20 or 21	56	17	14	12	1	100	668
22–25	62	15	10	12	1	100	182
26 and over	72	13	4	7	4	100	136
No answer	(100)	—	—	—	—	100	4
All	57	17	13	11	2	100	1413
Postgraduates							
20 or 21	54	12	17	17	—	100	41
22–25	67	11	12	9	1	100	457
26 and over	79	10	5	3	3	100	323
No answer	(100)	—	—	—	—	100	5
All	71	11	10	7	1	100	826

Note : ' Other ' includes ' don't remember ' and no answer.

Thus, 46% of undergraduates aged less than nineteen sat in for some time on at least one day, compared with 24% of those aged twenty-six or more. However, among undergraduates under twenty-six, the proportion of extreme activists who sat in on 7-9 days was independent of age. Postgraduates participated less in the sit-in than undergraduates of the same age, except those aged twenty or twenty-one. This group of forty-one postgraduates was particularly active in the sit-in. Participation in the boycott showed a similar relationship with age among undergraduates and postgraduates.

Differences in the attitudes and participation-rates of male and female undergraduates were very small and showed no consistency in direction. Among British students taking postgraduate degrees or diplomas, the women showed rather more support for the boycott and sit-in than the men, both attitudinally and in their actions. The greatest difference was in regard to participation in the boycott: 51% of women, compared with 33% of men, reported that they missed lectures in support of the boycott. Among foreign postgraduates the differences in the support of men and women were smaller, and proportionately more men than women participated in the sit-in.

Nationality

Both at the time of the demonstrations at L.S.E. and later it was suggested that American students had played a disproportionately important role in them. Differences in the support of British and overseas students have already been shown to be small (see Chapter 8). An analysis of attitude and participation by nationality enabled the hypothesis of disproportionately high American support to be tested.

The percentage of each nationality sub-group of undergraduates regarding the boycott as wholly justified ranged from a high of 47% of the British students, through 42% of Americans, to a low of 38% of the Africans. The corresponding range for the sit-in was from 49% of Americans, through 44% of British students, to 43% of Africans. Thus, attitudinal differences of undergraduates of different nationalities were small. Among postgraduates these differences were larger. The percentage of students believing the boycott to be wholly justified ranged from 50% of the (non-British) Europeans to 18% of Asians: 41% of the British and 48% of Americans were in the category. On the sit-in the percentage saying 'wholly justified' had a maximum of 57% for Europeans, a minimum of 28% for

Australasians and Canadians, and values of 45% and 52% for the British and Americans respectively.

Table 9.3 Participation in the boycott: by nationality

Percentages

Attendance at lectures, classes, etc.

Nationality	Same as usual	Less in support of boycott	Less for other reasons	Total	N
Undergraduates					
British	26	56	18	100	1206
Asian	14	61	25	100	66
African	26	47	27	100	47
American	16	61	23	100	43
European	34	50	16	100	32
Other	(16)	(63)	(21)	100	19
All	26	56	18	100	1413
Postgraduates					
British	37	40	23	100	400
Australasian/Canadian	51	26	23	100	86
Asian	44	24	32	100	66
African	31	41	28	100	51
American	38	45	17	100	147
European	15	52	33	100	46
Other	37	47	16	100	30
All	37	39	24	100	826

Table 9.3 shows that amongst undergraduates participation in the boycott was geatest (61%) in the case of Asians and Americans, and least (47%) among the Africans. Similarly Table 9.4 shows American and Asian undergraduates to have taken part in the sit-in slightly more frequently than the British, but differences are very small. The extent of participation in the boycott by British and American postgraduates was very similar and was lower than that of the European students. In the case of the sit-in the highest participation was claimed by the African postgraduates. The patterns

Table 9.4 Participation in the sit-in: by nationality

Percentages

Nationality	Number of days of participation in sit-in					Total	N
	None	1–3	4–6	7–9	Other		
Undergraduates							
British	57	16	14	12	1	100	1206
Asian	53	26	12	8	1	100	66
African	55	21	2	13	9	100	47
American	53	19	9	19	0	100	43
European	65	16	16	3	0	100	32
Other	(53)	(26)	(16)	(5)	0	100	19
All	57	17	13	11	2	100	1413
Postgraduates							
British	69	10	12	9	0	100	400
Australasian/ Canadian	85	11	2	1	1	100	86
Asian	86	8	2	3	1	100	66
African	59	22	12	2	5	100	51
American	67	11	13	9	0	100	147
European	65	15	7	9	4	100	46
Other	77	0	7	7	9	100	30
All	71	11	10	7	1	100	826

of degree of participation in the sit-in of British and American post-graduates are remarkably similar.

The survey data, while showing quite large differences in participation by nationality, thus provide only negligible support for the hypothesis that a disproportionately great part in the demonstrations was played by Americans. Both the large group of American postgraduates and the small group of undergraduates behaved in a very similar way to their British counterparts, though their involvement in both the boycott and the sit-in was marginally greater. Regrettably the survey did not enable us to provide any evidence on the crucial matter of leadership.

Father's occupation

The coincidence of the rapid growth of the student population in Britain with student unrest has led many to suggest that the unrest is due to the very different types of young people now entering universities. Two Bristol academics put this argument forcibly in a memorandum to the Commons select committee on student relations.

More students now come from homes with limited intellectual and cultural backgrounds. When they were only a minority it mattered little. Others set the tone of the intellectual and social climate and at the end of three years any first-generation entrant who had made the most of the opportunities provided by the university was indistinguishable from his colleagues. Now the 'Yahoos' in the undergraduate population, although a minority still, tend to be quite satisfied to remain as such and they are sufficiently numerous to keep one another in countenance. They are anti-establishment because they have no respect for the values that a university accepts and teaches.[1]

David Martin,[2] starting from the same assumption of a disproportionate degree of activism among students from working-class backgrounds, attempted to explain this in terms of the 'alienated migrants adrift between cultures'.

Although superficially plausible, there is no evidence, referring to any student population, in support of the hypothesis that students from less educated families are more likely than others to become activists. At Berkeley in 1964[3] attitudinal support for the Free Speech Movement was shown to be the same among students at both ends of the social scale. Participants in student sit-ins, both at Berkeley and on other American campuses, have, however, been found to be drawn disproportionately from better-educated, higher-income homes.[4]

In the L.S.E. survey we looked for a relationship between father's occupation and support for the protest. As Table 9.5 shows, the attitudes of home undergraduates showed only slight variations with father's occupation. Among postgraduates, differences were larger, those in the 'own-business' group being, rather surprisingly, most in favour of both boycott and sit-in. Among both undergraduates and postgraduates, least support was expressed by those whose fathers were retired or dead.

Participation in the boycott and sit-in showed a similarly irregular variation with father's occupation. Among British undergraduates differences were slight, participation in the sit-in being greatest among those in the 'professional' group, and participation in the boycott greatest in the 'manual' group. Postgraduate participation

Table 9.5 Attitudes to the boycott and sit-in: by father's occupation

Home students

Percentages

| Father's occupation | Percentage saying wholly justified | | | | | |
| | Undergraduates | | | Postgraduates | | |
	Boycott	Sit-in	N	Boycott	Sit-in	N
Professional	49	47	290	45	51	114
Managerial	46	40	217	43	43	54
Own business	45	46	144	51	58	45
Clerical	48	47	119	(50)	(64)	28
Manual	52	45	219	40	39	43
Retired or dead	36	43	151	32	35	105
Other	43	33	66	(27)	(18)	11
All	47	44	1206	41	45	400

in both boycott and sit-in was greatest for the 'own-business' group.

Among foreign students, both at the undergraduate and post-graduate levels, the same tendency for those whose fathers were retired or dead to be more opposed to, and less involved in, the demonstrations was found. As for the British students, no other clear relationship between attitude or participation and father's occupation was observable. The survey thus provided no evidence that support for the boycott and sit-in was drawn in a disproportionate way from students of a working-class or lower-middle-class background.

School and university background

The attitudes to the boycott and sit-in of British undergraduates

Table 9.6 Attitudes to the boycott and sit-in: by type of school

Home undergraduates

Percentages

| Secondary school | Percentage saying wholly justified | | |
	Boycott	Sit-in	N
Grammar	46	43	793
Other maintained	51	51	105
Direct grant	50	48	117
Independent	41	37	153
Other or no answer	50	61	38
All	47	44	1206

from different types of schools are shown in Table 9.6. Differences
are fairly small.

Those from independent schools were least in favour of either
sit-in or boycott whereas those from 'other maintained schools'
were most in support. When participation rates were examined
(Table 9.7), those from direct-grant schools were found to have
participated in the sit-in to a slightly greater extent than any other
group. In the case of the boycott, those from 'other maintained
schools' had the highest rate of participation.

Table 9.7 Participation in the sit-in: by type of school

Home undergraduates

Percentages

Secondary school	Number of days of participation in the sit-in					Total	N
	None	1-3	4-6	7-9	Other		
Grammar or senior secondary	58	16	15	10	1	100	793
Other maintained	55	13	16	14	2	100	105
Direct grant	47	17	14	21	1	100	117
Independent	61	14	10	12	3	100	153
Other or no answer	60	21	8	11	0	100	38
All	57	16	14	12	1	100	1206

Among postgraduates who had obtained their first degree at a
British university, support for the demonstrations showed only a
small amount of variation with the university attended. Thus, participation in the sit-in was lowest (26%) among those forty-three
students whose first degree was from a London college other than
L.S.E. and greatest (36%) in the group of eighty from Oxford or
Cambridge. L.S.E. graduates participated marginally less than the
latter group. Participation in the boycott showed a similar pattern.
Academic achievement
In most studies of American student protest a fairly strong positive relationship has been found between academic achievement and
activism.[5] We therefore investigated the relationship between
academic achievement and support for the demonstrations among
L.S.E. students, although no measure of achievement as satisfactory
as the cumulated grade-point average, used in the States, was avail-

H*

able. For undergraduates as a whole, 'A' level grades provided the best available information on academic achievement. Because, however, of the relatively narrow range of 'A' level performance of students accepted by the School, and the difficulty of devising any completely satisfactory rank-ordering of results due to the variation in the number of subjects and attempts, they must be regarded as a somewhat unsatisfactory measure.

Appendix C, Table 9.1A, shows the variation in participation in the sit-in of those with different 'A' levels. No grouping of grades has been attempted as this would disguise the basic irregularities. Although participation in the sit-in was greatest (57%) for the seventy-five students with the relatively poor 'A' levels of no A and one B, the group of lowest participants (36%) were not those with the best ' A ' levels but those with one A and two Bs. Participation in the boycott showed a similar pattern. Thus, although there was no regular relationship, the results suggest that students with good 'A' levels were slightly less likely to have participated in the demonstrations than were those with poorer 'A' levels.

In the case of the B.Sc.(Econ.) students who were in their second year at the time of the survey and graduated in 1968, a measure of eventual academic achievement was provided by the class of their degree.[6] Table 9.8 shows no consistent relationship between attitudes to the sit-in and achieved degree-class. Attitudes to the boycott varied in a similar way though differences were smaller.

Table 9.8   Attitudes to the boycott and sit-in: by class of degree
B.Sc.(Econ.) second years

Percentages

Class of degree (1968)	Wholly unjustified	Partly justified	Wholly justified	Other	Total	N
	Attitudes to the sit-in					
First or upper second	31	22	44	3	100	101
Lower second	26	16	52	6	100	114
Third, pass, fail	27	21	47	5	100	47
All	27	21	47	5	100	262

Note: The table covers all respondents to the 1967 survey who took the B.Sc.(Econ.) final examination in 1968.

Those who obtained lower seconds more frequently regarded both boycott and sit-in as wholly justified than those who obtained either better or worse degrees.

Similarly, as Table 9.9 shows, participation in the sit-in was highest amongst the lower seconds, though differences are small, and the group of those with the best degrees contains the highest percentage (18%) of extremists, who sat in on seven to nine days.

Table 9.9   Participation in the sit-in: by class of degree
B.Sc.(Econ.) second years

Percentages

Class of degree (1968)	Number of days of participation in the sit-in				Total	N
	None	1-3	4-6	7-9		
First or upper second	61	13	8	18	100	101
Lower second	52	20	18	10	100	114
Third, pass, fail	62	19	11	8	100	47
All	57	17	13	13	100	262

Note: Coverage as in Table 9.8.

For postgraduates with a first degree from a British university the class of this degree provided the best available measure of academic achievement. Attitudinal support for the boycott and sit-in was found to be least among those with lower seconds or thirds and most among the small group of twenty-five with firsts. Participation was, however, greatest among those with upper seconds. Thus, 38% of the latter group, compared with 25% of those with a lower second or third, and 20% of those with a first, participated in the sit-in.

The survey therefore provided no evidence of any consistent relationship between academic achievement and support for the demonstrations in the student body as a whole.

Political views
Party allegiance of British students

Systematic studies of attitude and participation in student revolt have so far been mainly confined to the American scene. For the most part, the studies have reported a strong positive relationship between radicalism and protest. For example, one study[7] of the

Berkeley revolt found that approval for the Free Speech Movement increased from 37% of Republican students to 73% of Democrats and 93% of Socialists. Another study of the same campus, in this case of the participants in a demonstration,[8] found that the demonstrators were generally more liberal in their political views than the university population as a whole and that a majority of the most seasoned protesters amongst them classified themselves as revolutionary socialists. Our own data for British students at L.S.E., relating party allegiance to involvement in the sit-in and boycott, confirm the existence of a similar relationship between political outlook, attitude and participation. In summary, we found that the more to the left was the student's party, the more likely it was that he supported the boycott and sit-in and that he took an active part in both: conversely, the more to the right his party preference, the more probable it was that he was unsympathetic to the demonstrations, abstained from participation himself and tried to persuade others against giving their support.

Table 9.10   Attitudes to the boycott and sit-in: by party allegiance

Home students

Percentages

| Party allegiance | Percentages saying wholly justified | | | | | |
| | Undergraduates | | | Postgraduates | | |
	Boycott	Sit-in	N	Boycott	Sit-in	N
Conservative	17	19	243	7	13	47
Liberal	42	39	194	23	29	56
Labour	52	51	507	48	54	213
Left-wing groups	88	74	103	75	78	36
Don't know, other	51	46	159	46	34	48
All	47	44	1206	41	45	400

Table 9.10 illustrates clearly the extent of the differences in attitude between the supporters of the four main political parties. Amongst the undergraduates, unqualified support for the boycott and sit-in was given by less than one in five Conservatives, but increased leftwards in the political spectrum to about two in five of the Liberals, half the Labour students and three-quarters of the Left-wing Groups students. It has already been noted that postgraduates in general gave less support to the boycott and sit-in

than undergraduates. It is interesting to see from the table that the lower level of support was confined mainly to Conservative and Liberal postgraduates.

The same steep climb in support as one moves from political right to left is found when we turn from data on attitudes to those on participation.

Table 9.11 Participation in the boycott: by party allegiance

Home students

Percentages

Attendance at lectures, classes, etc.

Party allegiance	Same as usual	Less in support of boycott	Less for other reasons	Total	N
Undergraduates					
Conservative	45	30	25	100	243
Liberal	30	50	20	100	194
Labour	23	62	15	100	507
Left-wing groups	4	92	4	100	103
Don't know, other	20	58	22	100	159
All	26	56	18	100	1206
Postgraduates					
Conservative	72	4	24	100	47
Liberal	39	30	31	100	56
Labour	29	47	24	100	213
Left-wing groups	25	64	11	100	36
Don't know, other	40	40	20	100	48
All	36	40	24	100	400

Table 9.11 shows that, although the postgraduates of all political parties were less active than the undergraduates, the differences between parties were maintained. For example, amongst both undergraduates and postgraduates about sixty percentage points separate the Conservative minority at one extreme from the Left-wing Groups majority at the other.

Table 9.12 Participation in the sit-in: by party allegiance

Home students

Percentages

Party allegiance	Number of days of participation in the sit-in					Total	N
	None	1–3	4–6	7–9	Other		
Undergraduates							
Conservative	84	8	5	3	—	100	243
Liberal	62	20	11	6	1	100	194
Labour	52	19	16	11	2	100	507
Left-wing groups	15	14	33	34	4	100	103
Don't know, other	50	14	13	20	3	100	159
All	57	16	14	12	1	100	1206
Postgraduates							
Conservative	98	2	—	—	—	100	47
Liberal	80	9	7	2	2	100	56
Labour	67	12	14	7	0	100	213
Left-wing groups	28	11	25	36	—	100	36
Don't know, other	70	10	10	10	—	100	48
All	69	10	12	9	0	100	400

The data presented in Table 9.12 suggest that not only did participation in the sit-in increase from right to left in the political spectrum but that the commitment of those who sat in, measured by the number of days they were involved, also increased in the same direction. In the extreme case of the Left-wing Groups supporters, more students sat in for the longest period of seven to nine days than for either of the two shorter periods.

Predictably, the political parties with the highest proportion of students opposed to the sit-in also had the highest proportion of those who tried to persuade others not to take part in it. Thus, amongst the undergraduates, 41% of Conservative students said they had tried to persuade other students not to take part, compared with only 1% of the supporters of Left-wing Groups. Comparison of the numbers of those wholly opposed to the sit-in and the numbers of those who said they had tried to dissuade others from participation suggested that a surprisingly high proportion of the undergraduates who were against the sit-in had been prepared to act on their beliefs in this way. This was true whichever political party they supported. Thus, 41% of Conservative undergraduates said they had tried to dissuade other students from taking part in the sit-in, compared with 48% who thought the tactic wholly unjustified. The proportions of dissuaders and of those wholly opposed in the other parties were 20% and 23% of the Liberals, 16% and 18% of Labour students, and 1% and 2% of Left-wing Groups supporters. The data on postgraduates, however, once again give witness to a lower level of involvement. Only 36% of Conservative postgraduates said they had tried to dissuade others, compared to the 51% who felt the sit-in was wholly unjustified. The corresponding proportions for supporters of other parties were 16% and 27% of the Liberals, 12% and 14% of Labour students, and 0% and 8% of the Left-wing Groups students.

Students' political views were also measured in terms of their answers to five questions on current political issues. The relationships of these measures to party allegiance were discussed in Chapter 3. It seemed probable that, for students of a given party allegiance, the more radical their political views, as expressed by their attitudes on the political issues, the more likely they were to have supported the boycott and sit-in. Table 9.13 shows that this was in fact the case.

Table 9.13 Attitude to sit-in: by attitude to Vietnam war and party allegiance

Home undergraduates

Percentages

| | | | Sit-in wholly unjustified | | | | | |
| Attitude to U.S. involvement in Vietnam | Conservative | | Liberal | | Labour | | Left-wing groups | |
	%	N	%	N	%	N	%	N
Strongly support	63	43	(57)	7	(22)	9	0	0
Support	48	117	40	38	23	74	0	5
Oppose	44	46	13	80	19	214	0	13
Strongly oppose	(38)	16	19	42	12	175	2	80
Other or no opinion	(38)	21	(30)	27	34	35	0	5
All	48	243	23	194	18	507	2	103

Among undergraduate Conservatives, Liberals, or Labour Party supporters, those supporting the American involvement in Vietnam were more likely to be wholly opposed to the sit-in than other students. Some evidence of the same relationship was found among postgraduates. Thus, 27% of the Labour postgraduates who supported the American intervention in Vietnam regarded the sit-in as wholly unjustified, compared with 11% of those who were wholly opposed to the intervention.

Although the support of British students for the boycott and sit-in was strongly related to their political views, it showed only a small relationship with their interest in national politics. For example, of those Labour undergraduates who were very interested in national politics, 18% thought the sit-in wholly unjustified, compared with 24% of those with little or no interest. For Conservative Party supporters the relationship between support and interest, though again fairly small, was, not surprisingly, in the opposite direction; those very interested in national politics were rather more opposed to the sit-in than other Conservatives.

Political views of overseas students

It has already been noted in Chapter 8 that, in terms of the proportions in support and opposition, the over-all reaction of overseas students to the boycott and sit-in resembled that of the home students quite closely. Examination of the relationship of political views and reactions to the demonstrations shows a very similar pattern to that described in the case of the home students. Thus, the attitudes of overseas students with conservative political views were divided in much the same way as those of home students giving allegiance to the Conservative Party, the replies of overseas liberals resembled those of home Liberal Party supporters, and those of overseas socialists matched those of home Labour Party supporters. Given these similarities, discussion of the different tables is confined to the few cases where they were not found and to some exploration of the variations in attitude and participation of those of the same political views but of different nationalities.

Comparison of Table 9.14 with Table 9.10 illustrates clearly that differences of attitude to the boycott and sit-in between home and overseas students holding comparable political views were small. For example, the percentages of overseas undergraduates finding the boycott wholly justified were 16% of the conservatives, 39%

Table 9.14 Attitudes to the boycott and sit-in: by political views

Overseas students

Percentages

| | Percentage saying wholly justified | | | | | |
| | Undergraduates | | | Postgraduates | | |
	Boycott	Sit-in	N	Boycott	Sit-in	N
conservative	(16)	(21)	19	19	10	31
liberal	39	46	72	33	41	176
socialist	49	53	74	49	51	132
Don't know, other	38	45	42	43	44	87
All	40	46	207	39	43	426

of the liberals and 49% of the socialists, while the figures for home students were 17% of Conservatives, 42% of Liberals and 52% of Labour students. However, if overseas students in the different political categories are separated by nationality, it is found that the over-all figures conceal substantial differences of attitude amongst students choosing the same political label to express their views. Restricting our attention to the overseas postgraduates, since undergraduate numbers are too small to make this kind of analysis viable, we find that the American and European students within each political category were considerably more likely to believe the boycott and sit-in wholly justified than were students from other countries. For example, 50% of European and 46% of American liberals said the boycott and sit-in were wholly justified, compared with 37% of African and Asian liberals, taken together, and 26% of Commonwealth liberals. The same kind of differences were found amongst socialists, although in this case the Americans were the strongest supporters of the demonstrations. Thus, 83% of American socialists said the boycott and sit-in were wholly justified, compared with 56% of the Europeans, 45% of Asians and Africans, and 36% of Commonwealth socialists.[9]

The over-all similarity of response of home and overseas students of corresponding political views extended to the character of their participation in both sit-in and boycott, as can be seen by comparing Tables 9.15 and 9.16 with Tables 9.11 and 9.12 above. When nationality is introduced into the analysis the same kind of differences are again found in levels of participation within each

Table 9.15 Participation in the boycott: by political views

Overseas students   Percentages

Attendance at lectures, classes, etc

Political views	Same as usual	Less in support of boycott	Less for other reasons	Total	N
Undergraduates					
conservative	(37)	(21)	(42)	100	19
liberal	26	54	20	100	72
socialist	11	67	22	100	74
Don't know, other	19	53	28	100	42
All	20	56	24	100	207
Postgraduates					
conservative	55	13	32	100	31
liberal	43	34	23	100	176
socialist	28	47	25	100	132
Don't know, other	39	39	22	100	87
All	38	38	24	100	426

Table 9.16 Participation in the sit-in: by political views

Overseas students   Percentages

Political views	Number of days participation in the sit-in					Total	N
	None	1–3	4–6	7–9	Other		
Undergraduates							
conservative	(79)	(16)	(5)	—	—	100	19
liberal	61	29	3	7	—	100	72
socialist	43	23	18	11	5	100	74
Don't know, other	57	10	12	19	2	100	42
All	56	22	10	10	2	100	207
Postgraduates							
conservative	94	3	3	—	—	100	31
liberal	79	11	6	3	1	100	176
socialist	65	14	8	8	5	100	132
Don't know, other	67	12	10	8	3	100	87
All	73	11	8	5	3	100	426

political category as were noted in regard to attitudes. For example, data on participation in the sit-in showed that amongst postgraduates American liberals were more active than liberals of other nationalities. Twenty-seven per cent of the Americans in this category sat in for one or more days, compared with 19% of the Europeans, a similar percentage of Africans and Asians, and 8% of Commonwealth liberals. The gap separating American socialists from other socialists was even greater. Sixty-seven per cent said they had sat in at some time, compared with 38% of European socialists, 27% of the Asians and Africans, and 20% of Commonwealth socialists. These data, together with those on attitudes to the boycott and sit-in, provide further support for the conclusion in Chapter 3 that American socialists at L.S.E. were markedly more radical in outlook than those from Asia, Africa and the Commonwealth.

A much smaller percentage of overseas students than of British students had attempted to dissuade others from sitting in, and the relationship between attempts to dissuade and political views was small, although in the same direction as for the British students.

Student activities and attitudes
Field of study

An important role has been played by students of sociology and related subjects in many of the recent expressions of student unrest in Europe and the United States. Social scientists as a whole have frequently been reported as being the category of students on a campus most involved in a particular series of demonstrations. Thus, in the 1965 Berkeley study,[10] support for the protest movement ranged from 75% of social-science majors to 42% of majors in business administration, engineering and architecture. No breakdown within the social sciences was provided.

At the L.S.E. the degree of specialisation within the B.Sc. (Econ.) is such that students of very different interests and abilities, such as those specialising in sociology and accounting, qualify for the same degree. The full range of undergraduate degrees available in 1967 for students of the School is shown in Appendix C, Table 5.1. Both because of our knowledge of the widely differing nature of the courses available, and the evidence already discussed on the different views on politics, student representation and satisfaction with the School of students following different courses, we expected to find considerable variation in support for the boycott and sit-in by field of study. In analysing the data, fields of study were grouped as in earlier chapters.

Table 9.17   Attitudes to the boycott and sit-in: by field of study

Percentages

Field of study	Percentage saying wholly justified		N
	Boycott	Sit-in	
Undergraduates			
Sociology and anthropology	65	62	249
International relations and international history	48	49	129
General course, other	48	49	127
Government	48	38	109
Economics	44	44	220
Economic history, history	42	40	83
Law	42	40	160
Geography	33	33	124
Industry and trade, accounting, statistics, computing	33	32	212
All	46	44	1413
Postgraduates			
Sociology, anthropology, social psychology	59	56	119
Government	43	43	56
Economic history, international history, international relations	43	41	94
Law	42	46	48
Social administration	42	41	192
Economics	36	47	130
Industrial relations, philosophy and other	34	39	38
Statistics, accounting	21	37	67
Geography	(18)	(25)	28
None given	32	43	54
All	40	44	826

Table 9.17 shows attitudes to the boycott and sit-in by fields of study, the latter having been ordered according to the proportion of students thinking the boycott 'wholly justified'. Among under-

graduates, the difference between the levels of support of the sociologists at one extreme and those specialising in industry and trade,
accounting, statistics, computing or geography, at the other is very
large. Roughly two out of every three sociologists thought both
boycott and sit-in wholly justified, whereas students of accounting,
etc., were only half as likely to be of this view. There was a
corresponding though much smaller divergence in the percentage of

Table 9.18 Participation in the sit-in: by field of study

Percentages

Field of study	Number	of	days of	participation in the sit-in		Total	N
	None	1–3	4–6	7–9	Other	Total	N
Undergraduates							
Sociology, anthropology	38	17	21	23	1	100	249
International relations and international history	52	18	12	16	2	100	129
General course, other	59	13	13	11	4	100	127
Government	56	21	15	5	3	100	109
Economics	59	20	13	7	1	100	220
Economic history, history	66	18	5	10	1	100	83
Law	54	15	16	12	3	100	160
Geography	75	10	10	5	—	100	124
Industry and trade, accounting, statistics, computing	67	16	10	6	1	100	212
All	57	17	13	11	2	100	1413
Postgraduates							
Sociology, social psychology, anthropology	56	15	15	14	—	100	119
Government	63	16	14	5	2	100	56
Economic history, inter-national history, inter-national relations	82	4	8	6	—	100	94
Law	75	15	4	2	4	100	48
Social administration	69	9	11	10	1	100	192
Economics	70	11	9	6	4	100	130
Industrial relations, philosophy and other	87	3	2	5	3	100	38
Statistics, accounting	75	12	10	2	1	100	67
Geography	(82)	(7)	(7)	—	(4)	100	28
None given	80	13	5	2	—	100	54
All	71	11	10	7	1	100	826

the two groups in the 'wholly unjustified' category: this ranged from 12% to 35%. In the case of postgraduates, the extreme groups are roughly comparable to those found for the undergraduates, statisticians, accountants and geographers being least in support and sociologists, anthropologists and social psychologists most in support. The difference between the views of the extreme groups is even larger among the postgraduates.

The percentage of students, within each field of study, who participated in the sit-in is shown in Table 9.18.

The percentage of undergraduates within each field of study who reported some participation is similar to, though usually less than, the percentage who considered it wholly justified. Only in the fields of government and law were there slightly higher percentages of participants in the sit-in than of those who later regarded it as wholly justified. Among postgraduates the difference between attitude and action was substantial in every department, and although the sociologists showed the highest participation-rate the lowest participation was reported not by the accountants and statisticians, but by those studying industrial relations. Active support for the boycott showed a similar variation by field of study; 73% of undergraduate sociologists, compared with 40% of the accountants and statisticians, reported that they missed lectures in support of the boycott. Among postgraduates active support ranged from 52% of the sociologists to 25% of the statisticians and only 11% of the small group of geographers.

The relationship between support for the boycott and sit-in, and field of specialisation is interesting in that it shows how varied were the reactions of specialists in the different social sciences, whilst providing strong support for the hypothesis that sociologists tend to be more active than other students in protest actions. The most plausible explanation of this appears to be that the subject attracts those interested in the analysis and reform of society, and such students are more ready than others to criticise the social structure of their own university.[11] Whether their predisposition to involvement in protest action is in any way affected by their course of study is not clear. We found a slightly higher level of support for the protest among first-year sociologists than among second or third years.

The strong relationship between support for the boycott and sit-in, and political views suggested the possibility that the relationship between field of study and support might be due to the differing political views of those in different fields of specialisation. We attempted to investigate this hypothesis by examining the level of support of those British students with the same party allegiance in differing fields of specialisation. The results are shown in Table 9.19 for the three largest subject-groups of undergraduates.

Table 9.19 Attitude to sit-in: by field of study and party allegiance

Home undergraduates

Percentages

Percentage saying sit-in wholly justified

Party allegiance	Sociologists		Economists		Accountants, etc.	
	%	N	%	N	%	N
Conservative	(33)	18	30	40	13	70
Liberal	(52)	27	(47)	24	19	32
Labour	66	110	49	68	47	62
Left-wing groups	82	34	(61)	13	(80)	10

The table shows that, of students with a given party allegiance, the sociologists were more likely to support the sit-in than either the economists or accountants. There appears, therefore, to be a relationship between support and field of study, independent of party allegiance. The relationship between field of study and party allegiance acts in the same direction, increasing the difference between the sociologists at one extreme and the accountants and statisticians at the other.

Year of course

Attitudinal support for the sit-in and boycott varied very little among undergraduates in differing years. The percentage thinking the sit-in wholly justified decreased from 46% of first years to 41% of third years. The corresponding range for the boycott was from 49% to 44%. Participation varied slightly more, although the relationship was still small. Thus, 60% of first years missed some lectures in support of the boycott, compared with 51% of third years; and 46% of first years participated in the sit-in, compared with 36% of third years.

Among postgraduates, attitudinal support for the boycott showed practically no variation with years at the School in the case of the boycott, but students in their third year were less frequently in support of the sit-in. Participation in the boycott decreased with year of study, from 29% of first years to 15% of third years, and participation in the sit-in decreased from 41% of first years to 18% of third years. When comparing postgraduates in different course-years we are, however, comparing students registered for different types of degrees. Although the majority of students in their first year are taking the one-year M.Sc., most third-year post-graduates are registered for a Ph.D. Support for the demonstrations showed considerable variation by degree among postgraduates. For example, the percentage of those thinking the sit-in wholly justified varied from 57% of the M.Phil. students, through 48% of the M.Scs, 39% of those on diploma courses and 37% of the Ph.Ds, to 34% of research-fee students.

The survey evidence on the relationship between years at the School and support for the demonstrations, among undergraduates, showed that new-comers and third years differed more in their willingness to participate than in their attitudes. The postgraduate data suggest a continuation of these trends. One can only speculate on the extent to which the difference between attitude and partici-pation reflects the greater involvement of students in their studies.

Accommodation

Support for the boycott and sit-in showed some variation with the type of accommodation in which the student was living. Among undergraduates, those in rented accommodation without board were more in support of the protest than were any other students. These differences, illustrated in Table 9.20 by attitude towards the boycott, were found still to exist among British students of the same political views. Similar though much larger differences were found among the Berkeley students.[12]

The data suggest that ideological differences between students are to some extent reflected in their choice of accommodation. Not only do a considerably higher proportion of Labour Party than Conservative Party supporters choose to live in the type of accom-modation which allows a maximum of freedom, but also the most

Table 9.20 Attitude to boycott: by accommodation and party allegiance

Home undergraduates

Accommodation	Boycott wholly unjustified							
	Conservative		Liberal		Labour		Left-wing groups	
	%	N	%	N	%	N	%	N
Parental home	53	76	33	39	27	107	(8)	12
Hall or hostel	50	52	31	49	19	103	(0)	12
Rent with board	46	41	29	34	20	49	(0)	8
Rent without board	42	67	27	64	17	223	4	66
All	48	236	30	186	22	482	4	92

Note: The table excludes thirty students in their own houses or flats and fifteen no answers.

radical of the supporters of each party are more likely to be living in this category of accommodation. The attitudes of those living at home may, of course, have been influenced by those of their parents.

Participation in student activities

The involvement of students in the activities of the Union and of other student societies was discussed in Chapter 4. In this section the relationship between measures of participation in student life and support for the boycott and sit-in is examined. Frequency of attendance at union meetings was found, as expected, to be strongly associated with all measures of support. Table 9.21 shows that, among undergraduates, participation in the sit-in ranged from 75% of those attending union meetings very frequently to only 8% of those never attending.

Among postgraduates the range is seen to be even greater. The actual extent of participation, measured in terms of the number of days on which students took part in the sit-in, is also seen to be strongly related to frequency of union attendance, both among postgraduates and undergraduates.

The small relationship between year of course and support for the demonstrations completely disappeared when frequency of

Table 9.21 Participation in the sit-in: by attendance at union meetings

Percentages

| Attend union meetings | Number of days of participation in the sit-in | | | | | | N |
	None	1–3	4–6	7–9	Other	Total	
Undergraduates							
Very frequently	23	15	16	44	2	100	195
Fairly frequently	40	19	26	13	2	100	455
Occasionally	69	18	8	3	2	100	458
Rarely	86	12	1	0	1	100	237
Never	91	8	0	0	1	100	67
Other	(100)	—	—	—	—	100	1
All	57	17	13	11	2	100	1413
Postgraduates							
Very frequently	6	12	18	58	6	100	33
Fairly frequently	33	18	28	18	3	100	115
Occasionally	66	15	11	6	2	100	224
Rarely	82	9	7	1	1	100	214
Never	94	4	1	0	1	100	231
Other	(89)	—	(11)	—	—	100	9
All	71	11	10	7	1	100	826

union attendance was held constant. Appendix C, Table 9.2A, shows that of undergraduates attending union meetings frequently 64% of first years, 64% of second years and 63% of third years participated in the sit-in, and a greater proportion of second years than of first years sat in on 7–9 days.

Active opposition to the sit-in showed no consistent relationship with frequency of attendance at the Union. Sixteen per cent of undergraduates attending very frequently reported that they had attempted to dissuade others from sitting in, compared with 24% of those attending rarely. Similarly, among postgraduates, this percentage ranged from 9% to 16%. However, a smaller percentage of those never attending union meetings than of the very frequent attenders had shown active opposition to the sit-in. Thus those students least involved in union activities were characterised not only by their low degree of support for the boycott and sit-in but also by the fact that they rarely showed active opposition.

The joint relationship of support for the demonstrations, frequency of union attendance and political views was also examined. Table 9.22 shows, for British students, the percentage participation in the sit-in of those in each party-allegiance and union-attendance sub-group.

Table 9.22 Participation in the sit-in: by frequency of union attendance and party allegiance

Home students

Percentages

Sat-in on one or more days

Attend union meetings	Conservative		Liberal		Labour		Left-wing groups	
	%	N	%	N	%	N	%	N
Undergraduates								
Very frequently, or frequently	33	93	55	82	69	249	88	76
Occasionally	11	68	34	64	44	159	(74)	19
Rarely or never	3	82	6	48	12	99	(38)	8
All	16	243	38	194	48	507	85	103
Postgraduates								
Very frequently, or frequently	(20)	10	(91)	11	65	52	(95)	21
Occasionally	(6)	18	(25)	20	35	74	(57)	7
Rarely or never	3	37	10	41	16	96	(44)	9
All	2	47	20	56	33	213	72	36

Note: The table excludes ten other answers on union attendance.

The table shows that party allegiance and union attendance, though related, were each also independently related to participation in the sit-in. Within each attendance-category participation increased the further left the political views. Similarly, among those of a given party allegiance, participation increased with frequency of union attendance. The same pattern was found among home postgraduates. Among overseas students also, the same interrelationships were found. For example, among undergraduate

socialists attending union meetings frequently, 71% participated in
the sit-in, compared with 38% of the socialists who rarely or
never attended. The corresponding percentages among postgraduates were 70% and 15%. Participation in the boycott was similarly
independently related to political views and union attendance.

Turning from union attendance to office-holding in the Union,
support for the demonstrations was, as expected, greater among
those students who had ever held a union post, though the differences were not large. Among undergraduates 58% of officials, compared with 41% of non-officials, thought the sit-in wholly justified
and, as Table 9.23 shows, 58% and 37% respectively of each
group participated in it.

**Table 9.23 Participation in the sit-in: by union office-holding
Undergraduates**

Percentages

| Union office-holding | Number of days of participation in the sit-in | | | | | Total | N |
	None	1-3	4-6	7-9	Other		
Ever held office	39	22	14	22	3	100	245
Never held office	61	15	13	9	2	100	1154
Other	(50)	(22)	(14)	(14)	(0)	100	14
All	57	17	13	11	2	100	1413

No relationship was found between support for the boycott and
sit-in and membership of the committees of other student societies.
Although a slightly smaller proportion of committee members than
of other students regarded the demonstrations as wholly justified, a
rather larger proportion participated. This absence of relationship
is not surprising in view of the wide variety of societies, ranging
from those of a political or academic nature to sports clubs.

Attitude towards the Union

Although frequency of attendance at union meetings was very
strongly related to support for the demonstrations, there was only
a slight relationship between support and satisfaction with the
Union's operation.

Table 9.24 shows that among undergraduates there was practically no difference in attitudinal support for the boycott and sit-in
between those who regarded the representation of student opinion

Table 9.24 Attitudes to the boycott and sit in: by adequacy of union representation of student opinion

Percentages

| | Percentage saying wholly justified | | | | | |
| Union | Undergraduates | | | Postgraduates | | |
representation	Boycott	Sit-in	N	Boycott	Sit-in	N
Adequate	47	45	465	59	58	269
Inadequate	45	43	834	36	42	298
Don't know	45	44	89	25	30	218
No answer	(60)	(60)	25	27	39	41
All	46	44	1413	40	44	826

by the Union as adequate and those regarding it as inadequate. Among postgraduates, although those who were satisfied with the Union were more in support of the demonstrations than those who were dissatisfied, least support was expressed by the large 'don't know' group of infrequent attenders.

Satisfaction with L.S.E.

The relationships between the measures of satisfaction with the School, discussed in Chapter 5, and support for the boycott and sit-in were examined. The strongest relationship was found in the case of satisfaction with staff contacts. Table 9.25 shows that among both undergraduates and postgraduates attitudinal support for both boycott and sit-in increased with dissatisfaction with staff contacts.

Table 9.25 Attitudes to the boycott and sit-in: by satisfaction with staff contacts

Percentages

| | Percentage saying wholly justified | | | | | |
| Staff | Undergraduates | | | Postgraduates | | |
contacts	Boycott	Sit-in	N	Boycott	Sit-in	N
Very satisfactory	30	28	213	27	34	241
Fairly satisfactory	40	38	465	43	45	327
Fairly unsatisfactory	54	51	377	48	49	142
Very unsatisfactory	56	56	309	55	60	84
Other	39	43	49	38	38	32
All	46	44	1413	40	44	826

Of those who were very satisfied with staff contacts, however, as many as one in three thought the sit-in wholly justified. Twenty-five per cent of the undergraduates and 15% of the postgraduates, in the very satisfied group, participated in the sit-in. Participation increased with dissatisfaction to 54% of the undergraduates and 34% of the postgraduates, who found staff contacts very unsatisfactory.

Table 9.26   Attitude to the sit-in: by party allegiance and satisfaction with staff contacts

Home undergraduates

Percentages

Staff contacts	Sit-in wholly justified					
	Conservative		Liberal		Labour	
	%	N	%	N	%	N
Very satisfactory	15	46	18	33	33	72
Fairly satisfactory	16	88	39	70	46	166
Fairly unsatisfactory	19	67	49	45	62	151
Very unsatisfactory	31	35	45	40	56	112
All	19	243	39	194	51	507

Note: The table excludes eighty-one students giving other answers on staff contacts.

The relationship between support and dissatisfaction was found to hold for British undergraduates of each party allegiance. Thus, as Table 9.26 shows, support for the sit-in increased with dissatisfaction with staff contacts, independently of political views. In the light of these data, the theory that dissatisfaction with various aspects of the School was one of the contributory causes of the student demonstrations remains tenable. The fact that dissatisfaction was measured only after the demonstrations implies, however that the evidence is weak.

Desire for student representation

Student reaction to the sentences passed on their leaders by the Board of Discipline was undoubtedly one of the main reasons for support for the boycott and sit-in. It was therefore expected that a student's attitude towards student participation in disciplinary matters would be strongly related to support for the demonstrations. Table 9.27 shows that this was in fact the case, both among undergraduates and postgraduates. The greater the extent to which a student thought disciplinary decisions should be in the hands of students, the more likely he was to think the boycott and sit-in wholly justified.

Table 9.27   **Attitudes to the boycott and sit-in: by desire for representation on discipline**

Percentages

Attitude to representation on discipline	Percentage saying wholly justified		N
	Boycott	Sit-in	
Undergraduates			
Representation with:			
Student majority	84	78	165
Student equality	57	55	594
Student minority	34	34	413
Consultation only	10	12	128
No representation or consultation	6	5	85
Other	32	32	28
All	46	44	1413
Postgraduates			
Representation with:			
Student majority	78	74	99 .
Student equality	53	59	338
Student minority	21	28	240
Consultation only	12	14	73
No representation or consultation	4	4	47
Other	(41)	(41)	29
All	40	44	826

Participation in the boycott and sit-in showed a similar strong and consistent relationship with views on representation on discipline. Among undergraduates, 90% of those wanting a student majority on discipline missed lectures in support of the boycott, compared with only 6% of those against any form of student participation. Comparable figures for the postgraduates were 68% and 4%. Table 9.28 shows the same pattern in the case of the sit-in.

Two out of every three undergraduates and roughly half of the postgraduates who believed in majority representation on discipline had sat in on at least four days, compared with only one of the 132 students opposed to any form of student participation. Because of the relationships already discussed, between views on

Table 9.28   Participation in the sit-in: by desire for representation
on discipline

Percentages

| Attitude to representation on discipline | No of days of participation in the sit-in | | | | | | N |
	None	1-3	4-6	7-9	Other	Total	
Undergraduates							
Representation with:							
Student majority	13	18	26	42	1	100	165
Student equality	46	20	18	13	3	100	594
Student minority	71	17	8	3	1	100	413
Consultation only	92	6	1	1	–	100	128
No representation or consultation	93	6	–	1	–	100	85
Other	(68)	(7)	(11)	(11)	(3)	100	28
All	57	17	13	11	2	100	1413
Postgraduates							
Representation with:							
Student majority	40	14	25	21	–	100	99
Student equality	60	17	12	8	3	100	338
Student minority	87	6	4	1	2	100	240
Consultation only	95	3	1	–	1	100	73
No representation or consultation	98	2	–	–	–	100	47
Other	(69)	–	(10)	(21)	–	100	29
All	71	11	10	7	1	100	826

student participation and party allegiance, and between party allegiance and support for the demonstrations, we tried to discover whether attitude towards representation on discipline was related to support for the demonstrations independently of party allegiance.

Table 9.29 suggests that support for the sit-in was indeed independently related to both views on representation on discipline and party allegiance. Participation increases as we move from right to left in the political spectrum, within each of the representation categories. Similarly, for students of a given party allegiance, participation increases as the extent of desired student participation increases. Comparable data for postgraduates are not given as the basic numbers become very small in most of the categories.

The desire for student participation in some of the other areas of decision-making was also related to support for the demonstra-

Table 9.29 Participation in the sit-in: by representation on discipline and party allegiance

Home undergraduates

Attitude to representation on discipline	Sat in on one or more days							
	Conservative		Liberal		Labour		Left-wing groups	
	%	N	%	N	%	N	%	N
Representation with:								
Student majority or equality	23	69	50	102	60	302	84	85
Student minority	16	89	27	60	31	147	(67)	12
Consultation only	0	39	(17)	23	8	36	(100)	2
No representation or consultation	2	41	(11)	9	(8)	13	–	0
All	16	243	38	194	48	507	85	103

Note: The table excludes eighteen students who expressed no views on representation on discipline.

tions independently of party allegiance, but the relationships were smaller. Among Labour Party supporters, 61% of the 183 under-graduates who wanted some student representation on the appoint-ment of the Director had participated in the sit-in, compared with 38% of those who were against any representation on this appoint-ment. Similar figures for Conservative undergraduates were 45% of those in favour of some representation compared with 12% of those opposed to any representation involved in the sit-in.

The survey data thus suggest that, both in the student body as a whole and among those of a given party allegiance, the desire for an increased level of student participation in the decision-making processes at the School was a factor highly correlated with support for the demonstrations.

Discussion

In interpreting the survey findings on the variables correlated with support for the protest, it is important to identify those determined at a prior point in time. Prior variables related to support are highly relevant to any discussions of the causes of student unrest, whereas attitudinal measures taken after the protest, although they illuminate the *ex post facto* differences between participants and non-participants, cannot be used to test causal hypotheses.

I

Background characteristics of the students constituted the main category of prior variables, but among these no strong relationships were found. Neither sex nor the home or school background of British students showed more than a small irregular relationship with support, and foreign students differed little from the British, although there were some variations by nationality. Both among undergraduates and postgraduates, however, support showed a steady, though relatively small, decline with age.

Two prior variables more strongly related to support were field of study and frequency of attendance at Students' Union meetings. Sociologists were considerably more likely than specialists in any other field of study to have been in support of the protest. Similarly, those attending union meetings frequently were more likely to have participated in the boycott and sit-in. Prior academic achievement showed little relationship with support, although those in the middle ranges appeared to have participated slightly more than other students. The accommodation in which a student was living showed a small relationship with support, those living at home being least involved.

Political views at the time of the survey, though less certain to have been unaffected by the period of protest, can reasonably be regarded as prior to it. Among undergraduates and postgraduates, home and foreign students, the more radical their political views the more likely were they to have supported the protest. Whether measured in terms of views on specific issues or in terms of party allegiance, the relationships were very strong and regular. Similarly, those with no religious beliefs were considerably more likely to have participated in the protest than were those with religious beliefs.

Attitudes towards aspects of the School and the Students' Union and views on student participation in school decision-making, measured after the protest, cannot be assumed to have been unaffected by it. Whether or not such attitudes were to any extent contributory causes of support for the protest can remain only a matter for speculation.

From the survey data one can therefore infer that the values and attitudes of L.S.E. students which caused them to support the 1967 protest were equally likely to be found in students from any type of home and school background and in those of differing levels of academic achievement. They occurred more frequently among sociologists than among specialists in other subjects and were very strongly related to political views and to attendance at union meetings. They were also strongly related, after the protest if not before, to views on student representation and less strongly related to dissatisfaction with the School, particularly in regard to contacts with staff.

Experience of student life at L.S.E. appeared to have little effect upon the motivating attitudes, although they were apparently less dominant the older the student. Actual participation in the protest, which presumably depended upon attitudinal support and a complex of other variables, was more strongly dependent upon both years at the School and age. Young first-year undergraduates were more likely than any other group to have participated, although the majority had examinations at the end of the year.

A detailed summary of the findings on support for the protest is given in Chapter 10, where they are discussed in the light of research on American student activism and current hypotheses on the causes of student protest.

Chapter 10
Summary and discussion

The object of the study forming the basis of this report was to provide a factual record of the first major student protest in a British university in recent years. We neither hoped nor expected to be able to explain as a result of the survey why the protest had taken place. Nevertheless, in view of the spread of student unrest in Britain since 1967 and the numerous explanatory hypotheses based upon little or no empirical evidence which have been proffered, we shall discuss the relevance of the survey data to explanations of student unrest. The chapter consists of two sections. In the first our findings on the extent and nature of student support for the 1967 protest at L.S.E. are summarised. The second section discusses in the light of American research the many factors which are potentially relevant in tracing the sources of student protest and the nature of the contribution which can be made by student surveys.

Summary of findings

1. The different methods available for the expression of student protest, most of which were used at L.S.E. in 1967, commanded differing levels of attitudinal support. At the time of the survey between 80% and 69% of all students regarded petitions, protest meetings and the lobbying of members of staff as having been wholly justified; between 54% and 42% viewed protest marches, a sit-in without immobilising the School, a boycott of lectures and classes and picketing as having been wholly justified and 22% would have regarded a sit-in immobilising the School as wholly justified.

2. Differences in the attitudes of undergraduates and postgraduates towards the actual sit-in and boycott were very slight, rather more undergraduates than postgraduates believing the boycott to have been wholly justified. Home and overseas students also differed little in their attitudes, overseas undergraduates being slightly more in favour of the sit-in though less in favour of the boycott than home undergraduates.

3. Seventy-nine per cent of all students regarded either the sit-in, the boycott or both as having been either wholly or partly justified.

4. During the week in which the boycott and sit-in took place attitudes towards the boycott changed very little, though there was a small net increase in approval. Attitudes towards the sit-in showed more change: 17% of students changed to approval and 10% to disapproval.

5. Thirty-six per cent of all students participated in the sit-in on one or more days, 22% on four or more days. More undergraduates (41%) than postgraduates (28%) and more home (39%) than overseas students (30%) participated in the sit-in. Eighteen per cent of all students stayed in the School at least one night.

6. Forty-nine per cent of all students participated in the boycott, most of this group missing all their lectures and classes. Again, more undergraduates (56%) than postgraduates (37%) participated and more home (52%) than overseas students (45%). Twenty per cent of all students, 24% of undergraduates and 14% of postgraduates, claimed to have picketed at some time during the week.

The relationship of student characteristics and attitudes to their support for the demonstrations were examined in terms of their retrospective attitudes towards the justification of the boycott and sit-in and their participation in the boycott and the day-time sit-in. In addition, comparisons were made between two extreme groups and the entire student body. The extreme supporters of the protest (208 students) were defined as those who had sat in on four or more days and thought a sit-in immobilising the School would have been wholly justified. The extreme opposers were the 213 students who thought the sit-in without immobilising the School wholly unjustified and had attempted to dissuade others from supporting it. The two extreme groups have been labelled the activists and the opposition throughout the remainder of the summary. Twenty-two per cent of the activists, 13% of the opposition and 28% of all students were foreign. Thirty per cent of the activists, 22% of the opposition and 37% of all students were postgraduates.

7. Younger students were rather more likely than older students to have regarded both the boycott and the sit-in as wholly justified and to have participated in each. The extreme-groups comparison shows, however that both extremes were on average rather younger than all students. Thus 62% of the activists, 66% of the opposition and 51% of all students were under twenty-two years of age.

8. Variations were found in the support of students of different nationalities. American and British undergraduates and post-graduates showed very similar levels of support, although American participation-rates were marginally higher than those of British students. Seventy-eight per cent of the activists, 87 per cent of the opposition and 72 per cent of all students were British: 12% of the activists, 4% of the opposition and 9% of all students were American. African and Asian postgraduates gave less support to the protest than the British, but least support came from the group of postgraduates from Australasia and Canada.

9. Among British students support showed only small variations with father's occupation. Among undergraduates those classifying their father's occupation as professional participated most in the sit-in, whereas the 'manual' group's participation-rate in the boycott was highest. Among postgraduates the 'own-business' group had the highest participation-rate in both boycott and sit-in. Thirty per cent of the activists, 25% of the opposition and 26% of all students came from the 'professional' group: 17% of the activists, 9% of the opposition and 13% of all students came from the 'manual' group.

10. The school background of the British undergraduates similarly bore only a small relationship to support for the protest. The participation-rate of those from direct-grant schools was the highest (52%) for the sit-in, whereas those from non-grammar maintained schools had the highest participation-rate (66%) in the boycott. Those from independent schools gave less support than any other group to both boycott and sit-in but, nevertheless, 36% of this group took part in the sit-in and 47% in the boycott. The British students in both extreme groups closely reflected the population distribution in regard to secondary schooling.

11. Academic achievement, measured in different ways, showed no regular relationship with support, although there was some evidence of slightly greater participation on the part of those of middling ability. Among home students 46% of the activists compared with 54% of the opposition had at least one A and one B at 'A' level.

12. A strong and regular relationship was found between political party allegiance and support. Thus, among home undergraduates 19% of Conservatives, 51% of Labour and 74% of the supporters of groups left of Labour regarded the sit-in as wholly justified.

For home postgraduates these percentages were 13%, 54%, and 75% respectively. Participation in the sit-in varied in a similar way. Among home students 72% of the activists, compared with 29% of the opposition and 55% of all students, were supporters of the Labour Party or of groups left of Labour. A strong relationship was also found between the political views of overseas students and their support for the demonstrations.

13. Students' views on various political issues were similarly found to be strongly related to their support for the protest. For example, 71% of the activists, 15% of the opposition and 37% of all students strongly opposed the American involvement in Vietnam. Among the supporters of each political party, support for the demonstrations increased with radicalism, measured in terms of attitudes towards the political issues.

14. Among home students the political party for which their parents had voted in 1966 was related to their own voting preference and to their support for the protest. Thus, among home students, 48% of the activists, compared with 20% of the opposition and 30% of all students, said their mother had voted Labour in 1966.

15. The religious beliefs of students were also quite strongly related to support. Seventy-three per cent of the activists, compared with 31% of the opposition and 49% of all students, had no religious beliefs.

16. There were large differences in the degree of support for the boycott and sit-in of those specialising in different subjects. Among undergradutes, 61% of sociologists compared with 32% of statisticians and accountants, and 25% of geographers took part in the sit-in. Among postgraduates these figures were 44%, 24% and 14% respectively. The differences persisted among British students when party allegiance was held constant. Thirty-three per cent of the activists, compared with 6% of the opposition, and 16% of all students were specialising in sociology, social anthropology or social psychology.

17. Year of course showed a small regular relationship with support, differences in participation being greater than attitudinal differences. Thus, among undergraduates 46% of first years compared with 41% of third years regarded the sit-in as wholly justified, whereas 46% and 36% respectively of each year-group had taken part in it. The differences disappeared when frequency

of union attendance was held constant. Forty-six per cent of the activists, compared with 48% of the opposition, and 37% of all students were in their first year at the School.

18. Differences were found in the support for the protest of students living in different types of accommodation. Those living in rented flats were more likely than other students to have taken part in the boycott and sit-in whereas those living at home were least likely to have participated. Twenty-one per cent of the activists, compared with 47% of the opposition and 35% of all students, lived either at home or in a hall or hostel; 69% of the activists, 39% of the opposition and 51% of all students lived in rented flats.

19. Frequency of attendance at union meetings was very strongly related to support. Thus, 75% of undergraduates and 88% of postgraduates who attended union meetings very frequently regarded the sit-in as wholly justified compared with 8% and 5% respectively of those of each group who never attended. The more frequently students attended union meetings, the more likely were they to have taken part in the sit-in on several days and to have missed all their lectures in support of the boycott. This relationship was independent of party allegiance. Seventy-nine per cent of the activists, compared with 31% of the opposition, and 36% of all students attended union meetings very or fairly frequently.

20. Among undergraduates, attitudes towards the adequacy of the Union's representation of student opinion was unrelated to support. Postgraduates who regarded the Union as adequately representative of student opinion were, however, considerably more likely to have supported the protest than were those regarding the representation as inadequate. The extreme groups diverged markedly in their attitude to the Union: 57% of the activists, compared with 9% of the opposition, and 33% of all students regarded the Union's representation of student opinion as adequate.

21. Dissatisfaction with various aspects of the School was related to support for the protest, the strongest relationship being with dissatisfaction with staff contacts. Thus, 56% of the undergraduates who were very dissatisfied with staff contact, compared with 28% of those who were very satisfied, regarded the sit-in as wholly justified. Among postgraduates these percentages were 60% and 34% respectively. Forty-one per cent of the activists, compared with 69% of the opposition and 55% of all students, were satisfied with staff contacts. Forty-five per cent of the activists, compared

with 79% of the opposition and 68% of all students, were satisfied with lectures.

22. Support for the protest was also related to attitudes towards student representation on school committees, the strongest relation being with the desire for representation on disciplinary committees. Thus, 77% of those wanting a student majority on disciplinary committees, compared with 5% of those wanting neither consultation nor representation on discipline, regarded the sit-in as wholly justified. The extreme groups showed large differences in their desire for student representation on discipline, course-content and the appointment of the director. Eighty-eight per cent of the activists, compared with 21% of the opposition and 54% of all students, wanted at least equal numbers of students on disciplinary committees. Sixty-four per cent of the activists, compared with 13% of the opposition and 30% of all students, wanted at least equality in regard to course content. Forty-six per cent of the activists, compared with 1% of the opposition and 13% of all students wanted at least equality on the appointment of the Director.

23. The extreme groups differed markedly in regard to their answers to several items taken from a scale of authoritarianism. (See Appendix A, question 53.) Fifty-eight per cent of the activists, compared with 9% of the opposition and 26% of all students, strongly disagreed with the statement: 'Young people sometimes get rebellious ideas but as they grow up they ought to get over them and settle down.' Fifty-five per cent of the activists compared with 16% of the opposition and 28% of all students, strongly disagreed with the statement: 'If people would talk less and work more everybody would be better off.' Seventy-two per cent of the activists, compared with 22% of the opposition and 42% of all students, strongly disagreed with the statement: 'Obedience and respect for authority are the most important virtues that children should learn.'

Sources of student unrest[1]
The origins of the wave of student protest which started in the United States in 1964 and reached Britain in 1967 are undoubtedly many. And the relative importance of the different factors accounting for the protests in different countries and in different institutions within each country can be expected to vary considerably. In

r*

considering the sources of student protest within any country, however, factors of four distinct types are potentially relevant:

1. Student characteristics, such as family and educational background, academic ability, values, expectations, motivations, political ideology and fields of specialisation.

2. University characteristics such as size, location, material conditions, governing structure, decision-making procedures, reputation, degrees, curricula, teaching-methods, attitudes of the academics and administrators, and the general nature of the educational and social environment provided.

3. The cultural and political climate prevailing in the country, particularly in regard to the status of youth and the extent of social criticism and protest on both national and international issues.

4. Historical events and trends both in the country and in the world.

Students

Most explanations of student unrest in Britain start from an assumption that it is due either wholly or in large part to the different attitudes and values of many of today's students compared with those of earlier generations. Variations in the incidence or scale of protests at different universities are assumed to be largely due to the different extent to which they attract activists or potential activists. Evaluations of the nature of the changes in students and of their causes are many and various. Burns[2] provides a sample ranging from those assuming unrest to be largely due to a small core of activists, through a-political explanations assuming anomie, a particularly large generation-gap or an increasing dissatisfaction with the university system to those who see the unrest in a broader ideological and cultural context.

No data are available to test the extent to which students have changed in any of the hypothesised ways, but the theories necessarily assume not only change but also a relationship between the changed values and attitudes and support for protest. Surveys of students, particularly in universities where protest has occurred, enable the identification of those attitudes, values and characteristics of students most strongly associated with support for protest. Such studies as the L.S.E. survey may therefore provide support for causal hypotheses or throw doubt on their general validity, to the extent that relevant questions have been asked. Only by repeated studies, however, based on different student populations and focused on different aspects of activists could an adequate body of evidence eventually be accumulated.

In the United States very many studies of students have already been carried out and much is known about the activists on American campuses. In the first place the percentage of students on any campus who have actively participated in any one protest has rarely exceeded 5%. Peterson's investigations[3] of the issues over which organised protest occurred in 1967/8 showed, however, that 38% of institutions had experienced protest against the Vietnam war; 34% on living-group regulation; 29% on civil rights; 27% on student participation in campus policy-making; 25% on the draft; 25% on military recruitment; and 15% on curriculum inflexibility.

Students participating in demonstrations concerned with living group regulations may well be considerably different from those who protest against the war in Vietnam. Most researchers in the States have studied participants in student demonstrations or group activities concerned with some matter of general political or ethical principle. From the large number of studies already completed, covering students activists at different universities and at different times in the period 1964-8, with varying degrees of methodological sophistication, remarkably consistent results have emerged.[4]

American student activists are usually those with above-average grades: the higher the student's grade-point average, the more likely it is that he will become involved in any 'political' demonstration. Activists are more politically radical than other students, and their parents are more liberal than those of other students. A disproportionate number of the activists come from professional and intellectual families of upper-middle-class status, with incomes well above average. Activism is related to a complex of values which tend to be shared by the students and their parents. Thus, the activists have been found to place greater stress than other students on involvement in intellectual and aesthetic pursuits, humanitarian concerns and opportunity for self-expression. They tend to disvalue personal achievement, conventional morality and conventional religiosity, and are anti-authoritarian. Once at university they drop out less frequently than other students and a disproportionately large number of them continue on to graduate school and later to academic careers.

At university, they tend to specialise in the social sciences and humanities, and to express more dissatisfaction than other students, not so much with their education as with the defects of the college administration. There is, however, evidence of differences between activists and other students in their approach to the educational process and their preferred emphases in methods of teaching.[5] They are also much more concerned than other students in participating in university decision-making.[6] And finally, in Keniston's words, ' It is primarily perceived injustice or the denial of student rights by the Administration that agitates the activist.'[7]

This profile of the American student activist has played an important role in explanations of American student protest. It is therefore significant that L.S.E. activists in 1967 showed only some of the same characteristics. The main similarities were their predominantly radical political views, their lack of religious beliefs, their concentration in certain fields of study, their concern for student participation in university decision-making and their anti-authoritarianism. The essential differences were twofold: there is no evidence from the L.S.E. survey that either extreme activists or all participants in the protest came disproportionately from upper-middle-class families with higher-than-average incomes; there is similarly no evidence that they were drawn disproportionately within the School from a category of students of above-average ability. In view of suggested explanations of British student protest, we must also stress that the L.S.E. data would not support any hypotheses assuming activists to be less academically able or from more limited educational and social backgrounds than other students. At L.S.E. the 1967 protest appears to have been supported by a roughly representative cross-section of the students in terms of their home and school backgrounds and their academic ability.

The L.S.E. findings on the characteristics of the activists may not be replicated in studies of activism in other British universities. The unique nature of the student population at the School in regard to fields of study, together with the high entrance-standards, is such that we would not expect findings elsewhere to be closely similar. For example, the relationships between home background, academic ability and activism, found in the States, may operate in universities covering all faculties but not within the social sciences. It is, however, equally plausible that British student activism differs markedly from American activism in this way.

Universities

No empirical studies have as yet been made in Britain of the relationship between student protest and institutional characteristics. Although most universities have increased considerably in size in the last ten years and there is more diversification than previously in their material amenities, student accommodation, curricula and methods of teaching, such differences as exist do not appear *prima facie* to be associated with the occurrence of protest.

Analysts of American student activism, drawing on the evidence of studies of the relationship between institutional characteristics and protest such as those of Cowan[8] and Peterson[9] have concluded that certain institutions which are, typically, large urban universities with high academic standards tend to recruit selectively a greater proportion of protest-prone students. Keniston[10] suggests that such institutions act as magnets for potential activists not so much because of their reputations for political radicalism as because they are noted for their academic excellence. He sees the greater incidence of protests in universities of this type as resulting, primarily, from their ability to sustain an activist sub-culture with sufficient mass and potency to generate a demonstration or action programme, and discounts, to a large extent, their impersonality or the nature of their teaching-arrangements as causes of protest. Other writers such as Flacks[11] have attached greater importance to the increasing rationalisation of the educational process in American high schools and universities as a cause of student unrest.

If British protest only occurred at universities of the size typifying the American 'protest-promoting' institution there would be no protest. However, if Keniston's thesis is correct, the largeness of the 'protest-promoting' university in the States is relevant, mainly because of the small proportion of activists or potential activists on any campus. Assuming Berkeley activists to constitute 5% of the student population, they would number roughly 1400 students. The number of L.S.E. students who participated either in the sit-in or boycott in 1967 was at least 1300. It would certainly appear obvious that frequent or sustained protest only occurs in universities where there are enough activists to organise, participate in and provide the leadership for demonstrations. How large an institution this requires will depend upon the nature of its students.

The question of leadership is one to which the L.S.E. survey can provide no answers. American writers have stressed the important role frequently played by teaching-assistants, graduate students and young faculty-members. At L.S.E. there are now some teaching-assistants on the American model, and a growing number of part-time postgraduates and ex-students employed in other London colleges maintain close contacts with the School. There is evidence that this group made a significant contribution to the leadership of the 1967 protest. The number of young members of staff has increased at L.S.E., as in other British universities, and there are undoubtedly some who sympathise at least with many of the aspirations of the activists if not with all their methods.

It seems probable that in Britain, as in the States, different universities attract potential activists and their leaders in varying proportions related to the degree courses offered and to their reputation. Once a university has attracted large numbers of such students, the occurrence or scale of protest may be to some extent dependent upon material conditions, teaching-methods, staff attitudes or the nature of student participation in decision-making, but on this there is no evidence. Less tangible aspects of the social and educational environment, and in particular the extent of informal contacts between students and academic staff may be of fundamental importance. Students' expectations of the university environment have been investigated in the States[12] and in Britain the Marris[13] data showed fairly widespread disappointment among students. The discrepancy between expectations and experience is seen by some as an important contributory factor in student unrest. Whether or not this is the case, there is ample evidence that the extreme radicals want to bring about fundamental changes in their universities and that in some of their demands they have the support of many more moderate students.

Whatever may be the relative importance of other factors, when a university contains large numbers of potential activists who are to some extent dissatisfied with the institution, the role of the administration becomes central in importance. The extent to which protests have been stillborn because of skilful handling on the part of administrators necessarily remains unknown. It is, however, relatively uncommon for a major student protest to occur without the actions of the university authorities coming under some form of attack from outside as well as from within the institution. Few would disagree with Keniston that:

'Skilful handling of student complaints, the maintenance of open channels of communication between student leaders and faculty members and administrative willingness to resist public and political pressures in order to protect the rights of students—all minimise the likelihood of organised protest. Conversely a university administration that shows itself unduly sensitive to political, legislative or public pressures, that treats students arrogantly, ineptly, condescendingly, hypocritically or above all dishonestly, is asking for a demonstration.[14]

The situation is, however, made complex by the differences which frequently exist between the views of students, governors, administrators and academics on student rights.

Socio-cultural and historical factors

Historically, as Flacks[15] suggests, students and young intellectuals appear to have become actively involved in protest movements within a society under two sets of interrelated conditions: when they have been marginal in the labour market because their numbers exceed the number of suitable job-opportunities (typically in underdeveloped countries), and when the traditional values of a society no longer seem appropriate due to the impact of Westernisation, industrialisation or modernisation. The second of these conditions may apply in some degree to countries of Western Europe in the 1960s. Many other theories relating current student unrest to the nature of the societies in which it has occurred, have, however, been advanced.

Student protest may be seen as only one variant of a youth culture running counter to the established order of the adult middle-class world, which has developed in many countries as a particularly articulate, visible and militant form of the 'generation gap'. Teddy boys, mods and rockers, provos and hippies are all seen as part of the same phenomenon. Many commentators relate this behaviour of youth to the over-permissive societies in which they have grown up. The post-1945 era of economic affluence and parental gentleness in many Western countries is said to have resulted in a generation of young people who regard the individual's impulses and sentiments as sacred and anything which thwarts them as repressive.

Another hypothesis links student unrest to the 'bankruptcy of the left'. Then dissatisfaction with current trends in a society or its apparent stagnation can find no outlet in support for any political doctrine or party policy, it is expressed in militancy and the rejection of order. A further interpretation, related to this, is that the momentum of para-political activities such as C.N.D., the anti-Vietnam movement and the American Civil Rights movement, in which many students participate, has flooded over into action against university authorities who do not ally themselves with these causes. Unrest is seen as largely due to the belief on the part of many students that the universities are not properly fulfilling their political and moral role in society.

Keniston,[16] discussing the characteristics of the cultural climate in which American student protest is most likely to occur, suggests that protest activities must appear meaningful either in an expressive or instrumental sense and that the anticipated consequences of activism must not be seen by the students as overwhelmingly damaging to themselves. The importance of the prevailing climate of social criticism and cynicism, both in the States and in Britain, as a stimulus to student protest would appear undeniable. And, as increasing numbers of students in each country see protest and direct action as both legitimate and effective, more participate. The communicatons media and, in particular, television, usually play an important part in convincing students that protest pays, both in terms of the publicity obtained for their causes and the importance assumed by the activists and their leaders.

The role of the mass media as 'an overlooked member of the total academic and community picture of unrest and activism' has been stressed by Sampson[17] and others. No doubt most members of the staffs of universities which have experienced major protests believe with Sampson that the mass media significantly perpetuate and escalate conflicts, whether by their accurate or inaccurate reporting or by their frequently highly biased comment. Also, in serving as a channel of communication between students and university authorities, they frequently create new issues and cause positions to harden, making resolution of the conflict increasingly difficult.

Television has probably played an important role of a different type in increasing the sensitivity of students and others to world events. At the very least it has to a large extent abolished all sense of the distances separating countries such as Britain, the United States, Vietnam, Czechoslovakia, Biafra and Rhodesia. Students demonstrating in London, Paris, Berlin or Chicago tend to feel a shared identity and common purpose, however disparate their immediate objectives may be. Keniston[18] sees this as part of a general trend towards the 'internationalisation of identity' brought about by the unique conditions of the twentieth century. Rapid developments in communications and the world-wide threat of nuclear war have resulted in the emergence in many countries of vanguard groups in which parochial and national allegiances have been weakened in favour of a more inclusive sense of affinity with people of other nations. Thus, many recent conflicts between students and univerisity authorities have been triggered off by disputes over the methods chosen by students to express their concern for the insecure and underprivileged, not only in their own society but also in other countries.

Future research
It seems probable that current student protest in Britain and other Western countries is due to the interaction of a large number of individual, institutional, cultural and historical factors of the type discussed. The relative importance of the different factors no doubt varies considerably from country to country, but that protest is more likely to occur in one country while it continues in another seems certain. Sanford[19] has predicted an increase in American student activism throughout the 1970s. If activism continues or increases in Britain, then the need for further research is overwhelming and the potential scope very wide.

Student surveys in other universities, similar to the L.S.E. survey, would indicate the shared characteristics of student activists in Britain. More detailed investigations of the expectations, perceptions, motivations and values of students are also needed both in universities where protests have occurred and elsewhere. Similiar studies of pupils in their final years at school and, in particular, a longitudinal study following a sample of sixth formers through their university years and first jobs would be of great interest. More should also be known about university administrations and administrators. Similarly, the attitudes, expectations and practices of academic staff should be studied in relation to how these are perceived by their students. In some of these areas, American researchers have already led the way, but British data are non-existent.

Only by a better understanding of the nature and sources of British student unrest can appropriate changes in the structure and functioning of universities be evolved. Without research, protest in particular institutions is likely to continue to be 'explained' in terms of small bands of student revolutionaries leading their gullible supporters into deliberate confrontations with authorities. That there are students who seek confrontations with university authorities we do not dispute. But the hypothesis that without them unrest would not exist, nor protests occur, appears to be unduly naïve.

Appendix A
The questionnaire

L.S.E. STUDENT SURVEY

Please answer each question by *ringing* the most appropriate number category: give details where appropriate. If you wish to make any additional comments or to qualify your answers, please write on the back of the appropriate page.

Attitudes to the sit-in and boycott, 13-21 March 1967.

1. Which of these ways of expressing student grievances do you now think were justified and which unjustified at L.S.E. last term? (Ring *one* number in each *row*.)

	Wholly unjustified	Partly justified	Wholly justified	Undecided	No opinion
lobbying staff	1	2	3	4	9
petitions	1	2	3	4	9
protest meetings	1	2	3	4	9
protest marches	1	2	3	4	9
boycott of lectures	1	2	3	4	9
picketing	1	2	3	4	9
sit-in without immobilising the School	1	2	3	4	9
sit-in immobilising the School	1	2	3	4	9

2. What was your attitude to the *sit-in* (*a*) when it first started, Monday, March 13, and (*b*) at the end of term?

(*a*) *at the start of the sit-in*		(*b*) *at the end of term*	
strong disapproval	1	strong disapproval	1
mild disapproval	2	mild disapproval	2
mild approval	3	mild approval	3
strong approval	4	strong approval	4
undecided	5	undecided	5
no opinion	9	no opinion	9
don't remember	0	don't remember	0

3. What was your attitude to the *boycott* (*a*) when it first started, Monday, March 13, and (*b*) at the end of term?

(*a*) *at the start of the boycott*		(*b*) *at the end of term*	
strong disapproval	1	strong disapproval	1
mild disapproval	2	mild disapproval	2
mild approval	3	mild approval	3
strong approval	4	strong approval	4
undecided	5	undecided	5
no opinion	9	no opinion	9
don't remember	0	don't remember	0

4. Did you at any time:

	Yes	No
try to dissuade others from supporting the sit-in	1	2
try to dissuade others from supporting the boycott	1	2
wear a white badge to show disapproval of the boycott	1	2
show opposition in any other way (please specify):		

Political attitudes

5. What is your attitude to the United States' involvement in Vietnam?

strongly support	1
support	2
oppose	3
strongly oppose	4
no opinion	9
other (please specify):...............	
....	

6. Which of the following solutions to the Rhodesian situation would you most prefer?

indefinite continuation of white minority rule	1
majority rule at some fixed date beyond 10 years	2
majority rule within 10 years	3
majority rule now	4
no opinion	9

7. Do you think that everyone in Britain should accept some reduction in their standard of living so as to increase aid to developing countries?

yes	1
no	2
undecided	3
no opinion	9

8. What is your attitude towards existing legislation against racial discrimination in this country?

should be extended	1
is adequate	2
should be reduced	3
should be repealed	4
no opinion	9

U.K. students only, answer 9 to 13. Foreign students go to 14.

9. Are you in favour of, or opposed to, replacing the existing system of grammar and secondary modern schools by comprehensive schools?

strongly in favour	1
in favour	2
opposed to	3
strongly opposed to	4
undecided	5
no opinion	9

10. How interested are you in national politics?

very interested	1
moderately interested	2
slightly interested	3
not interested	4

11. Which political party or group most nearly reflects your own political views?

Conservative	1
Liberal	2
Labour	3
Communist	4
other (please specify)	
.... 5	
no opinion	9

12. Are you a *member* of a political party?

Conservative	1
Liberal	2
Labour	3
Communist	4
other (please specify)	
....	
none	6

13. If there were a general election tomorrow and you had a vote, for which party would you vote?

Conservative	1
Liberal	2
Labour	3
Communist	4
other (please specify)	
....	5
none	6
don't know	9

Foreign students only, answer question 14.

14. How would you describe your political views?

conservative	1
liberal	2
socialist	3
communist	4
other (please specify)	
....	
....	5
none	8
don't know	9

15. On how many *days* did you sit in at any time between 9.30 a.m. and 10.30 p.m.?

none	1
1-3	2
4-6	3
7-9	4
don't remember	0

16. On how many *nights* did you stay *all* night (from 10.30 p.m. to 7 a.m.) in the School?

none	1
1 or 2	2
3 to 6	3
7 or 8	4
don't remember	0

17. On how many *nights* did you stay in the School for *part* of the night, between 10.30 p.m. and 7 a.m.?

none	1
1 or 2	2
3-6	3
7 or 8	4
don't remember	0

18. (a) Did you take part in the march on Friday 17 March?

yes 1
no 2

(b) Did you attend the subsequent meeting in Lincoln's Inn Fields?

yes 1
no 2

19. Did you take part in picketing at any time between Monday 13 March and Tuesday 21 March:

(a) At one of the entries to the School?

yes 1
no 2

(b) Outside lecture rooms or classrooms?

yes 1
no 2

20. Did you attend as many lectures, classes and seminars as usual during the week Monday 13–Friday 17 March? (i.e. you went and the lectures, etc., were given)

yes 1
no 2
don't remember 0

If no
(a) Approximately how many did you miss?

all 1
half or more, but not all 2
less than half 3
not applicable Y

(b) What was the *main* reason you missed lectures, etc.?

lectures, etc., were not held 1
you wanted to attend but were dissuaded by those supporting boycott 2
you supported the boycott 3
other (please specify) ....
....
not applicable Y

21. Did you attend and/or vote at the meeting of the Students' Union on Monday 13 March, at which it was decided to hold the boycott and sit-in?

attended and voted 1
attended without voting 2
did not attend 3
don't remember 0

If you did not attend
Were you in the School on that afternoon?

yes 1
no 2
don't remember 0
not applicable Y

22. Did you attend and/or vote at the meeting of the Students' Union on Monday 20 March, at which it was decided to suspend the boycott and sit-in?

attended and voted	1
attended without voting	2
did not attend	3
don't remember	0

If you did not attend
Were you in the School on the evening of Monday 20 March?

yes	1
no	2
don't remember	0
not applicable	Y

23. Did you speak at *any* of the union meetings held between Monday 13 March and Tuesday 21 March?

yes	1
no	2
don't remember	0

24. During the boycott and sit-in did you use the library more or less than usual?

more than usual	1
as much as usual	2
less than usual	3
not at all	4
don't remember	0

25. During the boycott and sit-in did you study at home more or less than usual?

more than usual	1
as much as usual	2
less than usual	3
not at all	4
don't remember	0

Aspects of L.S.E.
26. How would you express your personal level of satisfaction with each of the listed aspects of L.S.E.? (Ring *one* number in each *row*.)

	satisfactory		unsatisfactory		no
	very	fairly	fairly	very	opin.
your lectures	1	2	3	4	9
your classes or seminars	1	2	3	4	9
tutorial arrangements	1	2	3	4	9
the structure of your degree	1	2	3	4	9
you contacts with staff	1	2	3	4	9
the main library	1	2	3	4	9
the teaching library	1	2	3	4	9
the location of L.S.E. in central London	1	2	3	4	9
your living accommodation	1	2	3	4	9

Which *one* of the above do you consider to be:
    (*a*) most satisfactory ....
    (*b*) most unsatisfactory ....

27. By what method, if any, do you think student views should be taken into account in school decision-making on each of the following: (Ring *one* number in each *row*.)

	representation on relevant school committees with students in:			consultation without representation	neither consultation nor representation	no opinion
	majority	*equality*	*minority*			
admission of students	1	2	3	4	5	9
teaching-arrangements	1	2	3	4	5	9
course-content	1	2	3	4	5	9
examinations	1	2	3	4	5	9
discipline	1	2	3	4	5	9
library	1	2	3	4	5	9
careers advisory service	1	2	3	4	5	9
academic appointments	1	2	3	5	5	9
appointment of director	1	2	3	4	5	9
senior administrative appointments	1	2	3	4	5	9
any other matters (please specify)	1	2	3	4	5	9

28. Have you attended the meetings or taken part in the activities of any L.S.E. societies (including athletic societies) during this academic year?

yes 1
no 2

29. List below the names of any L.S.E. societies (including athletic societies) of which you are a member. If you do not belong to any, write ' none '.

30. Have you ever been on the committee of any L.S.E. society?

yes 1
no 2

31. Have you ever been on Union Council, an official of the Graduate Students' Association, a member of a Union Committee or an officer of the Union? (Includes offices held on Beaver, A.I.E.S.E.C., Clare Market Review.)

yes 1
no 2

32. How frequently do you attend union meetings?

very frequently	1
fairly frequently	2
occasionally	3
very rarely	4
never	5

33. How adequate do you think the following are at L.S.E.? (Ring *one* number in each *row*.)

	very adequate	fairly adequate	rather inadequate	very inadequate	don't know
accommodation for union offices	1	2	3	4	9
accommodation for union meetings	1	2	3	4	9
accommodation for society meetings	1	2	3	4	9
accommodation for other activities including common rooms	1	2	3	4	9
union housing bureau	1	2	3	4	9
NUS travel facilities	1	2	3	4	9
union social activities	1	2	3	4	9
the representation of student opinion by the Union	1	2	3	4	9

34. Do you think presidents of the Students' Union should be given a sabbatical year?

as a matter of principle	1
at the School's discretion	2
not at all	3
no opinion	9

35. Do you think it is important or unimportant for the Union to have complete control over its premises?

important	1
unimportant	2
no opinion	9

Background characteristics

36. Are you:

male	1
female	2

37. What was your age last birthday?

19 or under	1
20 or 21	2
22-5	3
26 and over	4

38. Are you:

single	1
married	2
widowed/divorced/separated	3

39. What are your religious beliefs:

none	1
Anglican	2
Roman Catholic	3
Non-conformist	4
Jewish	5
other (please specify)	
....	

40. Are you:

British (from U.K.)	1
Australian or a New Zealander	2
Canadian	3
Asian	4
African	5
American (from U.S.A.)	6
European	7
other (please specify)	
....	

41. Please list below the *U.K. ' A ' level* subjects you have passed, the grade obtained in each and the year in which you sat the examination. (If you sat the same subject more than once give the highest grade obtained.) If none write ' none '.

subject	grade	year

42. Did you enter L.S.E. to study for your *present* degree, diploma, etc., within 6 months of leaving your last secondary school (high school, etc.)?

yes	1
no	2

If no, then please give below details of any full-time or part-time education received and any full-time occupation followed, during the period between leaving your last school and entering your *present* course of study at L.S.E.

(*a*) education

name of institution*	qualification obtained (if any) with class of degree	subject of study

* L.S.E. graduates please provide information on first degree, diploma, etc.

(*b*) full-time employment

How long did you spend in full-time employment (i.e. more than 30 hours per week) during this period? (Exclude vacation jobs.)

none	1
less than 1 year	2
1 but less than 2 years	3
2 or more years	4

43. For which of the following are you registered at L.S.E.?

undergraduate degree or diploma 1
postgraduate degree or diploma 2
general course 3
research fee 4
other (please specify) ....
....

If undergraduate student

(a) For which degree, etc., are you studying? ....
(b) What is your special subject? ....
(If B.Sc. (Econ.) Part I give the special subject you intend studying next year.)

If postgraduate student

(a) For which of the following degrees/diplomas are you studying?

Ph.D. 1
M.Phil. 2
M.Sc. (by examination) 3
postgraduate diploma 4
other (please specify) ....
....

(b) Which department are you in? ....

44. Which year of your present course are you in? (A preliminary year to an M.Sc. counts as a year in your M.Sc. course.)

1st 1
2nd 2
3rd 3
4th or more 4

45. During this term (summer 1967) are you living:

at home of parents or guardian 1
in a hall of residence or hostel 2
in rented accommodation with board (evening meal) included in rent 3
in rented accommodation without board (flat or room)
other (please specify) ....
....

46. Do you have adequate facilities for studying at your accommodation?

yes 1
no 2

47. How long on average does it take to travel from your present term-time address to L.S.E.?

less than 15 mins 1
15 mins but less than 30 mins 2
30 mins but less than 45 mins 3
45 mins but less than 60 mins 4
60 mins but less than 90 mins 5
90 mins or more 6
don't know 9

48. Do you have a grant, scholarship, fellowship, etc., for the current academic year?	yes	1
	no	2

If yes please specify:
(a) the source ....
(b) the amount paid to you ....
(c) whether your fees are included in the sum given above

	yes	1
	no	2

49. In which of the following categories would you put your father's or guardian's occupation at present?	professional	1
	managerial	2
	own business	3
	clerical	4
	skilled manual	5
	semi-skilled manual	6
	unskilled manual	7
	father retired or dead	8
	other (please specify occupation)	
	....	
	don't know	9

U.K. students only, answer 50 to 52. All students answer 53

50. In which of the following income-categories would you estimate your father's or guardian's income fell last year (1966), before tax?	less than £500	1
	£500 but less than £1000	2
	£1000 but less than £1500	3
	£1500 but less than £2000	4
	£2000 but less than £2500	5
	£2500 but less than £5000	6
	over £5000	7
	father dead	8
	don't know	9

	father	mother
51. Which political party did your father and mother vote for in the last general election (spring, 1966)? (Ring *one* number in *each* column.)		
Conservative	1	1
Liberal	2	2
Labour	3	3
Communist	4	4
other (please specify)		
parent dead	5	5
....		
did not vote	6	6
don't know	9	9

52. What type of secondary school did you *last* attend full time before entering university for the first time?

grammar, senior secondary	1
technical, central	2
secondary modern or junior secondary, elementary	3
comprehensive, bilateral, multi-lateral	4
direct grant	5
independent (public or private)	6
school or college overseas	7
other (please specify) ....

....

All students answer 53

53. Please indicate whether you Strongly Agree (SA), Agree (A), Disagree (D), or Strongly Disagree (SD) with the following statements:

	SA	A	D	SD
(a) Young people sometimes get rebellious ideas, but as they grow up they ought to get over them and settle down.	1	2	3	4
(b) Wars and social troubles may some day be ended by an earthquake or flood that will destroy the whole world.	1	2	3	4
(c) Every person should have a complete faith in some supernatural power whose decisions he obeys without questions.	1	2	3	4
(d) It is to be regretted that there are so many young people today who do not feel a great love, gratitude or respect for their parents.	1	2	3	4
(e) If people would talk less and work more, everybody would be better off.	1	2	3	4
(f) Obedience and respect for authority are the most important virtues that children should learn.	1	2	3	4

When you have completed the questionnaire would you please check that you have answered all the questions. Then return the questionnaire to us in the enclosed envelope, either by placing it in one of the boxes labelled *L.S.E. Student Survey*, provided near the porters' lodges of the School, or through the post.

Thank you for your co-operation

Appendix B
Methodology

Population coverage

The population covered by the survey comprised all students registered for a full-time course at the London School of Economics in May 1967. At the request of the school authorities no sampling was attempted and the survey thus covered all 2806 students on the lists provided by the Registry and the Postgraduate School. Of these students, 1692 were undergraduates registered for a first degree or taking a one-year school-course, 268 were registered for school diplomas and 846 for higher degrees or as research-fee students.[1]

Field procedure

Questionnaires were sent out on 11 May to the London address of each student. In a covering letter signed by the four authors and the President of the Student Union, the purposes of the survey were explained, together with the special procedure being used to guarantee anonymity. This procedure, which was agreed with the union officers, was felt to be necessary because of the nature of the information being sought. The questionnaires were sent out bearing index numbers corresponding to the numbered population, but on receipt of a completed questionnaire, after registering the reply, the original index number was removed and a new one, which merely recorded the order in which the questionnaire had been returned, was placed upon it. In this way non-respondents could be followed up, but after the checking-in procedure no identification of respondents was possible. In the case of B.Sc. (Econ.) second years, index numbers from an earlier survey were also placed on the returned questionnaires in order that information obtained in the two surveys could be related. A reminder letter was sent out on 29 May and a second questionnaire on 16 June.

It seems likely that the anonymity problem was not exaggerated as, even with the assurances given, a number of questionnaires were returned with the index numbers removed. These questionnaires were discarded in order to avoid the possibility of one respondent completing two questionnaires. Other students, although returning the questionnaire without removing the index number, did not provide information (such as the name of the previous university they had attended, in the case of overseas postgraduates) which might have made their identity known.

Response-rates
The total number of returned questionnaires was 2269. However, as Table 1 shows, thirty questionnaires were discarded either because the index number had been removed or a large proportion of the questionnaire had been left uncompleted. Thus the total number of questionnaires used in the analysis was 2239, giving an overall response-rate of 80%.

Table 1 Over-all response-rate

Total returned questionnaires	2269
Questionnaires not used	
Index numbers removed	16
Very incomplete	14
Total usable questionnaires	2239
Total population	2806
Effective response-rate	80%

A total of ninety-seven other replies were received: sixty-one from students indicating that they did not wish to participate in the survey and thirty-six returns through the G.P.O. because the student was not found at the given address.

As students were grouped within courses of study on the population lists, it was possible to calculate the response-rate for each course-of-study sub-group. These are shown in Table 2. The eighty-two students registered for the two-year diploma in social administraion have been classified as postgraduates, although most are non-graduates and all are classified by the School as undergraduates. This procedure was found to be necessary in analysing the survey data as responses to the course-of-study question proved inadequate for the separation of those taking the one-year (postgraduate) or two-year (undergraduate) diplomas in social administration.

The over-all response-rate for undergraduates was 83% and only in the case of one small group was the rate below 7%. As the course of study was not shown on the list of postgraduates no separate response-rates were able to be calculated by type of higher degree. Postgraduates and diploma students had an overall response-rate of 75%, a very low response being obtained from the sixty-seven students registered for diplomas in business studies, development administration and personnel management.

Table 2 Response rate: by course of study

Course of study	Population	Effective response	Response-rate (%)
Undergraduates			
B.Sc. (Econ.)	1056	906	96
Ll.B.	211	160	76
B.A./B.Sc. anthropology	12	9	(75)
B.A./B.Sc. geography	68	53	78
B.A. history	42	31	74)
B.A. philosophy and economics	22	15	(68)
B.A./B.Sc. sociology	179	142	79
Degree not given		11	
All first-degree students	1590	1327	83
Other undergraduate courses	102	86	83
All undergraduates	1692	1413	83
Postgraduates			
Postgraduates degrees and research fee	846	622	74
School diplomas			
Applied social science	32 ⎫		
Mental health	31 ⎪	1176	84
Social administration (1-yr)	56 ⎬		
Social administration (2-yr)	82 ⎭		
Business studies	17 ⎫		
Development administration	19 ⎬	18	27
Personnel management	31 ⎭		
All school diplomas	268	204	76
All postgraduates	1114	826	75
All full-time students	2806	2239	80

Notes: 1. B.A./B.Sc. anthropology includes B.Sc. (special) anthropology.
2. B.A./B.Sc. geography includes B.Sc. (special) geography.
3. Other undergraduate courses includes overseas service, trade union and general.

Checks on representativeness

As the list of undergraduates showed the year of course of each student it was possible to compare the population and respondent distributions on this factor within each first degree. The data are given in Table 3. As was expected because of the timing of the survey, there was in each group a very slight under-representation of the third-year students who were taking their final examination during the period of the survey.

Table 3   Year of course of first-degree students

| Degree | Source of data | Year of course | | | | No year given | Total number |
		1st	2nd	3rd or later	All		
B.Sc. (Econ.)	respondents	35	35	30	100	59	906
	population	33	33	34	100	—	1056
Ll.B.	respondents	38	37	25	100	4	160
	population	37	34	29	100	—	211
B.A./B.Sc.	respondents	38	39	23	100	2	142
Sociology	population	37	37	26	100	—	179
other first	respondents	34	37	29	100	4	108
degrees	population	34	34	32	100	—	144
All first	respondents	35	36	29	100	69	1316
degrees	population	34	35	31	100	—	1590

Note: The table excludes students on one-year courses and eleven respondents who did not give their degrees.

A similar comparison was made of the percentage of males in the respondent sample and in the population. Again, as Table 4 shows, only very small differences were found. In each degree course, women appear to have been slightly more willing to respond than men. However, for undergraduates as a whole and for all students, there was the same percentage of men among the respondents as in the population.

Time trend in response

The index numbers placed on the completed questionnaires identified the order in which they had been returned and it was therefore

Table 4 Response: by sex

Course of study	Percentages of men	
	Population	Respondents
Undergraduates		
B.Sc. (Econ.)	87	86
Ll.B.	83	79
B.A./B.Sc. sociology	41	38
other first degrees	58	56
other undergraduates	85	83
All undergraduates	78	78
Postgraduates		
Postgraduate degree	79	77
School diploma	44	41
All postgraduates	70	68
All full-time students	75	75

Note: All except twelve respondents gave their sex.

possible to analyse responses by date of return. This was done separately for undergraduates and postgraduates on questions related to the boycott and sit-in, satisfaction with the School and representation on school committees.

Table 5 shows attitude to the sit-in by five date-of-return categories. The categories were chosen in such a way as to group the total returns in batches of roughly 500.

Differences are extremely small and there appears to be no time trend in the nature of attitudes to the sit-in except for a small increase in the percentage of those in the 'other' category which included 'undecided', 'no opinion' and 'no answer'. Attitudes to the boycott showed a similar lack of trend.

Participation in the boycott and sit-in was also analysed in this way and found to show no trend over time. Thus, among undergraduates 45% of the first respondents and 46% of the last respondents reported day-time participation in the sit-in. Among postgraduates the corresponding percentages were 31% and 25%. Similarly, the proportions of early and late respondents who had attempted to dissuade others from sitting in were very close. These results suggested that non-respondents were likely to differ little

Table 5   Attitude to sit-in: by date of reply

Percentages

Date of return of questionnaire	Attitude to sit-in					
	Wholly unjustified	Partly justified	Wholly justified	Other	All	N
Undergraduates						
12–15 May	21	27	48	4	100	362
16–18 May	26	28	41	5	100	322
19–25 May	22	24	46	8	100	320
26 May–15 June	24	25	42	9	100	267
16 June–7 July	18	29	43	10	100	142
Postgraduates						
12–15 May	19	25	49	7	100	134
16–18 May	18	33	41	8	100	175
19–25 May	18	26	49	7	100	175
26 May–15 June	23	25	40	12	100	229
16 June–7 July	18	22	43	17	100	113

from respondents in regard to their support for the student protest.

The same absence of any significant trend over time was found in regard to attitudes towards aspects of the School and views on student representation. The last group of respondents appeared to differ consistently from the early respondents in only one respect; a slightly higher percentage of them expressed no definite views on each attitudinal question.

Appendix C
Additional tables

Table 2.1A Age distribution of students
Percentages

	Age (in years)					
	19 or under	20-1	22-5	26 or over	Total	N
Undergraduates						
Home	33	49	10	8	100	1203
Overseas	11	40	28	21	100	206
All	30	47	13	10	100	1409
Postgraduates						
Home	0	7	66	27	100	400
Overseas	0	3	47	50	100	421
All	0	5	55	39	100	821
all students	19	31	29	21	100	2230

Note: The ages of a few students are not known. They are excluded from
the table.

Table 2.2A Age distribution of overseas students: by country of origin
Percentages

Country of origin	Undergraduates Age (in years)						Postgraduates	
	19 or under	20-1	22-5	26 or over	Total	N	Percentage aged 26 years or over	N
Africa	—	15	30	53	100	47	54	50
Asia	14	43	34	9	100	65	74	66
Australasia/ Canada	(14)	(48)	(14)	(14)	100	7	55	85
Europe	13	16	47	25	100	32	73	46
U.S.A.	14	81	5	—	100	43	29	145
Other	(8)	(33)	(33)	(26)	100	12	(51)	29

Note: The ages of a few students are not known. They are excluded from
the table.

Table 2.3A Percentage of married students

Percentages

	Home	Overseas	All
Undergraduates	7	14	8
Postgraduates	25	38	32
All	12	31	17

Table 2.4A Percentage of students with fathers in professional or/and manual occupations

Home students

	Percentage with father in:	
	Professional occupation	Manual occupation
Undergraduates		
Men	26	23
Women	40	20
Postgraduates		
Degree		
Men	31	21
Women	51	10
Diploma		
Men	47	10
Women	48	9
All		
Men	34	19
Women	49	10

Note: See note to Table 2.4.

Table 2.5A Voting of students' mothers and fathers in the 1966 General Election

Home students

Percentages

	Conservative	Liberal	Labour	Other	Total	N
Fathers' vote						
Undergraduates	45	11	43	1	100	890
Postgraduates	46	11	41	2	100	265
Undergraduates	48	13	37	2	100	967
Postgraduates	45	15	39	1	100	304
Mother's vote						

Note: The table includes only parents who students reported as having voted in the national election of March 1966.

Table 2.6A Percentage of university entrants in October 1964 who had 'good' 'A' levels: by faculty and university

	Social science		Law
University	Percentage with 'good' 'A' levels	University	Percentage with 'good' 'A' levels
L.S.E.	89	L.S.E.	77
Sheffield	87	Kings, London	73
Birmingham	79	Bristol	67
Manchester	75	Nottingham	61
Leicester	73	Birmingham	59
Leeds	72	Manchester	57
Southampton	66	Aberystwyth	53
Hull	59	University College, London	50
Newcastle	58	Exeter	47
Nottingham	58	Hull	47
Sussex	56	Sheffield	45
All universities	62	All universities	51

Source: University Central Council for Admissions, *Second Report 1963/4* (U.C.C.A., 1966).

Notes: 1. The data are based on a sample of about 80% of all candidates finally admitted and cover only those applying through the U.C.C.A. scheme.

2. The coverage is effectively confined to universities in England and Wales, since Scottish entrants, who provide the large majority of Scottish university students, are accepted on the basis of the Scottish Leaving Certificate. In addition Oxford and Cambridge are excluded.

3. A good 'A' level performance is defined as at least three grade Cs (if three subjects had been passed) or an A and a B (if two).

4. The 'faculties' in the table are those for which candidates originally applied. In some cases they may have been finally accepted in another.

5. The table does not cover all universities—it excludes those with social-science faculties when fewer than 55% of entrants had good 'A' levels and/or fewer than fifty entrants; and it excludes universities with law faculties where fewer than 45% had good 'A' levels and/or fewer than thirty entrants.

Table 2.7A   Grades obtained at 'A' level: by sex, secondary schooling, father's occupation, degree and field of study.

	Home undergraduates			Percentage
	Percentage with at least this number of 'A' levels at grades A or B			
	3 or more	2	Total	N
Men	38	86	100	865
Women	31	76	100	249
Secondary schooling				
Maintained	38	85	100	857
Direct grant	32	83	100	110
Independent	31	79	100	138
Father's occupation				
Non-manual	37	84	100	720
Manual	44	89	100	203
Degrees				
B.Sc.(Econ.)	39	87	100	760
Other degrees	32	78	100	374
Field of study				
Economics	40	89	100	336
Geography	32	84	100	122
Law	33	81	100	139
Politics	37	85	100	285
Sociology	34	78	100	216
Other	31	86	100	36

Note: The data exclude those 3% of students who did not have any 'A' levels and also those whose father's occupation, secondary schooling, degree or field of study is not known.

Table 2.8A   Travelling time from accommodation to the School
All students

Type of accommodation	Median travelling-time (in minutes)	Percentage of students travelling for over an hour
Parents' home	49	21
Hall	20	0
Lodgings	41	4
Flat	33	2
Other	36	38
All	33	6

Table 2.9A Father's occupation: by country of origin

Overseas students

Percentages

	Professional	Managerial	Own business	Clerical	Manual	Total	N
			Non-manual				
Country of origin							
Africa	24	13	44	7	11	100	50
Asia	36	22	35	4	3	100	88
Australasia/ Canada	50	15	17	5	14	100	70
Europe	37	8	41	6	8	100	52
U.S.A.	40	23	28	2	7	100	152
Other	(52)	(13)	(17)	(9)	(9)	100	23
All	42	18	29	4	8	100	435
Undergraduates	37	17	38	2	5	100	139
Postgraduates	43	18	25	5	9	100	296

Note: In 25% of cases, the father had either died or retired; a further 2% of answers were not classifiable, and 2% of students gave no answer. These are excluded in the above table.

Table 3.1A Attitude to American involvement in Vietnam

Home students

Percentages

	Strongly support	Support	Oppose	Strongly oppose	Don't know No answer	Total	N
		Attitude to American involvement					
Undergraduates	6	21	33	31	9	100	1206
Postgraduates	2	11	30	46	11	100	400
All	5	19	32	34	10	100	1606

Table 3.2A   Attitude to majority rule in Rhodesia

Home students

Percentages

Attitude to majority rule in Rhodesia

	Indefinite continuation of white minority rule	beyond 10 years	within 10 years	Now	Don't know No answer	Total	N
Undergraduates	3	19	57	18	3	100	1206
Postgraduates	1	13	55	29	2	100	400
All	2	17	57	21	3	100	1606

Table 3.3A   Attitude to legislation against racial discrimination

Home students

Percentages

Attitude to legislation against racial discrimination

	Extended	Adequate	Reduced	Repealed	Don't know No answer	Total	N
Undergraduates	70	16	2	6	6	100	1206
Postgraduates	76	12	2	3	7	100	400
All	72	15	2	5	6	100	1606

Table 3.4A   Attitude to comprehensive schools

Home students

Percentages

Attitude to comprehensive schools

	Strongly in favour	In favour	Oppose	Strongly oppose	Undecided	No answer	Total	N
Undergraduates	34	31	15	9	10	1	100	1206
Postgraduates	41	37	9	4	8	1	100	400
All	36	32	14	8	9	1	100	1606

Table 3.5A Attitude to aid to underdeveloped countries

Home students

Percentages

Attitude to aid to underdeveloped countries

	Yes	No	Undecided	Don't know No answer	Total	N
Undergraduates	28	49	20	3	100	1206
Postgraduates	40	39	15	6	100	400
All	31	46	18	5	100	1606

Table 3.6A Attitude to American involvement in Vietnam: by party allegiance

Home students

Percentages

Attitude to American involvement

Party allegiance	Strongly support	Support	Oppose	Strongly oppose	Don't know No answer	Total	N
Conservative	17	47	20	6	10	100	290
Liberal	3	17	40	25	15	100	250
Labour	2	13	40	38	7	100	720
Left-wing groups	—	4	11	82	3	100	139
Other	(4)	(12)	(25)	(42)	(17)	100	24
Don't know	4	10	37	37	12	100	123
No answer	3	12	13	44	28	100	60
All	5	19	32	34	10	100	1606

Table 3.7A Attitude to majority rule in Rhodesia: by party allegiance

Home students

Percentages

Party allegiance	Indefinite continuation white minority rule	Majority rule beyond 10 years	Majority rule within 10 years	Now	Don't know No answer	Total	N
Conservative	7	37	48	4	4	100	290
Liberal	1	20	64	13	2	100	250
Labour	—	11	64	23	2	100	720
Left-wing groups	—	2	40	56	2	100	139
Other	(8)	(17)	(42)	(25)	(8)	100	24
Don't know	6	18	46	23	7	100	123
No answer	3	20	40	25	12	100	60
All	2	17	57	21	3	100	1606

Table 3.8A   Attitude to legislation against racial discrimination: by party allegiance

Home students

Percentages

Attitude to legislation against racial discrimination

Party allegiance	Extended	Adequate	Reduced	Repealed	Don't know No answer	Total	N
Conservative	49	27	6	10	8	100	290
Liberal	67	17	3	6	7	100	250
Labour	80	13	1	3	3	100	720
Left-wing groups	86	7	0	1	6	100	139
Other	(50)	(17)	(0)	(17)	(16)	100	24
Don't know	63	11	4	7	15	100	123
No answer	73	5	0	10	12	100	60
All	72	15	2	5	6	100	1606

Table 3.9A Attitude to comprehensive schools: by party allegiance

Home students

Percentages

Attitude to comprehensive schools

Party allegiance	Strongly in favour	In favour	Oppose	Strongly oppose	Don't know No answer	Total	N
Conservative	3	19	37	28	13	100	290
Liberal	16	44	16	6	18	100	250
Labour	51	35	6	1	7	100	720
Left-wing groups	71	22	1	1	5	100	139
Other	(33)	(21)	(21)	(17)	8	100	24
Don't know	29	35	15	6	15	100	123
No answer	28	37	7	7	21	100	60
All	36	32	14	8	10	100	1606

Table 3.10A Attitude to aid to underdeveloped countries: by party allegiance

Home students

Percentages

Attitude to aid to underdeveloped countries

Party allegiance	Yes	No	Undecided	Don't know No answer	Total	N
Conservative	12	72	13	3	100	290
Liberal	36	40	20	4	100	250
Labour	35	42	20	3	100	720
Left-wing groups	48	28	112	12	100	139
Other	(29)	(59)	(8)	(4)	100	24
Don't know	23	51	20	6	100	123
No answer	37	35	13	15	100	60
All	31	46	18	5	100	1606

Table 3.11A   Student's party allegiance: by father's occupation

Home students

Percentages

Father's occupation	Student's party allegiance					Total	N
	Conservative	Liberal	Labour	Left-wing groups	Don't know No answer		
Undergraduates							
Professional	21	20	35	7	17	100	290
Managerial	26	13	42	7	12	100	217
Own business	27	15	36	9	13	100	144
Clerical	20	15	43	7	15	100	119
Skilled manual	8	19	52	11	10	100	131
Semi-skilled	4	15	65	13	3	100	48
Unskilled manual	15	10	45	10	20	100	40
Retired or dead	19	15	48	9	9	100	151
Don't know/ other	15	17	46	11	11	100	47
No answer	(37)	(5)	(16)	(10)	(32)	100	19
All	20	16	42	9	13	100	1606
Postgraduates							
Professional	8	17	57	8	10	100	114
Managerial	20	11	56	6	7	100	54
Own business	18	11	49	11	11	100	45
Clerical	(11)	(11)	(54)	(18)	(6)	100	28
Skilled manual	(7)	(7)	(50)	(11)	(25)	100	28
Semi-skilled manual	—	(33)	(22)	(11)	(34)	100	9
Unskilled manual	(12)	(12)	(66)	—	(10)	100	6
Retired or dead	10	13	54	9	14	100	105
Don't know/ other	(20)	(20)	(40)	(20)	—	100	5
No answer	(33)	(33)	(34)	—	—	100	6
All	12	14	53	9	12	100	400

Table 3.12A   Party allegiance: by field of study

Home students

Percentages

Field of study	Party allegiance					Total	N
	Conservative	Liberal	Labour	Left-wing groups	Other Don't know No answer		
Undergraduates							
Government	13	13	57	7	10	100	104
Anthropology, sociology	8	12	47	15	18	100	235
International relations, international history	17	17	46	10	10	100	111
History, economic history	15	13	39	14	19	100	82
Economics	24	14	41	8	13	100	166
Geography	20	28	37	6	9	100	123
Law	29	18	37	5	11	100	142
Industry and trade, statistics, accounts, computing	38	17	34	4	7	100	185
Other	10	15	44	17	14	100	48
No answer	(10)	0	(70)	—	(20)	100	10
All	20	16	42	9	13	100	1206
Postgraduates							
Government	(11)	(11)	(44)	(17)	(17)	100	18
Sociology, social psychology anthropology	3	13	53	19	12	100	64
Social administration	11	17	55	8	9	100	153
International history, international relations, economic history	12	9	52	6	21	100	33
Economics	13	16	51	—	20	100	45
Geography	(20)	(20)	(53)	—	(7)	100	15
Law	(20)	—	(60)	(20)	—	100	10
Statistics, accounting, demography	16	16	52	6	10	100	31
Industrial relations, philosophy, other	(17)	(6)	(59)	(18)	—	100	17
No answer	(29)	(7)	(50)	—	14	100	14
All	12	14	53	9	12	100	400

Table 3.13A Attitude to American involvement in Vietnam: by political views

Overseas students

Percentages

| | Attitude to American involvement | | | | | | |
Political views	Strongly support	Support	Oppose	Strongly oppose	Don't know No answer	Total	N
conservative	14	48	8	16	14	100	50
liberal	4	23	33	30	10	100	249
socialist	1	6	21	66	6	100	205
Other	—	11	20	60	9	100	35
Don't know/ no answer		21	21	36	22	100	94
All	3	19	25	43	10	100	633

Table 3.14A Attitude to majority rule in Rhodesia: by political views

Overseas students

Percentages

| | Attitude to majority rule | | | | | | |
| | Indefinite white majority rule | Majority rule | | | Don't know No answer | Total | N |
Political views		Beyond 10 years	Within 10 years	Now			
conservative	4	28	54	12	2	100	50
liberal	—	11	60	23	6	100	248
socialist	—	5	35	58	2	100	206
Other	—	9	51	40	—	100	35
Don't know/ no answer	1	7	34	36	22	100	94
All	—	10	48	36	6	100	633

Table 3.15A Attitude to legislation against racial discrimination: by political views

Overseas students

Percentages

Political views	Extended	Adequate	Reduced	Repealed	Don't know No answer	Total	N
	Attitude to legislation						
conservative	46	18	4	6	26	100	50
liberal	74	6	—	4	16	100	248
socialist	80	5	—	3	12	100	206
Other	74	9	3	—	14	100	35
Don't know/ no answer	55	12	2	4	17	100	94
All	70	8	1	4	17	100	633

Table 3.16A Attitude to aid to underdeveloped countries: by political views

Overseas students

Percentages

Political views	Yes	No	Undecided	Don't know No answer	Total	N
	Attitude to aid					
conservative	12	76	6	6	100	50
liberal	27	43	17	13	100	248
socialist	40	34	13	13	100	206
Other	43	43	2	12	100	35
Don't know/ no answer	19	48	7	26	100	94
All	29	44	13	14	100	633

Table 4.1A Attendance at union meeting: by membership of society committees

Percentages

Membership of Society committee	Attendance at union meetings				
	Frequently	Occasionally	Very rarely or never	Total	N
Undergraduates					
On committee	52	32	16	100	484
Not on committee	43	33	24	100	917
All	46	32	22	100	1413
Postgraduates					
On committee	30	38	32	100	101
Not on committee	16	26	58	100	718
All	18	27	55	100	826

Table 4.2A Attendance at union meetings: by membership of societies

Percentages

Membership of Societies	Attendance at union meetings				
	Frequently	Occasionally	Very rarely or never	Total	N
Undergraduates					
No societies	31	31	38	100	278
One society	40	37	23	100	324
Two societies	48	33	19	100	359
Three or more societies	58	30	12	100	449
All	46	32	22	100	1413
Postgraduates					
No societies	9	23	67	100	434
One society	21	32	46	100	220
Two societies	31	31	37	100	106
Three or more societies	46	36	19	100	59
All	18	27	55	100	826

Table 4.3A Attitudes towards aspects of student life: by type of student

Percentages

% of students saying accommodation for:	HUG	OUG	HPG	OPG	All UGs	All PGs
Union offices						
Very adequate	4	3	3	5	4	4
Fairly adequate	19	13	14	12	18	13
Rather inadequate	31	26	18	15	30	16
Very inadequate	19	10	10	2	17	16
Don't know or no answer	27	48	55	66	31	61
All	100	100	100	100	100	100
Union meetings						
Very adequate	6	7	5	6	6	5
Fairly adequate	27	25	22	25	27	24
Rather inadequate	32	30	26	21	32	24
Very inadequate	28	22	17	14	27	15
Don't know or no answer	7	16	30	54	8	32
All	100	100	100	100	100	100
Society meetings						
Very adequate	7	7	6	5	7	5
Fairly adequate	45	33	29	23	43	26
Rather inadequate	22	12	16	12	21	14
Very inadequate	9	6	6	4	8	5
Don't know or no answer	17	42	43	56	21	50
All	100	100	100	100	100	100
Common rooms						
Very adequate	2	3	4	3	2	3
Fairly adequate	8	16	14	22	9	18
Rather inadequate	30	33	33	32	31	33
Very inadequate	54	29	33	20	50	26
Don't know or no answer	6	19	16	23	8	20
All	100	100	100	100	100	100

Table 4.4A Control over union premises: by party allegiance

Home students

Percentages

| Party allegiance | Control over union premises | | | | |
	Important	Unimportant	Don't know	Total	N
Undergraduates					
Conservative	56	31	13	100	243
Liberal	65	21	14	100	194
Labour	72	18	10	100	507
Left-wing groups	88	7	5	100	108
Don't know or no answer	65	16	19	100	144
All	68	20	12	100	1206
Postgraduates					
Conservative	32	49	19	100	47
Liberal	55	32	13	100	56
Labour	69	20	11	100	213
Left-wing groups	92	3	5	100	36
Don't know or no answer	54	15	31	100	39
All	64	23	13	100	400

Table 4.5A Union representation: by political views

Overseas students

Percentages

Political views	Union representation			Total	N
	Adequate	Inadequate	Don't know		
Undergraduates					
conservative	(32)	(42)	(26)	(100)	19
liberal	36	53	11	100	72
socialist	43	35	22	100	74
Other	(23)	(69)	(8)	(100)	13
Don't know or no answer	(35)	(36)	(29)	(100)	29
All	37	45	18	100	207
Postgraduates					
conservative	26	48	26	100	31
liberal	32	31	37	100	176
socialist	40	28	32	100	132
Other	33	33	34	100	46
Don't know or no answer	37	19	44	100	41
All	35	30	35	100	426

Table 4.6A Sabbatical year for president: by political views
Overseas students

Percentages

Political views	Sabbatical year				Total	N
	In principle	At School's discretion	Not at all	Don't know		
Undergraduates						
conservative	(26)	(37)	(11)	(26)	(100)	19
liberal	60	24	5	11	100	72
socialist	72	10	9	10	100	74
Other	(84)	(16)	(0)	(0)	(100)	13
Don't know or no answer	(42)	(29)	(0)	(29)	(100)	29
All	60	20	7	13	100	207
Postgraduates						
conservative	23	26	32	19	100	31
liberal	34	17	23	26	100	176
socialist	45	20	14	21	100	132
Other	33	13	26	28	100	46
Don't know or no answer	34	12	27	27	100	41
All	37	18	21	24	100	426

Table 4.7A Importance of control of union premises: by political views

Overseas students

Percentages

| Political views | Control of union premises | | | | |
	Important	Unimportant	Don't know	Total	N
Undergraduates					
conservative	(21)	(53)	(26)	(100)	19
liberal	47	27	26	100	72
socialist	72	16	12	100	74
Other	(70)	(15)	(15)	(100)	13
Don't know or no answer	(44)	(28)	(28)	(100)	29
All	55	24	21	100	207
Postgraduates					
conservative	26	45	29	100	31
liberal	42	31	27	100	176
socialist	65	12	23	100	132
Other	44	26	30	100	46
Don't know or no answer	49	25	26	100	41
All	49	25	26	100	426

Table 5.1A Satisfaction: by course of study

Undergraduates

Course of study	Lectures	Classes	Tutorials	Staff contacts	Degree structure	N
B.Sc. (Econ.)[1]						
Economics A/D	67	64	58	36	53	109
Economics/Econometrics	(75)	(67)	(42)	(46)	(63)	24
Monetary economics	69	62	52	36	53	87
Industry and trade	84	54	44	46	51	57
Accounting	76	65	50	46	63	74
Economic history	75	65	69	67	58	52
Government	53	54	55	41	53	109
Sociology	61	44	58	29	42	80
Statistics	78	60	42	62	69	45
Computing	68	55	61	58	64	36
International relations	61	54	63	40	53	87
Sociology and anthropology	(50)	(67)	(56)	(56)	(44)	18
International history	76	52	48	38	58	42
Geography	76	61	51	44	46	71
Philosophy	(47)	(47)	(47)	(33)	(50)	15
Ll.B.	79	74	49	53	67	160
B.A./B.Sc. Anthropology	(100)	(78)	(89)	(78)	(78)	9
B.A./B.Sc. Geography	79	58	87	87	62	53
B.A. History	48	55	55	87	22	31
B.A. Philosophy and economics	(60)	(53)	(40)	(47)	(60)	15
B.A./B.Sc. Sociology	53	51	73	47	49	142
General Course, Trade Union studies, other	73	78	67	49	—	97
All undergraduates	68	61	59	48	53	1413

Notes: 1. All students registered for the B.Sc.(Econ.) were classified by special subject, although in the case of first years this was merely their intended field of specialisation.

2. Percentages shown in the table are for each group, the percentage of students saying the aspect was 'very' or 'fairly satisfactory.'

Table 6.3A Representation desired ... home (H) and overseas (O) students

Percentages

Area of decisions		Representation desired by undergraduates						Representation desired by postgraduates					
		At least student equality	Student minority	Only consultation	No consultation or representation	No opinion or no answer	All	At least equality	Student minority	Only consultation	No consultation or representation	No opinion or no answer	All
Student admissions	H	8	16	19	52	5	100	6	16	22	50	6	100
	O	15	24	15	40	6	100	7	20	20	45	8	100
Teaching arrangements	H	44	37	15	2	2	100	28	43	22	5	2	100
	O	39	34	19	3	5	100	24	36	26	8	6	100
Course content	H	35	39	21	4	1	100	24	41	27	6	2	100
	O	34	33	20	9	4	100	20	39	28	7	6	100
Examinations	H	27	31	27	13	2	100	20	27	28	22	3	100
	O	24	26	30	15	5	100	16	30	27	21	6	100
Discipline	H	53	29	9	7	2	100	53	28	11	7	1	100
	O	57	30	8	2	3	100	53	30	7	5	5	100
Library	H	69	24	5	1	1	100	57	33	8	0	2	100
	O	67	28	3	0	2	100	56	31	6	1	6	100
Careers service	H	43	27	15	4	11	100	44	32	15	2	7	100
	O	42	27	11	2	18	100	37	31	13	2	17	100
Academic appointments	H	8	19	27	43	3	100	7	18	24	47	4	100
	O	13	21	23	35	8	100	8	21	24	39	8	100
Appointment of director	H	12	21	32	33	2	100	13	20	29	35	3	100
	O	21	27	25	23	4	100	14	21	27	31	7	100
Senior administrative appointments	H	9	18	27	43	3	100	11	16	24	46	3	100
	O	14	25	17	37	7	100	10	19	24	37	10	100

Table 6.2A Percentage desire for some student representation: by 'A' levels

Undergraduates — Percentages

Issue	'A' level grades										No 'A' level or no answer
	3A	2A 1B	2A no B	1A 2B	1A 1B	1A no B	3B no A	2B no A	1B no A	No B no A	
Admissions	34	23	26	25	22	26	34	22	25	(21)	34
Teaching	87	82	81	82	80	78	85	80	81	(86)	72
Course-content	72	71	76	70	75	80	81	71	73	(79)	65
Examinations	63	53	62	49	61	58	67	53	61	(59)	47
Discipline	84	80	84	83	81	77	88	83	85	(86)	86
Library	92	94	94	93	94	92	97	93	93	(97)	92
Careers	76	66	71	67	70	69	74	70	65	(83)	72
Academic appointments	32	26	26	26	24	28	33	27	31	(34)	33
Director's appointment	37	33	34	32	32	32	38	33	43	(41)	40
Senior administrative appointment	26	29	26	26	25	22	32	28	36	(35)	37
No	82	141	107	151	264	88	73	229	75	29	174

Note: The table shows the percentage of each group desiring majority, equality, or minority representation.

Table 8.1A Retrospective opinions on the use of the sit-in and the boycott as means of expressing student grievances

Percentages

	Wholly un-justified	Partly justified	Wholly justified	Undecided	No opinion	No answer	Total
Sit-in:							
Undergraduates							
Home	24	26	44	4	1	1	100
Overseas	15	27	46	2	3	7	100
All	23	26	44	3	1	2	100
Postgraduates							
Home	20	25	45	5	2	3	100
Overseas	19	27	43	5	3	3	100
All	20	26	44	5	2	3	100
Boycott:							
Undergraduates							
Home	27	23	47	2	1	1	100
Overseas	22	28	40	6	2	2	100
All	26	23	46	3	1	1	100
Postgraduates							
Home	31	22	41	3	1	2	100
Overseas	28	24	39	4	2	4	100
All	29	23	40	4	1	3	100

The use made of these ways of expressing student grievances the previous terms was:

L

Table 8.2A Retrospective opinions of the sit-in: by opinions of the boycott

Percentages

The boycott and sit-in were

	Both wholly unjustified	Both wholly justified	Both partly or wholly justified	At least one was wholly or partly justified
Undergraduates				
Home	18	37	60	79
Overseas	10	28	58	83
Postgraduates				
Home	16	34	56	77
Overseas	14	31	54	79
All	16	34	58	79

Table 8.3A Percentage of students who approved of the sit-in and the boycott at their start and at the end of term

Percentages

	Percentage of students who approved of the			
	sit-in		boycott	
	Start	End of term	Start	End of term
Undergraduates				
Home	47	53	58	57
Overseas	60	66	57	59
All	49	55	58	58
Postgraduates				
Home	43	57	47	54
Overseas	49	56	48	50
All	46	57	48	51

Table 8.4A Students who sat-in on one or more days: by their attitude to the sit-in at its start and at the end of term

All students

Percentages

		Percentage of students with given attitudes who sat in	Percentage of those who sat in who held these attitudes
Attitude to sit in at		Column 1	Column 2
Start	*End*		
D	D	2	(—)
D	A	28	8
D	O	(5)	(—)
A	D	33	7
A	A	68	72
A	O	53	2
O	D	8	(—)
O	A	42	8
O	O	4	(—)
Other answers		(—)	(—)
			100

Note: D means either strong or mild disapproval. A means either strong or mild approval, and O means either no opinion, undecided or no answer.

Table 8.5A Percentage of students who sat-in: by their retrospective opinion of the sit-in

All students

Percentages

	Percentage of students who sat-in on at least one occasion		
	Undergraduates	Postgraduates	All
Retrospective opinion that the sit-in had been:			
Wholly unjustified	6	3	5
Partly justified	25	12	20
Wholly justified	71	50	63
Other answers	29	14	22

Table 8.6A Students who missed at least some lectures and classes in order to support the boycott: by their attitude to the boycott at its start and the end of term

All students

Percentages

Attitude to sit-in at		Percentage of students with given attitudes who boycotted lectures and classes	Percentage of those who boycotted who held these attitudes
Start	End	Column 1	Column 2
D	D	3	2
D	A	39	4
D	O	(7)	0
A	D	57	6
A	A	86	85
A	O	(80)	2
O	D	(17)	0
O	A	55	3
O	O	6	0
			100

Note: D means either strong or mild disapproval. A means either strong or mild approval, and O means either no opinion, undecided or no answer.

Table 8.7A Percentage of students who boycotted lectures by their retrospective opinions of the boycott

Percentages

	Percentage of students who boycotted at least some of their lectures and classes		
	Undergraduates	Postgraduates	All
Retrospective opinion that the boycott had been:			
Wholly unjustified	5	2	4
Partly justified	49	32	43
Wholly justified	91	74	86
Other answers	15	14	15

Table 8.8A Percentage of students who tried to dissuade others from supporting the sit-in and boycott

Percentages

| | Percentage who tried to dissuade others from supporting | | | |
	Sit-in	Boycott	Sit-in and boycott	Sit-in or boycott
Undergraduates				
Home	20	19	15	23
Overseas	9	8	5	10
Postgraduates				
Home	14	19	15	23
Overseas	8	9	7	10
All students	16	14	11	18

Table 9.1A Participation in the sit-in: by 'A' levels

Undergraduates

Percentages

| | Number of days of participation in the sit-in | | | | | | |
'A' level grades	None	1-3	4-6	7-9	Other	Total	N
3 A	60	16	13	11	0	100	82
2 A 1 B	59	15	13	12	1	100	141
2 A 0 B	56	20	11	9	4	100	107
1 A 2 B	62	13	16	7	2	100	151
1 A 1 B	58	18	11	12	1	100	264
1 A 0 B	60	15	14	8	3	100	88
No A 3 B	48	15	19	15	3	100	73
No A 2 B	53	17	15	14	1	100	45
No A 1 B	43	20	17	20	0	100	75
No A or B	(48)	(24)	(10)	(14)	(4)	100	29
No 'A' levels	62	17	10	9	2	100	144
No grades given	67	10	10	10	3	100	30
All	57	17	13	11	2	100	1413

Table 9.2A Participation in the sit-in: by year of course and attendance at union meetings

Undergraduates

Percentages

Year of course	Attend union meetings	Number of days of participation in the sit-in					Total	N
		None	1-3	4-6	7-9	Other		
1st	Frequently	33	20	24	20	3	100	249
	Occasionally	65	20	9	5	1	100	153
	Rarely/never	90	8	2	—	—	100	71
2nd	Frequently	35	16	21	27	1	100	232
	Occasionally	72	14	7	3	4	100	132
	Rarely/never	81	16	—	—	3	100	85
3rd	Frequently	36	18	25	20	1	100	123
	Occasionally	68	20	8	2	2	100	138
	Rarely/never	87	11	1	1	—	100	115

Bibliography

Abbot, J., 'Social Class in Three Northern Universities', *British Journal of Sociology*, vol. 16, no. 3 (1965).

Abrams, M., 'Social Trends in Electoral Behaviour', *British Journal of Sociology*, vol. 13, no. 3 (1960).

Ayob, I., *Clare Special on L.S.E.* (London School of Economics Student Union, 1967).

The Berkeley Student Revolt, ed. Seymour M. Lipset and Sheldon S. Wolin (New York; Doubleday, 1965).

Blackstone, T., and Hadley, R., 'Who Occupied L.S.E.?', *New Society*, 5 December 1968.

Blondel, J., *Voters, Parties and Leaders* (Penguin, 1967).

Brewster, B., and Cockburn, A., 'Revolt at the L.S.E.', *New Left Review*, no. 43 (1967).

Brown, D. R., 'Student Stress and the Institutional Environment', *Journal of Social Issues*, vol. 23, no. 3 (1967).

Burns, T., 'The Revolt of the Privileged', *S.S.R.C. Newsletter 4* (1968).

Butler, D. E. and King, A., *The British General Election of 1966* (Macmillan, 1966).

'The Caine Mutiny', *Solidarity*, vol. 4, no. 5 (1967).

Campbell, A. A., *et al.*, *The Voter Decides* (Evanston: Row, 1954).

Census of England and Wales (H.M.S.O., 1961).

Committee on Higher Education 1961-3, *Higher Education*, report and five volumes of appendixes, Cmnd 2154-11 (H.M.S.O., 1963).

Cowan, J. L., 'Academic Freedom, Protest and University Environments'. Paper read at the Association of Public Analysts, New York, in 1966.

Davis, P. D. C., 'The Troubles—A Chronology with Observations', *L.S.E. Magazine*, no. 33 (July 1967).

Decision of the Board of Discipline. Duplicated report issued on 13 March 1967 (London School of Economics).

Department of Education and Science, *Statistics of Education*. Published annually by H.M.S.O.

Department of Employment and Productivity, *Family Expenditure Survey Report*. Published annually by H.M.S.O.

Flacks, R., 'The Liberated Generation: Roots of Student Protest', *Journal of Social Issues*, vol. 23, no. 3 (1967).

Gales, K. E., 'A Campus Revolution', *British Journal of Sociology*, vol. 17, no. 1 (1966).

Glennerster, H., *Graduate School* (Edinburgh: Oliver & Boyd, 1967).

Gould, J., 'Politics and the Academy', *Government and Opposition*, vol. 3, no. 1 (1968).

Hadley, R., 'This Is Your Life', *Sphinx* (University of Liverpool Guild of Undergraduates, 1960).

Hatch, S. 'Student Survey', unpublished.

Heist, P., 'The Dynamics of Student Discontent and Protest'. Paper read at the Association of Public Analysts, New York, in 1968.

Hudson, L., *Contrary Imaginations* (Penguin, 1967).

Hyman, H., *Political Socialization* (Chicago: Free Press of Glencoe, 1959).

Keniston, K., 'The Sources of Student Dissent', *Journal of Social Issues*, vol. 23, no. 3 (1967).

'L.S.E.'s New Director: A Report on Walter Adams' (L.S.E. Socialist Society, 1966).

The L.S.E. What It Is: And How We Fought It (Open Committee, L.S.E. Socialist Society, 1965).

Lyonns, G., 'The Police Car Demonstration: A Survey of Participants', in *Berkeley Student Revolt*, ed. Lipset and Wolin.

'The Machinery of Government of the School'. An unpublished report submitted to the Academic Board of the L.S.E., December 1966.

Macoby, E., *et al.*, 'Youth and Political Change', *Public Opinion Quarterly*, no. 18 (Spring 1954).

Marris, P., *The Experience of Higher Education* (Routledge & Kegan Paul, 1964).

Mock, K. R., 'The Potential Activist and His Perception of the University'. Paper read at the Association of Public Analysts, San Francisco, in 1968.

Newcomb, T. M., *Personality and Social Change* (New York: Holt, Rhinehart and Winston, 1943).

Parkin, F., 'A Student Revolution', *New Society*, 23 March 1967.

Peterson, R. E., *The Scope of Organised Student Protest in 1967-68* (Princeton: Educational Testing Service, 1968).

Report by the Director, 1966-67 (London School of Economics, 1967).

Rose, R., *Students in Society* (University of Manchester Union, 1963).

Sampson, E. E., ' Student Activism and the Decade of Protest ', *Journal of Social Issues,* vol. 23, no. 3 (1967).

Sanford, N., *Campus 1980: the Shape of the Future in American Higher Education* (Delacarte Press, 1969).

Somers, R. H., ' The Mainsprings of the Rebellion: A Survey of Berkeley Students in November 1964 ', in *Berkeley Student Revolt,* ed. Lipset and Wolin.

Spiers, M., *Student Political Attitudes* (Bradford Institute of Technology. 1964).

Staff Manual, 1966 (London School of Economics).

Student Opinion in the University of Leicester (University of Leicester Conservative Association, 1965).

Student Political Attitudes (Bradford Institute of Technology, 1964).

Student Social Survey (University of Nottingham, 1962).

Student survey, *Gemini* (Winter 1957-8).

Student survey, *Isis,* 4 March 1961.

Student Survey (Bristol College of Science and Technology, 1962).

Student Survey, *Clare Market Review* (Winter 1962-3).

Trent, J. W., and Craise, J. L., ' Commitment and Conformity in the American College ', *Journal of Social Issues,* vol. 23, no. 3 (1967).

University Grants Committee, *Returns from Universities and University Colleges.* Published annually by H.M.S.O. until 1965/6.

University of Oxford, *Report of Commission of Inquiry* (Oxford University Press, 1966).

Watts, W. A., and Whittaker, D., ' Free Speech Advocates at Berkeley ', *Journal of Applied Behavioural Science,* vol. 2, no. 1 (1966).

Watts, W. A., Lynch, S., and Whittaker, D., ' Alienation and Activism in Today's College-age Youth: Socialisation Patterns and Current Family Relationships '. Unpublished paper.

L*

List of Notes

Chapter 1

[1] The events leading up to the boycott and sit-in, and the course of the strike itself are described in greater detail in Chapter 7.

[2] *Guardian,* 15 March 1967.

[3] *Daily Sketch,* 16 March 1967.

[4] *Clare Special on L.S.E.,* p. xi. The report does not explain how the calculations were made. In particular, the reader must speculate on how it proved possible to establish normal levels of attendance at lectures as attendance is not compulsory at the School.

[5] *L.S.E. Magazine,* No. 33 (July 1967), p. 12.

[6] *Sunday Times,* 19 March, 1967.

[7] A small study of participants in the 'occupation' of the School in October 1968 was carried out by two of the authors. Some of the findings were reported in Tessa Blackstone and Roger Hadley, 'Who Occupied L.S.E.?', *New Society,* 5 December 1968.

Chapter 2

[1] The data in this section are drawn from two sources: London School of Economics, *Digest of Statistics, No. 3* (L.S.E., 1968); Department of Education and Science, *Statistics of Education 1966,* vol. 6, *Universities* (H.M.S.O., 1969).

[2] In 1965/6 there were 3478 students, and in 1967/8, 3439.

[3] Students on part-time courses comprise those reading for a part-time degree or diploma and 'occasional' students—those who attend a limited number of lecture courses at the School without registering for a specific degree.

[4] London University as a whole attracts more overseas students than the average—in 1966/7 18% of its students came from overseas. These data are drawn from Department of Education and Science, op. cit; overseas students are defined in terms of their permanent residence being outside the United Kingdom.

⁵ In the student survey students were asked for their nationality. This partly accounts for the difference between the survey data and the Department of Education and Science's data in the proportion of overseas students at L.S.E.

⁶ Between 1961/2 and 1966/7 the total number of students at universities in the United Kingdom increased by 63%; during the same period, the numbers reading for social science increased by 177%. See University Grants Committee, *University Development 1962-7*, Cmnd. 3820 (H.M.S.O.,

⁷ University Grants Committee, *Returns from Universities and University Colleges, 1965/6*, Cmnd. 3586 (H.M.S.O., 1968).

⁸ A list of all degrees is given in Appendix B.

⁹ The definitions of fields of study are given in the note to Table 2.2. First-year students in the B.Sc.(Econ.) degree are not officially allocated to a department. In the student survey, these students were asked to indicate which department they intended to enter in their second year.

¹⁰ The ' general ' course is a one-year course designed specifically for overseas students and in particular for those in their ' junior ' year at a university in the United States.

¹¹ See Department of Education and Science, op. cit.

¹² See the note to Table 2.4.

¹³ Comparable data for overseas students is given in Appendix C, Table 2.9A. As one might expect, very few (8%) came from manual backgrounds. The majority came from professional (40%) or ' own-business ' (29%) families, and there was little difference between postgraduates and undergraduates.

¹⁴ See Committee on Higher Education 1961-3, *Higher Education*, Appendix II B.

¹⁵ See P. Marris, *The Experience of Higher Education*. A survey of third-year male students at Cambridge, Leeds, Southampton and City universities in 1961/3 showed that 11% of social-science students, compared with 23% of all students, came from manual backgrounds.

¹⁶ Students were asked to place their father's income before tax into one of a number of categories. The data are obviously subject to error, but the results do not appear unreasonable and do not conflict with what is known about the national distribution of incomes by social class. The student-survey data relate to the 78% of students who gave their father's income; in 10% of cases the father had died, 9% of students did not know their father's income and 3% did not answer.

¹⁷ Ministry of Labour, *Family Expenditure Survey, Report for 1965* (H.M.S.O., 1966).

[18] See the note to Table 2.6.

[19] The source of the national data is given in Table 2.7. The extent of the departure from the national pattern can be realised if one calculates the expected national voting, if, within social class, electors nationally had voted as did L.S.E. parents. Under these circumstances, Labour would have had 55% of the votes and Conservatives 33%, a lead of 22% compared with the actual voting of 48% and 42% respectively, a lead of only 6%.

[20] It could partly be a result of the 1966 election itself, in which Labour stressed the 'technological revolution' and apparently won the votes of the 'educated' middle class and particularly those in professions; these form a high proportion of L.S.E. parents.

[21] See, for example, Committee on Higher Education, op. cit. Broadly defined, in England and Wales, maintained schools are wholly financed by the State. Non-maintained schools can be divided into two categories: direct grant schools, which are partially financed by the State, and independent schools, which obtain no direct State aid; the Scottish system differs slightly from that of England and Wales.

[22] In 1961/2 65% of students leaving school with the intention of entering university came from the maintained sector; in 1965/6 the comparable proportion was 70%. See Department of Education and Science, *Statistics of Education 1962*. Part Three (H.M.S.O., 1964) and 1966 vol. (H.M.S.O., 1967).

[23] It is even more difficult to obtain data on the secondary schools attended by students within different faculties than for students in all faculties. Evidence on entrants to Oxford in 1965-6, however, shows that 40% of all entrants came from maintained schools, but only 22% of those in Social Studies. See University of Oxford, *Report of Commission of Inquiry, vol.* II.

[24] At present, all Examining Boards use an alphabetic grading A, B, C, D, E, with F for a failure; in the past some Boards used a percentage grading with 60% or over being equivalent to A or B, or a numerical grading with 2 or 3 being equivalent to A or B.

[25] Fifty-two per cent of overseas undergraduates had two or more 'A' levels; almost all these students were from Asia, Africa or Europe and were on degree courses. Almost all those without 'A' level passes were 'general'-course students.

[26] At L.S.E. there is a positive relationship between the quality of a student's 'A' levels and his degree result. The following data relate to all students who obtained a B.Sc.(Econ.) degree in 1964, 1965 or 1966:

Number of grades A or B	*Percentage gaining a first or upper second*
3	36
2	26
1 or 0	21

27 It is generally recognised that Oxford and Cambridge tend to attract students of a higher calibre than other universities. In 1965/6 39% of men entering Oxford to study Arts or Social Science had very good 'A' level qualifications. (See University of Oxford, *Commission of Inquiry*); 'very good' is defined as having three grade Bs or better with three passes, and at least one A and one B with two passes. The comparable proportion at L.S.E. second-year students in 1966/7 was 42%. It should, however, be remembered that some students enter Oxford on their performance in the scholarship examinations and either do not attempt 'A' level examinations, or consider them unimportant.

28 See University Central Council for Admissions, *Second Report 1963/4* (U.C.C.A., 1966).

29 A ' good ' 'A' level result was defined as at least three grade Cs (if three subjects had been passed) or an A and a B (if two). Note that at this time U.C.C.A. did not deal with applicants to Oxford and Cambridge, where competition is in any case linked to performance in college scholarship and entrance examinations rather than 'A' levels.

30 The percentages with three or more 'A' levels at grades A or B are:

Geography	B.Sc.(Econ.)	39%
	B.A./B.Sc.(Geog.)	23%
Sociology	B.Sc.(Econ.)	44%
	B.A./B.Sc.(Soc.)	33%

31 These data relate only to home students. If all postgraduate degree students are considered, then, as overseas students are in the majority, over a half of all students have first degrees from a foreign university.

In the survey, 20% of overseas students did not answer the question on previous university attended. Of those that did, 9% had a degree from a United Kingdom university or other institution, 86% a degree from a foreign university, and the remainder had other qualifications.

32 See Committee on Higher Education, *Higher Education*. Nationally, in 1961/2 55% of postgraduates in social sciences had graduated at their present university. The proportion for all faculties was 74%.

33 See H. Glennerster, *Graduate School,* app. VII.

34 ' Other ' universities is defined as universities in the United Kingdom other than London, Oxford and Cambridge.

35 See Glennerster, op. cit., app. VIII.

36 Thirty per cent of overseas undergraduates had come to L.S.E. on leaving secondary school. Of the remainder 42% had a degree or other qualification; 41% (mainly the ones with qualifications) had not been in employment. These proportions varied widely with the student's origin.

[37] See Committee on Higher Education, op cit.

[38] Forty per cent of overseas postgraduates had not been in employment, and 35% had been employed for two or more years.

[39] See Appendix C, Table 2.8A.

Chapter 3

[1] The 9% categorised as Left-wing Groups consisted of Communists (4%), Left-wing Labour (3%), Trotskyists and Marxists (1%), and Anarchists (1%). Apart from two students who said they were Fascists, there was no evidence of extreme right-wing allegiance.

[2] Data supplied by National Opinion Polls. A national sample of just under 2000 electors was interviewed. Voting-intention figures exclude 8% of interviewees made up of those who would not vote, those who were undecided and those who refused to disclose their political affiliation.

[3] *Census of England and Wales,* 1961

[4] See M. Abrams, ' Social Trends in Electoral Behaviour ', *British Journal of Sociology,* vol 13, no. 3 p. 223. The question was included in a survey carried out in 1960.

[5] J. Blondel, *Voters, Parties and Leaders,* p. 90, for proportion of Conservative and Labour supporters belonging to their party. The figure for Liberal members is based on data provided by the Information Department of the Liberal Party, in which total membership in 1966 is estimated at approximately 250,000, compared with a vote of 2,300,000 in the general election of that year.

[6] Analysis of the differences between party members and supporters was confined to undergraduates since the numbers of Conservative Party and Liberal Party members amongst postgraduates was very small. A higher proportion of Conservative Party members than other Conservative Party supporters were conservative in their attitude to each of the political issues. Almost as consistently, a greater proportion of Labour Party members and Liberal Party members than other Labour and Liberal supporters held radical views on the issues. For example, on the question of Vietnam, 28% of Conservative Party members strongly supported American involvement, compared with 13% of other Conservative supporters. On the same question, 43% of Labour Party members strongly opposed American involvement, compared with 33% of other Labour supporters. The figures for Liberal Party members and other supporters were 26% and 21% respectively.

The main differences in the background characteristics of party members and other supporters were found in religion, age and schooling. A higher proportion of Conservative Party members held a religious belief than other Conservative Party supporters (74% compared with 65%), and a higher proportion were Anglicans (55% compared with 31%). A higher proportion of Labour Party members than other supporters was drawn from the two higher age-groups (35% compared with 20%). A greater proportion of Conservative Party members than other supporters came from independent schools (25% compared to 17%). In contrast, a larger proportion of Labour Party members than supporters came from the other maintained schools category (18% compared with 11%).

7 Blondell, op. cit., pp. 75-9.

8 Abrams, op. cit.

9 The preliminary enquiry was conducted with a quota sample of students selected by subject of study, department, and undergraduate/postgraduate status. The students were asked which political issues they regarded as the most important (*a*) in international affairs, (*b*) in British politics.

10 The three issues are Vietnam, Rhodesia and comprehensive schools. Those taking a ' conservative ' attitude supported or strongly supported American involvement in Vietnam, wanted majority rule in Rhodesia delayed more than ten years or indefinitely, and opposed or strongly opposed comprehensives. A ' radical ' attitude meant opposition or strong opposition to the American involvement in Vietnam, preference for majority rule in Rhodesia immediately or within ten years, and support or strong support for comprehensive schools.

11 Data supplied to us by National Opinion Polls from a survey carried out in February 1967.

12 Data supplied to us by National Opinion Polls from a survey carried out in July 1967.

13 For examples of student data see *Student Opinion in the University of Leicester*, a survey by the University of Leicester Conservative Association in 1965, which found that 38% of the women, compared to 27% of the men, said they would vote Conservative, while only 40%, compared with 45% of the men, would vote Labour; and Richard Rose, *Students in Society*, which reports that at Manchester University in 1963 37% of women, compared with 31% of men, were Conservative supporters and 25% of women against 37% of men were Labour supporters. For a review of some national data see Blondel, op. cit., pp. 59-60.

14 M. Spiers, *Student Political Attitudes*.

15 Rose, op. cit.

16 See, for example, the summary of data in Herbert H. Hyman's *Political Socialization*, ch. iv.

17 See, for example, ibid, pp. 78-80; and Rose, op. cit., p. 8.

18 A. A. Campbell, *et al., The Voter Decides.*

19 For example, see Blondel, op. cit., pp. 60/1.

20 See, for example, E. Macoby, *et al.,* 'Youth and Political Change', *Public Opinion Quarterly,* No. 18 (Spring 1954), pp. 23/39, and Hanan C. Selvin and Warren O. Hagstrom, 'Determinants of Support for Civil Liberties', in *Berkley Student Revolt,* ed. Lipset and Wolin.

21 No surveys of political opinion at other universities or colleges in Britain are available for 1967, but a number of studies carried out between 1959 and 1965 show that Conservatives had substantially more support than Labour in most cases. At Oxford in 1957 the students were divided: Conservatives 39%, Labour 25%, Liberal 11% (*Gemini,* Winter 1957-8); Liverpool, 1959: Conservatives 58%, Labour 11%, Liberal 8% (*Sphinx,* Summer 1960); Oxford, 1961: Conservatives 40%, Labour 20%, Liberal 24% (*Isis,* 4 March 1961); Bristol College of Technology, 1962: Conservatives 37%, Labour 12%, Liberal 24% (*Student Survey,* Bristol College of Science and Technology, 1962); Nottingham, 1962: Conservatives 40%, Labour 22%, Liberal 15% (*Student Social Survey,* University of Nottingham, 1962, Manchester, 1963: Conservatives 33%, Labour 34%, Liberal 17% (Rose, *Students in Society*); Bradford Institute of Technology, 1964: Conservatives 44%, Labour 35%, Liberal 7% (Spiers, *Student Political Attitudes*); Leicester, 1965: Conservatives 32%, Labour 42%, Liberal 13% (*Student Opinion in the University of Leicester*). Nationally, opinion swung to Labour between 1965 and 1967, but even assuming this trend was reflected fully amongst university students it would have been insufficient to produce at other universities the kind of support for the left which was found at L.S.E. in 1967. Further, there is evidence from an earlier survey that the dominance of the left at L.S.E. was no passing phenomenon. In 1961 a comparative study of second-year students at four London colleges, including L.S.E., found that 49% of the L.S.E. students would vote Labour in a general election, compared with less than half the number at Imperial College, Queen Mary's College and University College. (See *Clare Market Review* (Winter, 1962-3), pp. 36-9. The distribution of support between the three main parties was as follows: L.S.E. Labour 49%, Liberals 19% and Conservatives 15%; U.C. 20%, 20% and 39% respectively; Imperial 15%, 19% and 43%; Q.M.C. 14%, 24% and 41%.)

22 Stephen Hatch, unpublished student survey.

23 Rose, op. cit. At Manchester University Labour voters made up 60% of social-studies students, 38% of geographers, historians and students of allied subjects, 30% of science students and 24% of engineering students.

24 Spiers, op. cit. At Bradford Institute of Technology 56% of the social scientists said they would vote Labour, compared with 36% of the engineers.

[25] See, for example, F. Parkin, 'A Student Revolution', *New Society*, 23 March 1967, and Rose, op. cit.

[26] T. M. Newcomb, *Personality and Social Change*.

[27] See especially *Contrary Imaginations,* passim.

Chapter 4

[1] A limitation is that it is only concerned with formally constituted student organisations, since no questions were asked about informal groups based on patterns of friendship. Nor does it provide information on students' social and political activities outside the School.

[2] The Union has negotiated with the governors of the School in order to secure their agreement to amend the constitution of the Union, so that the distinction between Union and Associated Societies is abolished. This is controversial, since it would allow the use of union funds for political activities, which might require an amendment to the objects clause in the constitution which states that the purpose of the Union is to further the welfare of students.

[3] Appendix A lists these questions in detail.

[4] The union council is the executive committee of the Union, and consists of the President and his Deputy, the General Secretary, Senior Treasurer and five Vice-Presidents who chair various union committees. The council is responsible for the co-ordination of policies and the day-to-day running of the Union.

[5] During 1967 the Union Structure Reform Commission was set up. The majority recommended retaining a reformed version of the present structure, but a minority advocated the setting up of a students' representative council. Its report has since been rejected by the Union.

[6] In many universities the Students' Union receives a *per capita* grant direct from local education authorities out of which it finances all its activities, including the upkeep of its premises, and which it is free to spend as it likes. In the case of L.S.E. the local education authorities have paid a block tuition-fee to the School (part of which is presumably supposed to cover student-union expenses) for the students they maintain. The School then reallocated part of this in a block grant to the Union. The criteria on which it based the size of this grant were not clear. Since the sit-in the Union has successfully negotiated a change to the *per capita* system. This means that the Union no longer has to take its budget to the school authorities for vetting and plead with them for extra money each year, although they may from time to time need to ask for an increase in the capitation grant.

7 In a survey (unpublished), carried out in 1966 by Stephen Hatch of a sample of second-year undergraduates at University College, London, Exeter and Nottingham, the proportions of students belonging to no societies were considerably lower. They were respectively 8%, 9% and 5%. The question was framed in a slightly different way to cover membership of 'University and Hall Clubs, societies and other organisations'. The broader coverage of this question may account for the differences between L.S.E. and the other institutions, and make any direction comparison invalid.

8 These percentages differ slightly from those in the table since they include those who belong to party political societies and other political societies, but count those who belong to both once only.

9 At first glance this claim seems high in view of the capacity of the Old Theatre. However, a more careful consideration of the figures indicates that it may be completely valid. On the assumption that 'frequently' means attendance at one meeting in every three, and this would seem a legitimate interpretation of 'frequent' attendance, 18% of undergraduates and 7% of postgraduates from this category would have been at any one meeting. This constitutes approximately 400 students. When the Old Theatre is filled to capacity it can hold 700 students.

10 There is some evidence from the survey by Hatch, quoted earlier, that student dissatisfaction with their Union exists elsewhere too. There were quite large minorities agreeing with the statement 'The Union is run by a scheming clique.' At Exeter 21% of the students agreed with this, and at University College, London, and Nottingham, the percentages were respectively 30% and 29%.

11 These exceptions were made since there was not reason to expect that the relationship between the variables listed above and participation in student life would vary much between undergraduates and postgraduates.

12 The relationship between holding a post on the Union and attitudes to various facilities was not investigated for postgraduates since so few were involved.

13 This is further useful evidence to that given in Chapter 5 on satisfaction with accommodation, for those concerned with policies on student housing.

14 Hatch, contrary to this evidence, found from his survey that 'at each university lodgings students who did not get evening meals in their lodgings were more inclined to use the campus in the evenings than those who did'. However, he also found that 'at each university the hall students were not particularly prone to use the campus. Their evenings are definitely centred on hall, since at each place they spent on average nearly four evenings there'. He also found that at two of the universities there was little difference between hall and non-hall students in the levels of participation in student life. However, at University College, London, they

found that ' hall seems to make for considerably greater participation '. The findings from previous research are not consistent. A survey at Birmingham showed that hall students took a more active part in student societies, which was supported by the evidence of another survey at Leeds and Southampton. However, at Cambridge this survey found no difference between those in college and those not. The explanation for the inconclusive nature of these findings may lie in different methods of selection in various universities for students in halls.

[15] This is consistent with the evidence on political-party membership of undergraduates given in Chapter 3: a higher proportion of Conservative students were members of their party than Labour students.

[16] Since 1967 these attitudes have hardened, and have given rise to the demand for the abolition of the present union structure, and its replacement by a General Assembly of staff, students and workers.

Chapter 5

[1] Marris, *Experience of Higher Education,* p. 32.

[2] Glennerster, *Graduate School,* p. 117.

[3] Marris, op. cit., p. 55.

Chapter 6

[1] *Guardian,* 21 June 1968.

[2] *The Times,* 14 June 1968.

[3] *The Times,* 8 October 1968.

Chapter 7

[1] In this section we have drawn in particular on four accounts of the boycott and sit-in and the events leading up to them: the *Clare Special on L.S.E.* by Ismail Ayob; the *Report by the Director 1966-67,* App. 1, ' The Student Disturbances ', pp. 17-29; P. D. C. Davis, ' The Troubles—A

Chronology with Observations ', *L.S.E. Magazine,* no. 33 (July 1967), pp. 8-19; and *The L.S.E., What It Is: And How We Fought It,* published by the Open Committee, L.S.E. Socialist Society. Other accounts referred to include: Julius Gould, ' Politics and the Academy ', *Government and Opposition,* vol. 3, no. 1 (1968), pp. 23/47; Ben Brewster and Alexander Cockburn, ' Revolt at the L.S.E.', *New Left Review,* no. 43 (1967); and, for events up to February 1967, ' The Caine Mutiny ' in *Solidarity,* vol. 4, no. 5 (1967).

We have also drawn freely on press reports, documents issued by administration and students, and our own experiences as members of the staff of the School at the time.

We are indebted to Mr Harry Kidd, School Secretary at the time of the sit-in and boycott, and Mr P. D. C. Davis, publications officer, for their detailed comments on the first draft of this chapter. We alone, of course, are responsible for any deficiencies in the account.

2 *Staff Manual 1966,* p. 14.

3 Report of a speech by the Director to a meeting of the Students' Union held on 2 December 1966, in *Beaver,* 8 December 1966. At the same meeting the President denied that contacts between himself and the Director had ceased to take place regularly and claimed to have seen the Director every two weeks in that term. It has been pointed out to us by Mr Harry Kidd, Secretary of the School at the time, that the statements were not contradictory. The practice of regular meetings at fixed times between the Director and President had been abandoned, but in the special circumstances of the Michaelmas term there had been frequent *ad hoc* meetings between the two.

4 *Staff Manual, 1966,* p. 17.

5 ' The Machinery of Government of the School ', submitted to the Academic Board in December 1966.

6 At the end of the summer term 1967, five student representatives were invited to join the Committee and took part in all subsequent discussions and the writing of the final report published in 1968.

7 *Guardian,* 2 November 1966.

8 Letter to *The Times,* 24 October 1966, from Mr Louis Blom-Cooper. Letter to *The Times,* 4 November 1966, from Dr Robert Birley.

9 ' The Caine Mutiny ', *Solidarity,* vol. 4, no. 5, p. 9.

10 *Report by the Director 1966-67,* p. 20.

11 *L.S.E. Magazine,* no. 33, p. 9.

12 *Clare Special on L.S.E.,* p. 2.

13 182 against, 141 for, 23 abstentions.

14 516 for, 118 against, 53 abstentions.

15 The Director decided not to remain on the Board because it appeared that there was a ' real possibility that an attempt would be made to take outside legal action to invalidate the proceedings if I were to serve ' (*Report by the Director, 1966-67*, p. 20).

16 *L.S.E. Magazine*, no. 33, p. 10.

17 *Beaver*, no. 66 (December 1966), p. 8.

18 *Report by the Director, 1966-67*, p. 21.

19 *Decision of the Board of Discipline*, 13 March 1967, p. 8.

20 *Report by the Director, 1966-67*, p. 22.

21 See, for example, an article entitled ' Bloom Must Go!' in *Free Speech*, no. 1 (7 February 1967), a duplicated news-sheet sub-titled ' Voice of the Student Moderate Co-ordinating Committee of the L.S.E.'.

22 The presidential elections took place on 9-10 March. Peter Watherston, ex-chairman of the L.S.E. Conservative Society and a member of the Bow Group, was elected. He was due to succeed David Adelstein at the end of the Lent term.

23 See, for example, the student broadsheet *What We are Doing and Why*, issued on 14 March 1967, and the two open letters sent by the students to the staff on 15 and 19 March.

24 *L.S.E. What It is: And How We Fought It*, p. 2.

25 *Report by the Director, 1966-67*, pp. 25-6.

26 *The Times*, 15 March 1967.

27 Ibid.

28 The students' proposed choice of charities was anti-apartheid and family planning.

29 At the same meeting the Union passed a resolution authorising ten students to meet ten members of the staff during the vacation to continue negotiations.

Chapter 8

1 In the survey a distinction was drawn between a sit-in which would and a sit-in which would not immobilise the School. In this and subsequent chapters, the term ' sit-in ' is used for the latter category, and the former is referred to in full.

[2] i.e. home undergraduates, home postgraduates, overseas undergraduates and overseas postgraduates.

[3] See Appendix C, Table 8.1A.

[4] In this context 'day' was defined as the hours during the School was officially open, i.e. 9.30 a.m. to 10.30 p.m.

Chapter 9

[1] *The Times,* 14 March 1969.

[2] *The Listener,* 7 March 1968.

[3] R. H. Somers, '*The Mainsprings of the Rebellion:* A Survey of Berkeley Students in November 1964, in *Berkeley Student Revolt,* ed. Lipset and Wolin.
K. E. Gales, 'A Campus Revolution', *British Journal of Sociology,* vol. 27, no. 1 (1966).

[4] See, for example, R. Flacks, 'The Liberated Generations: Roots of Student Protest', *Journal of Social Issues,* vol. 23, no. 3 (1967).

[5] See, for example, Somers, op. cit.; Gales, op. cit.

[6] This information was available due to the index-number link with the 1966 Part I B.Sc.(Econ.) survey.

[7] Gales, op. cit.

[8] G. Lyonns, 'The Police Car Demonstration: A Survey of Participants' in *Berkeley Student Revolt,* ed. Lipset and Wolin.

[9] See Chapter 3, p. 62 for a discussion of other differences in attitudes within political categories, by nationality, and a tentative explanation of these differences.

[10] Gales, op. cit.

[11] See Chapter 3, p. 57 for a discussion of explanations of the relationship between political views and field of study.

[12] Gales, op. cit.

Chapter 10

[1] Although developed independently, the framework of this discussion is similar to that of Kenneth Keniston in 'The Sources of Student Dissent', *Journal of Social Issues,* vol. 23, no. 3 (1967). We are considerably indebted to this evaluation of the sources of American student protest.

[2] T. Burns, 'The Revolt of the Privileged', *S.S.R.C. Newsletter 4,* 1968.

[3] R. E. Peterson, *The Scope of Organised Student protest in 1967/68.* The study covered 859 colleges and universities, and questionnaires were completed by deans of students.

[4] See, for example:
Somers, op. cit.
Gales, op. cit.
Flacks, op. cit.
P. Heist, 'The Dynamics of Student Discontent and Protest'. Paper read at the American Psychological Association, New York, in 1966.
W. A. Watts and D. Whittaker, 'Free Speech Advocates at Berkeley', *Journal of Applied Behavioural Science,* vol. 2, no. 1 (1966).
W. A. Watts, S. Lynch and D. Whittaker, 'Alienation and Activism in Today's College-age Youth: Socialisation Patterns and Current Family Relationships'. Unpublished paper.
J. W. Trent and J. L. Craise, 'Commitment and Conformity in the American College', *Journal of Social Issues,* vol. 23, no. 3 (1967).

[5] See in particular: K. R. Mock, 'The Potential Activist and His Perception of the University'. Paper read at the American Psychological Association, San Francisco in 1968.
D. R. Brown, 'Student Stress and the Institutional Environment', *Journal of Social Issues,* vol. 23, no. 3 (1967).

[6] See Mock, op. cit., and Gales, op. cit.

[7] Keniston, op. cit.

[8] J. L. Cowan, 'Academic Freedom, Protest and University Environments'. Paper read at the American Psychological Association, New York in 1966.

[9] Peterson, op. cit.

[10] Keniston, op. cit.

[11] Flacks, op. cit.

[12] Brown, op. cit.

[13] Marris, *The Experience of Higher Education.*

[14] Keniston, op cit.

[15] Flacks, op. cit.

[16] Keniston, op. cit.

[17] E. E. Sampson, 'Student Activism and the Decade of Protest', *Journal of Social Issues,* vol. 23, no. 3 (1967).

[18] Keniston, op. cit.

[19] N. Sanford, *Campus 1980: the Shape of the Future in American Higher Education.*

Appendix B

[1] These numbers do not correspond exactly with the Statistics of Students in the session 1966-7 given in the School Calendar (1967-8) because the Calendar data refer to registrations in the Michaelmas term of 1966.

Index

137 ; and class of first degree, 144 ; and satisfaction with lectures, 147

Course of study, and satisfaction with L.S.E., 115-6, 121-2 ; and support for the boycott and sit-in, 211-6 ; *see also*: field of study

Degrees, 109 ; satisfaction with, 112, 113, 114 ; *see also*: course of study, field of study

Degree results, full time students at L.S.E., 1965-8, 192-3

Director, position in government of the L.S.E., 151-2 ; *see also* Caine, Sir Sydney (Director 1956-7) and Adams, Dr Walter (Director, 1967-)

Director's appointment, students' desire for representation on, 135, 136, 137, 138 ; and nationality, 138-9 ; and father's occupation, 139-40 ; and year of course, 140-3 ; and field of study, 142-3 ; and academic achievement, 143-4 ; and political views, 144-6 ; and attendance at union meetings, 145-6

Disciplinary committees, actual student representation on, 133, 134 ;
students' desire for representation on, 132, 136-7 ; and nationality, 138-9 ; and father's occupation, 139-40 ; and year of course, 140-1 ; and field of study, 141-3 ; and course of study, 142-3 ; and academic achievement, 143-4 ; and political views, 144-6 ; and attendance at union meetings, 145-6

Discipline, Board of, 1-2, 156-8, 162-6

Examinations, students' desire for representation on, 136, 137 ; and class of degree, 144

Expectations, students', 110

Extreme groups, definition, 229 ; characteristics of, 229-33

Father's income, 21 ; and satisfaction with L.S.E., 119, 124

Father's occupation, 18, 19 ; and sex, 20 ; comparison with other universities, 20, 21 ; and previous university, 29 ; and party allegiance, (home students), 48-9 ; and political views (overseas students), 70-1 ; and participation in student life, 98 ; and satisfaction with L.S.E., 118, 124 ; and views on representation, 139-40 ; and participation in the boycott and sit-in, 198-200

Field of study, 15, 16, 17 ; and 'A' level qualifications, 28 ; and party allegiance (home students), 54-6 ; and political views (overseas students), 71-2 ; and participation in student life, 95-8 ; and satisfaction with L.S.E., 115-16

First degree, class of, *see* Class of first degree

Full-time employment before coming to L.S.E., 31, 32 ; and father's occupation, 32 ; and last secondary school, 32 ; and party allegiance (home students), 53-4 ; and participation in student life, 99

Generation gap, 234, 239

Governing bodies, student representation on in British universities, 132, 133, 134,